Modern Poems on the Bible

AN ANTHOLOGY

Modern Poems on the Bible

AN ANTHOLOGY

Edited with an Introduction by *David Curzon*

 THE JEWISH PUBLICATION SOCIETY

Philadelphia and Jerusalem   5754   1994

This second edition is
Dedicated in loving memory of
E V E L Y N   F U R M A N   R O S E N
1935–1971

No poem compares to your beauty
No words can describe your goodness

by David Rosen
and sons Joseph and Brian

Copyright © 1994 by David Curzon
First edition   All rights reserved
No part of this publication may be reproduced or
transmitted in any form or by any means, electronic or
mechanical, including photocopy, recording, or any
information storage or retrieval system, except for brief
passages in connection with a critical review, without
permission in writing from the publisher: The Jewish
Publication Society, 1930 Chestnut Street, Philadelphia,
PA 19103.
Manufactured in the United States of America

Library of Congress Cataloging-in-Publication Data
Modern poems on the Bible: an anthology /
edited with an introduction by David Curzon.—1st ed.
p.   cm.
Includes indexes.
ISBN 0–8276–0449–1
1. Poetry, Modern—20th century.
2. Bible O.T.—History of Biblical events—Poetry.
I. Curzon, David.
PN6110.B38M63   1993
808.81'04—dc20   93–31931
                                          CIP

Designed by Arlene Putterman
Typeset in Caslon 540 by Ruttle, Shaw & Wetherill, Inc.

10 9 8 7 6 5 4 3 2

In memory of my parents
LILLIAN CURZON and
MAURICE CURZON (CZERCHOWSKI)
and of the family in Poland
who were murdered

Sing Heav'nly Muse, that on the secret top
Of *Oreb,* or of *Sinai,* didst inspire
That Shepherd, who first taught the chosen Seed,
In the Beginning how the Heav'ns and Earth
Rose out of *Chaos:* or if *Sion* Hill
Delight thee more, and *Siloa's* Brook that flow'd
Fast by the Oracle of God; I thence
Invoke thy aid to my adventrous Song

John Milton
Paradise Lost

Wherever I had looked I had looked upon
My permanent or impermanent images

William Butler Yeats
"The Municipal Gallery Revisited"

And thou shalt visit thy habitation, and shalt miss nothing

Job 5:24 (Translation: JPS 1917)

Contents

Acknowledgments

Jeffrey Fiskin, whose judgments I trusted more than my own and sought for every choice and on all drafts; and others who helped and sustained my belief in the project: Stanley H. Barkan, Susan Bauman, Menachem Brinker, Deborah Brodie, Lynne Bundesen, Itzhak Galnoor, Bert Gross, Ya'acov Hanoch, Gabriel Preil, Jesse Rosenthal, Lori Seibel, Gail Holst Warhaft, Zellman Warhaft, and members of Minyan M'at who listened to and encouraged drashes using some of the poetry collected here. The anthology was started in the Writers Room, the urban writers' retreat in Greenwich Village.

Ellen Frankel, Editor-in-Chief at the Jewish Publication Society; Sharon Friedman, of John Hawkins and Associates; Herb Levine; Rebecca Mancini; Stephan Ip.

Many others have given advice, suggestions, corrections and information: Karen Alkalay-Gut, Maurice Clapisson, Ruth Feldman, Yael Feldman, John Felstiner, Norman Finkelstein, Ruth Frank, Serge Gavronsky, Louise Glück, Robert W. Greene, Linda Gutstein, Judith Hemschemeyer, John Hollander, Barry Holtz, Richard Howard, Jim Kates, Shirley Kaufman, Edna King-Smith, Elizabeth Macklin, Stephen Mitchell, Michèle Montas, Alicia Ostriker, Linda Pastan, Nicanor Parra, David Roskies, Shimon Sandbank, Harvey Shapiro, Adriana Valdés, Burton L. Visotzky, Chris Wallace-Crabbe, Ruth Whitman, Anne Winters, Leonard Wolf, Linda Zisquit.

Grateful acknowledgment is made to the following:

"In the Beginning" from *Collected Poems* by Primo Levi. English translation copyright © 1988 by Ruth Feldman and Brian Swann. Reprinted by permission of Faber and Faber, Inc. and Faber and Faber, Ltd., Publishers.

"The Great Explosion" from *The Beginning and the End and Other Poems* by Robinson Jeffers. Copyright © 1954, 1963 by Garth Jeffers and Donnan Jeffers. Reprinted by permission of Random House, Inc.

"Big Bang or Whatever" by Eugenio Montale, translated by Ruth Feldman. Reprinted by permission of the translator.

"When God First Said" reprinted by permission of Atheneum Publishers, an imprint of Macmillan Publishing Company, from *The Static Element:*

"Genesis" by Eva Tóth, translated by Peter Jay. Reprinted by permission of the translator.

"Adam" by Yevgeny Vinokurov from *Post-War Russian Poetry*, ed. by Daniel Weissbort. Reprinted by permission of the translator.

"As Yet Unborn" by Stanley H. Barkan from *The Blacklines Scrawl*. Reprinted by permission of Cross-Cultural Communications, Publisher.

"The Gift" copyright © 1976, 1977, 1978, 1979, 1980 by Louise Glück. From *Descending Figure* by Louise Glück, first published by The Ecco Press in 1980. Reprinted by permission.

"Spider" copyright © 1991 by Czeslaw Milosz Royalties, Inc. From *Provinces: Poems 1987–1991* by Czeslaw Milosz, first published by The Ecco Press in 1991. Reprinted by permission.

"Adam's Task" from *Selected Poetry* by John Hollander. Copyright © 1993 by John Hollander. Reprinted by permission of Alfred A. Knopf, Inc.

"Naming the Animals" from *The Transparent Man* by Anthony Hecht. Copyright © 1990 by Anthony Hecht. Reprinted by permission of Alfred A. Knopf, Inc.

"Eve Names the Animals" from *Eve Names the Animals* by Susan Donnelly. Copyright © 1985 by Susan Donnelly. Reprinted with the permission of Northeastern University Press, Boston.

"Linnaeus" copyright © 1991 by Czeslaw Milosz Royalties, Inc. From *Provinces: Poems 1987–1991* by Czeslaw Milosz, first published by The Ecco Press in 1991. Reprinted by permission.

"One Flesh" by Elizabeth Jennings from *Collected Poems*. Published by Carcanet, London. Reprinted by permission.

"Paradise" copyright © 1990 by Louise Glück. From *Ararat* by Louise Glück, first published by The Ecco Press. Reprinted by permission.

"Never Again Would Birds' Song Be the Same" from *The Poetry of Robert Frost* edited by Edward Connery Lathem. Copyright 1942 by Robert Frost. Copyright © 1969 by Holt, Rinehart and Winston. Copyright © 1970 by Lesley Frost Ballantine. Reprinted by permission of Henry Holt and Company, Inc., Jonathan Cape, Publishers, and the Estate of Robert Frost.

From "Silhouette of a Serpent" by Paul Valéry. Reprinted by permission of Princeton University Press.

"Ararat" by Dan Pagis from *Israeli Poetry: A Contemporary Anthology,* selected and translated by Warren Bargad and Stanley F. Chyet. Reprinted by permission of Indiana University Press.

"In the Tower of Babel" by Wislawa Szymborska from *Quarterly Review of Literature Poetry Series IV,* ed. by T. Weiss and R. Weiss. Reprinted by permission of the publisher.

"Genesis" by Jacob Glatstein, translated by Cynthia Ozick, copyright © 1987 by Cynthia Ozick. By permission of the translator and her agents, Raines and Raines.

"The Story of Abraham" by Alicia Ostriker first appeared in *5 PM.* Reprinted by permission of the author.

"Go Forth" by Amir Or. Reprinted by permission of the author.

"The Onus of Mercy" by Yehuda Amichai from *Israeli Poetry: A Contemporary Anthology,* selected and translated by Warren Bargad and Stanley F. Chyet. Reprinted by permission of the publisher, Indiana University Press.

"Covenant" by Allen Afterman from *Purple Adam.* Copyright © 1980 by Allen Afterman. Reprinted by permission of Angus & Robertson, publishers.

"The Destruction of Sodom" reprinted with permission of Atheneum Publishers, an imprint of Macmillan Publishing Company, from *Selected Poems of Daryl Hine,* and Daryl Hine. Copyright © 1960, 1980 by Daryl Hine.

"Gomorrah" reprinted by permission; copyright © 1992 by Christine Holbo. Originally in *The New Yorker.* All rights reserved.

"Lot Later" by Howard Nemerov. Reprinted by permission of the Estate of Howard Nemerov.

"Lot's Wife" from *Poems of Akhmatova.* Copyright © 1973 by Stanley Kunitz and Max Hayward. Permission granted by Stanley Kunitz and Darhansoff & Verrill Literary Agency.

"Lot's Wife" by Wislawa Szymborska from *Quarterly Review of Literature Poetry Series,* ed. by T. Weiss and R. Weiss. Reprinted by permission of the publisher.

"Lot's Wife" from *Poems 1956–1986* by James Simmons, published by The Gallery Press, Lougherew, Oldcastle, County Meath, Ireland.

"Lot and His Daughters II" by A. D. Hope from *Collected Poems.* Copyright © by A. D. Hope. Reprinted by permission of Angus & Robertson, publishers.

"Lot's Daughter" from *Confessions* by Enid Dame. Reprinted by permission of Cross-Cultural Communications, publisher.

"Lot's Son" by Stanley Moss. Copyright © by Stanley Moss. Reprinted by permission of the author.

"Sarah" by Edna Aphek, copyright © Edna Aphek. Translated by Yishai Tobin. Used by permission of Yishai Tobin. Translation copyright © 1979 Yishai Tobin.

"Hagar's Last Night in Abraham's House" by Itsik Manger from *The Treasury of Yiddish Poetry* edited by Irving Howe and Eliezer Greenberg. Copyright © 1969 by Irving Howe and Eliezer Greenberg. Reprinted by permission of Henry Holt and Company, Inc.

"Sacrifice" by H. Leivick, translated by Robert Friend. Reprinted by permission of Robert Friend.

"After Years of Feasting and No Sacrifice" by Linda Zisquit. Reprinted by permission of the author.

"The Parable of the Old Man and the Young" from *The Collected Poems of Wilfred Owen*. Copyright © 1963 by Chatto and Windus, Ltd. Reprinted by permission of New Directions Publishing Corp.

"The Akedah" by Aliza Shenhar. Used by permission of Linda Zisquit. Translation copyright © 1979 by Linda Zisquit.

"Photograph" copyright © 1985 by Zbigniew Herbert. From *Report from the Besieged City and Other Poems* by Zbigniew Herbert, first published by The Ecco Press in 1985. Reprinted by permission.

"The Sacrifice" by Chana Bloch. Copyright © by Chana Bloch. Reprinted by permission of Sheep Meadow Press.

"Isaac" from *The Light of Lost Suns: Selected Poems of Amir Gilboa*, translated by Shirley Kaufman, Persea Books 1979. Reprinted by permission of the translator.

"My Father Isaac" by Jacob Glatstein from *The Treasury of Yiddish Poetry* edited by Irving Howe and Eliezer Greenberg. Reprinted by permission of Henry Holt and Company, Inc.

"Esau's Letter" by Aharon Amir, translated by Gabriel Levin. Reprinted by permission of the translator.

"The Tune to Jacob" by Rivka Miriam, translated by Linda Zisquit. Reprinted by permission of the translator.

"Leah" from *From One Life to Another* by Shirley Kaufman, University of Pittsburgh Press, 1979. Reprinted by permission of the author.

"Israel" by Yitzhak Lamdan, translated by Ruth Finer Mintz from *Modern Hebrew Poetry: A Bilingual Anthology*. Reprinted by permission of University of California Press.

"Peniel" by Kevin Hart. Reprinted by permission of Golvan Arts, Publishers.

"Jacob and the Angel" from *Selected Poetry of Yehuda Amichai*, edited and translated by Chana Bloch and Stephen Mitchell. English language translation copyright © 1986 by Chana Bloch and Stephen Mitchell. Reprinted by permission of HarperCollins Publishers Inc.

"Last Words" first appeared in *The ThreePenny Review* and appears in the poetry collection *The Father* by Sharon Olds, published May 1992 by Alfred A. Knopf, NYC. Reprinted by permission of the author.

"Like Rachel" from *The Window* by Dahlia Ravikovitch, edited and translated by Chana Bloch and Ariel Bloch. Reprinted by permission of Sheep Meadow Press.

"Twelve Lines About the Burning Bush" by Melech Ravitch from *An Anthology of Modern Yiddish Poetry*, selected and translated by Ruth Whitman, was published by October House in 1966 and reprinted by the Workmen's Circle in 1979. Reprinted by permission of the translator.

"Exodus" by Harvey Shapiro from *Battle Report*, copyright © 1966 by Harvey Shapiro. Reprinted by permission of University Press of New England.

"Dead Men Don't Praise God" from *The Selected Poems of Jacob Glatstein*, translated by Ruth Whitman, was published by October House in 1972. Reprinted by permission of the translator.

"God of Mercy" by Kadya Molodovsky. Irving Howe, translator, from *The Penguin Book of Modern Yiddish Verse* by Irving Howe, Ruth R. Weisse and Khone Shmeruk. Copyright © 1987 by Irving Howe, Ruth Weisse, and Khone Shmeruk. Introduction and copyright notes copyright © 1987 by Irving Howe. Used by permission of Viking Penguin, a division of Penguin Books USA Inc.

"Biographical Note" by Gabriel Preil, translated by Howard Schwarz. Used by permission of Howard Schwarz.

"The Old Idea of Sacrifice" by D. H. Lawrence from *The Complete Poems of D. H. Lawrence* by D. H. Lawrence. Copyright © 1964, 1971 by Angelo Ravagli and C. M. Weekley, Executors of the Estate of Frieda Lawrence

Ravagli. Used by permission of Viking Penguin, a division of Penguin Books USA Inc., and Lawrence Pollinger Ltd.

"Manna" from *Collected Poems* by Samuel Menashe, published by The National Poetry Foundation of the University of Maine, Orono, Maine. Reprinted by permission of the author.

"Amalek" by Friederich Torberg. Translation copyright © 1979 by Erna Baber Rosenfeld.

"The Death of Moses" by Rainer Maria Rilke, from *The Unknown Rilke: Expanded Edition*, translated by Franz Wright. Reprinted by permission of Oberlin College Press, Field Translation Series.

"The Story of Joshua" by Alicia Ostriker first appeared in *Lilith*. Reprinted by permission of the author.

"Joshua at Shechem" copyright © 1976 by Charles Reznikoff. Reprinted from *The Complete Poems of Charles Reznikoff* by permission of Black Sparrow Press.

"Devorah" by Janet Ruth Heller from *Primavera*, copyright © 1975 by Janet Ruth Heller. Reprinted by permission of the author.

"His Mother" by Haim Gouri from *Israeli Poetry: A Contemporary Anthology*, selected and translated by Warren Bargad and Stanley F. Chyet. Reprinted by permission of Indiana University Press, Publisher.

"Ashkelon Beach" by Yehuda Amichai, translated by Karen Alkalay-Gut. Reprinted by permission of the translator.

"David" from *Poems: 1930–1960* by Josephine Miles. Reprinted by permission of Indiana University Press, Publisher.

From "Autobiography, New York" by Charles Reznikoff. Copyright © 1977 by Marie Syrkin Reznikoff. Reprinted from *The Complete Poems of Charles Reznikoff* with the permission of Black Sparrow Press.

"The Giant on Giant-Killing" by Richard Howard. Reprinted by permission of the author.

"Portrait of Saul" by Thomas W. Shapcott from *Selected Poems*. Copyright © 1978. Reprinted by permission of University of Queensland Press, publisher.

"And Perhaps Only Music" reprinted by permission of Atheneum Publishers, an imprint of Macmillan Publishing Company from *The Static Element: Selected Poems of Natan Zach*, translated by Peter Everwine and Shulamut Yasney-Starkman. Copyright © 1977, 1982 by Peter Everwine.

"Michal" by Anna Akhmatova is translated by Judith Hemschemeyer, and reprinted from Volume I of *The Complete Poems of Anna Akhmatova* (Zephyr Press, 1990), with permission of the publisher. Translation copyright © 1989 by Judith Hemschemeyer.

"Michal" by Rachel, translated by Robert Friend. Reprinted by permission of Robert Friend.

"Devotion to Duty" by Siegfried Sassoon. Reprinted by permission of George Sassoon.

"Abishag" by Rainer Maria Rilke from *New Poems* (1907) by Rainer Maria Rilke, translation copyright © 1984 by Edward Snow. Published by North Point Press and reprinted by permission of Farrar, Straus & Giroux, Inc.

"Abishag" from *Selected Poems of Yankev Glatshtyen*, translated by Richard J. Fein. Reprinted by permission of The Jewish Publication Society, publisher.

"Abishag" by Shirley Kaufman from *Claims*, The Sheep Meadow Press, 1984. Reprinted by permission of the author.

"Abishag Writes a Letter Home" by Itsik Manger from *An Anthology of Modern Yiddish Poetry*, translated by Ruth Whitman, was published by October House in 1966 and reprinted by the Workmen's Circle in 1979. Reprinted by permission of the translator.

"King David Old" from *History* by Robert Lowell. Copyright © 1973 by Robert Lowell. Reprinted by permission of Farrar, Straus & Giroux, Inc. and Faber and Faber Ltd., publishers.

"Provide, Provide" from *The Poetry of Robert Frost* edited by Edward Connery Lathem. Copyright 1942 by Robert Frost. Copyright © 1969 by Holt, Rinehart and Winston. Copyright © 1970 by Lesley Frost Ballantine. Reprinted by permission of Henry Holt and Company, Inc., Jonathan Cape, publishers, and the Estate of Robert Frost.

"O to Be a Dragon," copyright © 1957 by Marianne Moore, renewed 1985 by Lawrence E. Brinn and Louise Crane, Executors of the Estate of Marianne Moore, from *The Complete Poems of Marianne Moore* by Marianne Moore. Used by permission of Viking Penguin, a division of Penguin Books USA Inc.

"Solomon to Sheba" reprinted with permission of Macmillan Publishing Company from *The Collected Works of W. B. Yeats*, Vol. I: *The Poems*, revised, edited by Richard J. Finneran. Copyright 1919 by Macmillan Publishing Company, renewed 1947 by Bertha Georgie Yeats.

From "The Visit of the Queen of Sheba" from *Selected Poetry of Yehuda Amichai*, edited and translated by Chana Bloch and Stephen Mitchell. English language translation copyright © 1986 by Chana Bloch and Stephen Mitchell. Reprinted by permission of HarperCollins Publishers Inc. and the author.

"A Turtle from Oxford" copyright © 1989 by Paulina Wat, translation © 1989 by Czeslaw Milosz and Leonard Nathan. From *With the Skin: Poems of Aleksander Wat*, published by The Ecco Press in 1989. Reprinted by permission.

From "Elegy for the Queen of Sheba" from *The Collected Poetry* by Léopold Sédar Senghor (Charlottesville: Virginia, 1991). Reprinted by permission of the University Press of Virginia.

"On Woman" reprinted with permission of Macmillan Publishing Company from *The Collected Works of W. B. Yeats*, Vol. I: *The Poems*, revised, edited by Richard J. Finneran. Copyright © 1919 by Macmillan Publishing Company, renewed 1947 by Bertha Georgie Yeats.

"I Saw" by Natan Zach, translated by Gabriel Preil and David Curzon. Reprinted by permission of the author and translators.

"The Weariness of the Prophet Elijah" by Anna Kamenska. Reprinted by permission of Daniel Weissbort, *Modern Poetry in Translation*.

"Jezreel" from *The Collected Poems of Thomas Hardy*. New York, Macmillan 1978.

"Vacillation" reprinted with permission of Macmillan Publishing Company from *The Collected Works of W. B. Yeats*, Vol. I: *The Poems*, revised, edited by Richard J. Finneran. Copyright © 1919 by Macmillan Publishing Company, renewed 1947 by Bertha Georgie Yeats.

"Nachtwache" from *Collected Poems* by Primo Levi. English translation copyright © 1988 by Ruth Feldman and Brian Swann. Reprinted by permission of Faber and Faber, Inc. and Faber and Faber Ltd., publishers.

"You Be Like You" by Paul Celan, translated by John Felstiner. Reprinted by permission of the translator.

"Small Moment" by Howard Nemerov. Reprinted by permission of the Estate of Howard Nemerov.

"Just Think" by Paul Celan, translated by John Felstiner. Reprinted by permission of the translator.

"Like the Streams in the Negev" from *Even a Fist Was Once an Open Palm with Fingers* by Yehuda Amichai, selected and translated by Barbara and Benjamin Harshav. Copyright © 1991 by Yehuda Amichai. English translation copyright © 1991 by HarperCollins Publishers. Reprinted by permission of HarperCollins Publishers Inc.

"The Cosmos Is His Sanctuary" (Psalm 150) by Ernesto Cardenal, translated by Donald D. Walsh, from *Apocalypse and Other Poems*. Copyright © 1977 by Ernesto Cardenal and Danald D. Walsh. Reprinted by permission of New Directions Publishing Corporation.

"Proverbs 3:1" by David Curzon from *Midrashim*. Reprinted by permission of Cross-Cultural Communications, publisher.

"Homily" by Dan Pagis from *Points of Departure*, translated by Stephen Mitchell. Reprinted by permission of The Jewish Publication Society, publisher.

"Summary" by Wislawa Szymborska from *Quarterly Review of Literature Poetry Series*, volume 23, edited by T. Weiss and R. Weiss. Reprinted by permission of the publisher.

From "More Poems" from *The Collected Poems of A. E. Housman*. Copyright © 1936 by Barclays Bank Ltd., copyright © 1964 by Robert E. Symons, copyright © 1965 by Holt, Rinehart and Winston, Inc. Reprinted by permission of Henry Holt and Company, Inc.

"As the Sparks Fly Upward" from *The Night Mirror: Poems by John Hollander*. Copyright © 1972 by John Hollander. Reprinted by permission of the author.

"O the Chimneys" from *O The Chimneys* by Nelly Sachs. Copyright © 1967 by Farrar, Straus & Giroux, Inc. Reprinted by permission of Farrar, Straus & Giroux Inc., and Suhrkamp Verlag.

"Birds and Fishes" from *The Beginning and the End* by Robinson Jeffers. Copyright © 1963 by Steuben Glass. Reprinted by permission of Random House Inc.

From "The Second Happiness of Job" by Anna Kamienska. Reprinted by permission of Daniel Weissbort, *Modern Poetry in Translation*.

Extracts from "A Masque of Reason" from *The Poetry of Robert Frost* edited by Edward Connery Lathem. Copyright 1945, 1947 by Robert Frost. Copyright © 1969 by Holt, Rinehart and Winston. Copyright © 1973 by Lesley Frost Ballantine. Reprinted by permission of Henry Holt and Company, Inc., Jonathan Cape, publishers, and the Estate of Robert Frost.

"Poem of Explanations" from *The Window: Poems* by Dahlia Ravikovitch, translated and edited by Chana Bloch and Ariel Bloch. Reprinted by permission of the translators.

"Deathsfugue" by Paul Celan, translated by John Felstiner. Reprinted by permission of the translator.

"Song of Songs" by Iakovos Kambanelis, translated by Gail Holst Warhaft. Reprinted by permission of the author and the translator.

"The Book of Ruth and Naomi" from *Mars and Her Children* by Marge Piercy. Copyright © 1992 by Middlemarsh, Inc. Reprinted by permission of Alfred A. Knopf, Inc.

"Naomi" by Anna Kamienska. Reprinted by permission of Daniel Weissbort, *Modern Poetry in Translation.*

"Ecclesiastes 1:9" from *La Cifra* by Jorge Luis Borges. Copyright © 1988, 1989 by Emece Editores, S.A., Buenos Aires and Maria Kodama, Executrix, the Estate of Jorge Luis Borges. Translated from the Spanish by David Curzon and Leonor Maia-Sampaio. Reprinted by permission of the Estate of Jorge Luis Borges and the translators. All rights reserved.

Psalm 1 from the Revised Standard Version of the Bible, copyright © 1946, 1952, 1971 by the Division of Christian Education of the National Council of the Churches of Christ in the USA. Used by permission.

Psalm 126, translated by Ya'acov Hanoch and David Curzon. Used by permission of the translators.

Every effort has been made to contact the copyright holders for the works which appear herein. If any omissions are brought to our attention we will correct them in our next printing.

Modern Poems on the Bible

AN ANTHOLOGY

Introduction

THE GENRE OF MIDRASH: A LIVING TRADITION

> *God speaks:*
> *"I am not always fond of what I create.*
> *For instance, this man."*
> Alain Bosquet, "God's Torment"

> *My brother invented murder.*
> Dan Pagis, "Autobiography"

> *If I, like Solomon, . . .*
> *could have my wish—*
> Marianne Moore, "O to Be a Dragon"

This anthology offers a contemporary version of an old and serious pleasure, the name of which is midrash. In choosing the twentieth-century poems collected here, and in placing opposite them the short biblical passages to which they respond, I have been guided by my understanding of this genre, conceived at least 1500 years ago. Whether the poets knew it or not, and some of them did, they were writing midrash. Their reactions to biblical texts are both strikingly modern and within an ancient genre. The following introductory pages characterize those pleasures of midrash common to its new and old forms.

What did Adam think about when reminiscing in his old age? Why did Lot's wife look back? When Jacob discovered on his wedding night that he had Leah in his bed and not Rachel, what did Leah say? What did the manna taste like?

Some of these questions are answered in the rabbinic flights of interpretive imagination known collectively as the Midrash. And some are answered in the poems collected here. Both the rabbis and the poets fill in details of settings, thoughts, motives, and talk not given by the terse biblical narrative. And both also respond with speculation, argument, and wit to the psalms, proverbs, com-

3

mandments, and prophecies of biblical passages and books that are not narratives.

What was the rabbinic Midrash? The word *midrash* (plural: *midrashim*) is a Hebrew noun derived from a verb meaning to search out, to seek, to inquire. The midrashic literature consists of summaries of sermons and fragments of exposition and debate by rabbis living during the Roman period, edited anonymously between the fifth and eleventh centuries. Each of the five books of the Torah and each of many other books of the Hebrew Bible (known in the Christian tradition as the Old Testament) has an associated collection of these midrashim arranged in the order of the verses on which they comment.[1]

It occurred to me a few years ago that a similar collection could be made of midrashim by twentieth-century writers. I knew of many poems by well-known modern poets on the Creation, the Expulsion from Paradise, the Flood, the Tower of Babel. There were also dozens of poems on problematic biblical characters like Cain, Saul, David, and Jonah and on victims, particularly women such as Lot's wife, Hagar, Leah, and Abishag. Some poets manage to retain a contemporary sensibility while writing of biblical material, so that their poems on sacrifice and murder, and love and the lack of love, combine modernity with the resonance and depth of the ancient texts. "My brother invented murder," says the Israeli poet Dan Pagis in the name of Abel.

This engagement with biblical material, like all living traditions, assists the free imagination avoid solipsism. It permits the type of seriousness and wit possible only in relation to known stories and propositions, the fundamental wit of variance from what is established, of originality grounded in the familiar.

So, what did the manna taste like? The Midrash gives many answers, including this one:

> Another explanation of BEHOLD I WILL CAUSE TO RAIN BREAD FROM HEAVEN FOR YOU (Exodus 16:4). . . . When a man desired anything special to eat he had only to say "I wish I had a fat capon to eat" and the morsel of manna in his mouth immediately acquired the taste of fat capon. They had only to say the word and the Lord performed their will. Rabbi Abba said: They were even spared the utterance of their wish, for God fulfilled the thought still in their heart and they tasted their heart's desire.[2]

This typical midrash has three basic characteristics: it is a response to a specific and very short biblical text, the response is imaginative, and it makes a point.[3] The introductory phrase "another explanation" is also worth noting because it indicates that the genre is a tolerant one; a midrash is one response among many possibilities, not some definitive interpretation. This anthology is a collection of twentieth-century poems selected with these basic characteristics in mind.

MIDRASHIC TECHNIQUES OF TWENTIETH-CENTURY POETS

It is possible to respond to a biblical narrative by retelling or elaborating on the story; and to a biblical assertion or proposition by arguing against it, arguing in favor of it, or explaining its meaning. The ways in which the rabbis of the Midrash and twentieth-century poets used such techniques of response when applying their imagination to the text are illustrated in this section.

Narrative: Lot's Wife Looks Back

Most modern poets, like the rabbis, respond to the terse and archaic narrative style of the text with elaborations and anachronisms. The dove that Noah had sent forth returned with an olive leaf in its beak. Where on earth did the dove pick it up? Genesis 8:11 doesn't tell us, but the Midrash does: "Rabbi Levi said: She brought it from the Mount of Olives, for the land of Israel was not submerged by the Flood."[4] Similarly, in 1 Kings 10 we are told that the Queen of Sheba had "heard of Solomon's fame." But what exactly had she heard? The text doesn't linger over such ornamentation, but Yehuda Amichai, in his poem "The Visit of the Queen of Sheba," tells us that "She had been brought/a vague report/about circumcision." Why did Lot's wife look back while fleeing from Sodom? The text is silent on her motivations. The rabbis of the Midrash thought "Her mother love made her look behind," to see if her daughters were following.[5] In Wislawa Szymborska's poem "Lot's Wife," however, the wife speaks, and hints at quite different motives, such as "Not to look any more at the righteous nape/Of my husband, Lot." Both the rabbis and the poets have their agenda and bring them blatantly and fruitfully to the text.

What did the characters do outside their moments in the biblical narrative? Jorge Luis Borges apparently asked himself what Adam thought about in his old age—he lived to be 930—when, in a reflective mood, he mused on his salad days in the Garden of Eden and his subsequent disappointments after such a promising beginning. In Borges's poem "Adam Cast Forth," Adam speaks and, after allowing himself some bitterness concerning "the incestuous wars/Of Cains and Abels and their progeny," is led to this conclusion:

> Nevertheless, it means much to have loved,
> To have been happy, to have touched upon
> The living Garden, even for one day.

Like Borges and many of the other poets represented here, the rabbis of the Midrash also report the thoughts and talk omitted by the text. When Jacob found out that it was Leah and not Rachel in his bed, what did Leah have to say in her own defense? The rabbis tell us she retorted that she learned deceit from Jacob himself: "When your father called you Esau, just before he gave you his blessing, didn't you say, Here I am?"[6] Rivka Miriam, in "The Tune to Jacob Who Removed the Stone from the Mouth of the Well," presents a more diffident and subjective view: "He didn't know I was Leah/and I—I was Leah."

Sympathy with secondary characters often yields surprising and illuminating narrative viewpoints. And the characters don't even have to be human. Dan Pagis, reflecting on what happened as the Flood subsided, ends his poem "Ararat" with ruminations on the fish who had, admittedly, "lived/off the mishap like smooth speculators" but who were now "drowning in air."

The rabbis and the poets use the technique of an omniscient narrator to elaborate on matters left up to the imagination by the terseness of the text. For example, although the plants had been created on the third day, the Midrash states that "God did not permit them to sprout and appear above the surface of the earth until Adam prayed to Him to give them food, for God longs for the prayers of the pious."[7] What did Adam dream about after his first day in the Garden? Yevgeny Vinokurov, a Russian poet who fought in the Second World War, tells us by means of an omniscient narrator. Entering the Genesis narrative prior to the Eating of the Fruit gives Vinokurov a means of meditating on and representing a mind without knowledge of evil. His narrator informs us that Adam dreamed of "ditches filled with corpses" and

> in the bliss
> Of paradise, his face lit up.
> He slept, understanding nothing,
> Not knowing good and evil yet.

Edmond Jabès, in his prose poem "Adam, or the Birth of Anxiety," meditates on the related issue of Adam as a man "without childhood, without past." And W. H. Auden, in *Horae Canonicae*, "Prime," compares himself a moment after he wakes up in the morning to "Adam sinless in our beginning,/Adam still previous to any act."

The emblematic situations of the biblical stories invite not only elaboration but also application to the contemporary self. Eavan Boland, for example, is reminded of "The Serpent in the Garden" when she is putting on her makeup, noticing "the hood/I have made/for my eyes" and the tongue flicking over her lips. Louise Glück, in "The Gift," looks at her young son (after he has just begun to talk) standing at the screen door "welcoming each beast/in love's name." And by this allusion to Adam naming the beasts in Genesis 2:18–20, a small domestic scene in late twentieth-century America is made universal.

Proposition: Big Bang or Whatever

Both the rabbis of the Midrash and twentieth-century poets respond to the nonnarrative parts of the Bible as well as to its stories. Here, even more than with narrative, the need for midrash comes from the historic development of new circumstances, ideas, and values that, from at least the Hellenistic period onward, have appeared incompatible with much of the ancient biblical writings. For the sake of maintaining the continued vitality of the text, new interpretations have been needed every generation or so. The standard example is the early rabbinic interpretation of the law of compensation for damages in Exodus, 21:24 ("eye for eye, tooth for tooth, hand for hand") as meaning monetary compensation. In other cases the text contains a "dark saying" whose meaning has been lost or is otherwise in need of explication. Ecclesiastes 7:1, for example, reads: "The day of death [is better] than the day of one's birth." The rabbis interpreted this seemingly nihilistic remark by observing that "when the righteous are born nobody feels any difference, but when they die everybody feels it."[8]

The story of the Creation can, of course, be treated as a narrative, as is done by Alain Bosquet in his poem "God's Torment," where God, referring to " 'my strangest creatures:/the dragon, the angel and the unicorn,' " tells us that "to avoid certain misunderstandings/I thought it proper in any event to make them invisible.' " But the opening of Genesis can also be treated as a proposition about the origins of the universe. This is how Primo Levi responded in his poem "In the Beginning," using the biblical conception of a Creator:

> Twenty billion years before now,
> Brilliant, soaring in space and time,

There was a ball of flame, solitary, eternal,
Our common father and our executioner.
It exploded, and every change began.

In Primo Levi's poem, and in the poems by Eugenio Montale ("Big Bang or Whatever") and Robinson Jeffers ("The Great Explosion"), the proposition "God created heaven and earth" has been resisted by countering it with scientific understanding. Other poets in this anthology use the language and subject matter of biblical propositions more directly. Marianne Moore, for example, starts her poem "Blessed Is the Man" with a direct quotation from Psalm 1:1 and continues by elaborating, in her own terms, on the nature of persons who are blessed, producing an American version of the first psalm. The Australian poet A. D. Hope defends God's creation (and His aesthetic sense) with amiable rationality and poetic skill in "Protest to Fred Hoyle" by arguing against that astrophysicist's proposition that leaves would be more efficient if they were not green but black. And D. H. Lawrence, in "The Old Idea of Sacrifice," has written the one twentieth-century poem I could find that defends the slaughter of animals for sacrificial purposes, the laws of which are described at length in Leviticus and elsewhere.

Only some texts are propositions. But all texts can be treated as propositions, just as any text can be made part of a narrative. For example, Charles Reznikoff starts his poem "Autobiography, New York" by saying "I do not believe that David killed Goliath./It must have been—/you will find the name in the list of David's captains." Here, Reznikoff is reacting to the narrative as history. In other words, he was arguing against the implicit proposition that it actually was David who killed Goliath. Having informed his readers by this means that he considers the text to be an artful retelling of history, Reznikoff returns to the narrative ("But, whoever it was, he was no fool") and gently pushes it in the direction of an allegory about fighting with your own weapons in your own way. Similarly, Marianne Moore's poem "O to Be a Dragon" is based on the narrative of 1 Kings 3:5–15, where we are told that "At Gibeon the Lord appeared to Solomon in a dream by night; and God said, 'Ask, what shall I grant you?'" The implicit proposition (for those with the self-confidence to assume God is as pleased with them as He was with Solomon) is that God sometimes grants us our wishes. Marianne Moore's wish was to be a "felicitous phenomenon," a Chinese dragon. The Midrash reads propositions into biblical narrative very often since the rabbis assume that all biblical stories have an infinite number of lessons to teach us. The most sustained reading along these lines concerns the Song of Songs, called in some translations the Song of Solomon, which seems to the modern reader a collection of ravishing love lyrics strung together to make a slightly obscure story. But in the Midrash the Song of Songs is treated as a series of allegorical propositions. The man behind this *tour de force* of unlikely interpretation was Rabbi Akiva, who, to his everlasting credit, managed to get the Song of Songs into the sacred canon around 1900 years ago on the grounds that it was an allegory. And so exclamations such as "Thy lips, O my bride, drop honey" receive interpretations in the Midrash such as this from Rabbi Jose: "If one discourses on the Torah and his words are not as tasteful to his hearers as honey from the comb it were better that he had not spoken."[9]

Another way of responding to text as proposition is to ask: How could this apply to a contemporary such as myself? John Hollander's poem "As the Sparks Fly Upward," for example, is a meditation in a contemporary suburban setting on the great proposition in Job 5:7 that "man is born unto trouble as the sparks fly upward." Anthony Hecht's poem "Destinations" has as its epigraph Jeremiah's proposition "The harvest is past, the summer is ended, and we are not saved"; the poem is on the breakup of a marriage. And Dahlia Ravikovitch, in her "Poem of Explanations," picks up the Shulammite's warning in Song of Songs 2:7 to be careful about stirring up love, and comments:

> Some people know how to love,
> for others it's just not right.
> Some people kiss in the street,
> others find it unpleasant
> —and not only in the street.
>
> I think it's a talent like any other.

Comparison and Parable: A Reparations Agreement

A common rabbinic response to a difficult passage is to ask "To what may this be compared?" For example, Psalm 11:5 states, "The Lord trieth the righteous." Rabbi Jonathan said: "A potter does not test defective vessels." Rabbi Eleazer said: "When a man has two cows, one strong and the other feeble, upon which does he put the yoke? Surely upon the strong one."[10] For the rabbis, the biblical text is central and, where puzzling, in need of explanation by comparisons and parables drawn from daily life. But for contemporary poets it is usually daily life that is troubling and the biblical text that provides a comparison and clarification. The arrival of a sibling can be a trauma for the firstborn child. To what may this be compared? Louise Glück, in her poem "Paradise," compares it to God taking a rib from Adam to make Eve:

> Like Adam,
> I was the firstborn.
> Believe me, you never heal,
> you never forget the ache in your side,
> the place where something was taken away
> to make another person.

Yehuda Amichai, in his poem "Like the Streams in the Negev," describes his situation, in which sudden moments of happiness well up and then dissipate, and then recalls the simile in Psalm 126:4 referring to the sudden appearance and disappearance of streams in the Negev desert:

> I sit in a café in the afternoon hours.
> My sons are grown, my daughter is dancing somewhere else.
> I have no baby carriage, no newspaper, no God.
>
> . . .
>
> Sometimes suddenly tears of happiness well up in me
> as an empty street suddenly fills up with cars
> when the light changes at a distant intersection,
> or like the streams in the Negev
> that suddenly fill up with torrents of water from a distant rain.
> Afterward, again silence, empty
> *Like the streams in the Negev, like the streams in the Negev.*

Gabriel Preil makes similar use of the simplest of actions, described in Psalm 121:1 ("I will lift up mine eyes unto the mountains:/From whence shall my help come?") in his poem "Like David." Preil has a wonderful sense of continuity with King David, to whom tradition ascribes authorship of the Psalms:

> Like David the pursued I raise my eyes to the mountains:
> so slight are the differences of the valleys that indicate
> the map of helplessness in his days and in mine.

These three poets make use of biblical texts for explicit comparisons. But there is at least one example in this anthology of a modern parable based on an implicit comparison with a biblical text, Ezekiel's vision of the Valley of Dry Bones. In the vision, after sinews and flesh and skin have been restored to the bones and breath has entered them and they have stood up and been identified as "the whole House of Israel," God tells Ezekiel (chap. 37:12) to say: "I am going to open your graves, and lift you out of the graves, O My people, and bring you to the land of Israel." Dan Pagis, a survivor who emigrated to Israel after the Second World War, in his poem "Draft of a Reparations Agreement," has God agree to perform a miracle, like the one shown to Ezekiel, for those who perished in the Holocaust:

> Everything will be returned to its place,
> paragraph after paragraph.
> The scream back into the throat.
> The gold teeth back to the gums.
> The terror.
> The smoke back to the tin chimney and further on and inside
> back to the hollow of the bones,
> and already you will be covered with skin and sinews and you
>   will live,
> look, you will have your lives back,
> sit in the living room, read the evening paper.

Deconstruction: When Trouble Came

When God tells Abraham in Genesis 22:2 to sacrifice Isaac, He says "Take your son, your only son, whom you love, Isaac," and go to the land of Moriah. The rabbis noticed the circumlocution, and, assuming God had no need for circumlocution and imagining Abraham might be a little reluctant to understand these instructions, explained the apparent redundancy by means of the following dialogue:

GOD:	Take your son.
ABRAHAM:	I have two sons; I don't know which you mean.
GOD:	Your only son.
ABRAHAM:	One is the only son of his mother, and the other is the only son of his mother.
GOD:	Whom you love.
ABRAHAM:	I love this one and I love that one.
GOD:	Isaac.[11]

Such deconstruction of the text and interweaving of responses to each component is also used by modern poets. Anne Winters breaks up the opening of Genesis in her poem "The First Verse" and inserts her ruminations after each word of the text. Louis MacNiece uses phrases from Psalm 23 in a similar manner, as do other poets writing in response to the Psalms. MacNiece wrote his poem "Whit Monday" during the blitz of London in the Second World War:

> *The Lord's my shepherd*—familiar words of myth
> Stand up better to bombs than a granite monolith,
> Perhaps there is something in them. *I'll not want*—
> Not when I'm dead.

Even a single phrase, if it is recognizably biblical, can be handled in this way. For example, a well-known passage in Job, chapter 3, ends:

> [25]For the thing which I did fear is come upon me,
> And that which I was afraid of hath overtaken me.
> [26]I was not at ease, neither was I quiet, neither had
> I rest; But trouble came.

Shakespeare himself probably couldn't hold his own against Job 3:20–26, but A. E. Housman tries and, in his untitled poem on the same general subject matter as the Job passage, skillfully imitates the rhythmic isolation of the final words:

> The thoughts of others
>   Were light and fleeting,
>   Of lovers' meeting
>   Or luck or fame.
> Mine were of trouble,
>   And mine were steady,
>   So I was ready
>   When trouble came.

Implicit Proof-Texts

Traditional midrash draws on material from other parts of the canon as the primary evidence for interpretations of the text under discussion. The way this method works can be seen most easily if we look again at the example introduced a few pages back, this time with two proof-texts in place:

> Another explanation of BEHOLD I WILL CAUSE TO RAIN BREAD FROM HEAVEN FOR YOU (Exodus 16:4). It is written "Thou openest Thy hand, and satisfiest every living thing with favour" (Psalm 145:16). . . . It does not say every living

thing with "food" but with "favour", that is, He grants to each one his request. In the millennium, too, God will grant the request of each individual. Should you wonder at this, then see what He has done for Israel in this world, when He brought down for them the manna, in which all kinds of flavours lodged, so that each Israelite could taste therein anything he particularly liked, for it is written, "These forty years the Lord thy God hath been with thee; thou hast lacked nothing" (Deut. 2:7). What is the meaning of "thou hast lacked nothing"? When a man desired anything special to eat he had only to say "I wish I had a fat capon to eat" and the morsel of manna in his mouth immediately acquired the taste of fat capon. They had only to say the word and the Lord performed their will. Rabbi Abba said: They were even spared the utterance of their wish, for God fulfilled the thought still in their heart and they tasted their heart's desire.

This rabbinic explanation of the verse from Exodus starts by quoting a proof-text from Psalm 145 and discussing its meaning because it is in the light of this reading of the proof-text that the initial text is to be understood. Whoever created this midrash (the "darshan") understands Psalm 145:16 to mean that when God "opens His hand" He satisfies each individual's desires. If so, and if the manna falling from heaven is an example of God opening His hand, then it follows that the manna tasted different to each person and tasted like whatever that person wanted to eat. This understanding is reinforced by the second proof-text from Deuteronomy 2:7.

Modern poets, particularly those writing in Hebrew, quite often make allusions in one poem to texts from different parts of the biblical canon. For example, the following poem by Natan Zach has three of its six lines derived from biblical texts:

SONG OF A WOMANIZER

I have in my room
    a bed made of wood
which is always in bud.
Night unto night utters speech.   *Psalm 19:3*
From season to season
my couch is leafy.   *Song of Songs 1:16*
I shall not want.   *Psalm 23:1*

Having found this poem I looked up the Midrash and was delighted to discover that its first interpretation of Psalm 23:1 commences with a proof-text from the Song of Songs: "THE LORD IS MY SHEPHERD; I SHALL NOT WANT (Psalm 23:1). These words are to be considered in the light of the verse 'My Beloved is mine and I am His' . . . (Song 2:16)."[12] The anonymous darshan goes on to quote another proof-text from the Song of Songs, "Open to Me, My sister, My love" (5:2), and ends with yet another, "Thy navel is like a round goblet" (7:3; 7:2 in the King James Version). It is clear that both the rabbis and the poet consider the erotic relationship portrayed in the Song of Songs (interpreted by the rabbis allegorically) to be a suitable context in which to ponder the meaning of the opening proposition of Psalm 23:1, "I shall not want."

Few twentieth-century poems use biblical quotations as proof-texts for other biblical quotations. However, most modern midrashic poems draw on a different kind of evidence that does function in the same way as proof-texts in the Midrash. These poems, in other words, present an understanding of biblical texts in the light of something else that is introduced in evidence. In twentieth-century midrashic poems, such implicit proof-texts are drawn from virtually all domains of knowledge, including science, mathematics, history, other religious traditions, and personal experience. The easiest way to illustrate this is to reproduce in midrashic form two twentieth-century poems from the anthology. The examples I've chosen are Primo Levi's poem "In the Beginning" and "Draft of a Reparations Agreement," by Dan Pagis. Before quoting from the poems I have put in my own versions of standard rabbinic formulas used to introduce proof-texts:

> Another interpretation of IN THE BEGINNING GOD CRE-
> ATED THE HEAVEN AND THE EARTH (Gen. 1:1). Primo Levi
> opened his discourse: this is to be understood in terms of
> the current scientific theory of the creation of the universe,
> which assumes that "Twenty billion years before now,/Bril-
> liant, soaring in space and time,/There was a ball of flame,
> solitary, eternal,/Our common father and our executioner."

The reference verse and the function of scientific theory as a proof-text for the midrash on the verse, which were left implicit in the poem, are made explicit here.

> Another interpretation of THUS SAID THE LORD GOD: I AM
> GOING TO OPEN YOUR GRAVES AND LIFT YOU OUT OF YOUR

GRAVES, O MY PEOPLE, AND BRING YOU TO THE LAND OF
ISRAEL (Ezek. 37:12). Dan Pagis opened his discourse: this
is to be understood in the light of the Holocaust, the creation
of the State of Israel, and the concept of a reparations agree-
ment. Under a reparations agreement made by the God
speaking to Ezekiel in the Valley of Dry Bones, "Every-
thing will be returned to its place,/ . . . The scream back into
the throat./The gold teeth back to the gums./The terror./
The smoke back to the tin chimney and further on and
inside/back to the hollow of the bones,/and already you will
be covered with skin and sinews and you will live,/look, you
will have your lives back,/sit in the living room, read the
evening paper."

In this case the proof-texts used in the poem are drawn not from
science but from recent history.

The Verse from Afar

In the Midrash, the proof-text is sometimes located almost adjacent to
the text under consideration. For example, the Ten Commandments
are paired off and one used as a proof-text for the other: "The first
commandment, 'I am the Lord thy God,' corresponds to the sixth,
'Thou shalt not kill,' for the murderer slays the image of God."[13]
Normally, however, the proof-text is located much further away. And,
in a form of sermon summarized in the introductory parts of several
collections of midrashim, the proof-text selected was a "verse from
afar" that did not have any obvious connection to the initial text.[14]
Held in suspense, listeners marveled at the darshan's skillful mental
gymnastics as he spun out his comments on the proof-text without
giving away the denouement, which had to use the verse from afar to
provide an illumination of the initial text. In the following passage,
God plays the darshan with Moses as his audience. God has just told
Moses (Exod. 14:16) to divide the Sea of Reeds:

> Moses replied: "You commanded me to divide the sea, and
> lay bare the dry ground in the midst of it, and yet You
> Yourself made it a perpetual decree that the sand shall
> be the boundary of the sea."
> And again God spoke to Moses: "You haven't read the
> beginning of the Torah, where I said, 'Let the waters

under the heaven be gathered together in one place, and let the dry land appear.' "[15]

Here God applies a verse from afar (Gen. 1:9) directly, not needing to impress his audience by a lengthy buildup to the denouement.[16] The rabbis usually applied verses from even further away in the canon, such as the book of Psalms in the example of the previous section.

The Gospel narratives of the New Testament record many actions and statements of Jesus that allude to or quote texts in the Hebrew Bible. In Christian theology, these actions and statements are considered the fulfillment of such proof-texts, revealing their hidden meaning. Isaac placed on the altar for sacrifice by his father, for example, is seen as a foreshadowing or "type" of the Crucifixion. For those raised in the Christian tradition, the Crucifixion functions as an implicit but powerful mediation of their responses to the Isaac story. In fact, as the term "Old" Testament implies, the whole of the New Testament functions in this way in Christian readings of the Hebrew Bible.[17]

Virtually all the implicit proof-texts of the poems in this anthology are verses from afar, deriving in fact from totally different universes of discourse such as science, history, and personal experience. But some contemporary poets, like the ancient darshans in their sermons, spin out their discussion of, for example, a personal experience that functions as a verse from afar to produce a delayed and surprising relation to a biblical text quoted or alluded to at the end of the poem. Such a procedure is evident in Louise Glück's poem "Paradise" and in Sharon Old's poem "Last Words," where a daughter's meeting with her father on his deathbed is the surprising "context from afar" for the allusion in the last line to Jacob's nocturnal wrestling match in which Jacob says to his protagonist (Gen. 32:27) "I will not let thee go, except thou bless me":

I kept

going back to the mouth he would lift, his
forehead glittering with effort, his eyes
slewing back, shying, until
finally he cried out *Last kiss!*
and I kissed him and left. This morning his wife
called to tell me he has ceased to speak,
so those are his last words to me,
the ones he is leaving me with—and it is ending with a *kiss*—
a command for mercy, the offer of his cracked
creator lips. To plead that I leave,

my father asked me for a kiss! I would not
leave till he had done so, I will not let thee go except
    thou beg for it.

A radical reworking of traditional material has been one of the great
literary projects of the twentieth century, undertaken by Joyce, Eliot,
and Mann and, of course, by Yeats, Borges, Rilke, and all the other
poets whose works appear in this anthology.[18] For writers, a conscious
appropriation of tradition is not only compatible with the expression
of individuality but may often be the means by which it is most fully
realized, as T. S. Eliot argued early in the century in his widely quoted
essay "Tradition and the Individual Talent": "We dwell with satisfac-
tion upon the poet's difference from his predecessors . . . whereas if we
approach a poet without this prejudice we shall often find that not only
the best, but the most individual parts of his work may be those in
which the dead poets, his ancestors, assert their immortality most vig-
orously."[19] Many of the poems in this anthology illustrate Eliot's point.
Abishag, for example, speaks or thinks in strikingly different ways in
the half-dozen poems about her collected here.

Biblical material also provides a means of thinking about current
social and moral issues in fundamental terms. Several poems in the
anthology, for example, deal with the Holocaust. Genesis 1:27 permits
Dan Pagis to say of the murderers:

> No, no: they definitely were
> human beings: uniforms, boots.
> How to explain? They were created
> in the image.

Kadya Molodovsky, as well as others writing in Yiddish, approached
the subject through a bitter reconsideration of the covenant with Abra-
ham and the revelation at Sinai: "Choose—/another people./We are
tired of death, tired of corpses,/We have no more prayers." But most
Jewish and non-Jewish poets writing in Hebrew and other languages
preferred, like Pagis, more universal texts. The refrain in Paul Celan's
"Deathsfugue," surely one of the great poems of the century, alludes
to the Song of Songs; the title of Jaroslav Seifert's litany of names from
the Old Jewish Cemetery in Prague refers to the "Lost Paradise" of
Genesis. Nelly Sachs relates a text from Job to the smoke of "Israel's

body" issuing through "the chimneys/On the ingeniously devised habitations of death."

Another contemporary issue examined by many poems in this anthology is the treatment of women, as is obvious from quotations in prior sections of the introduction. One standard example of a biblical text that is problematical from this perspective is Exodus 19:15, in which Moses gives instructions to all the assembled children of Israel to prepare for the revelation to come: "Be ready for the third day: do not go near a woman." This text invites midrash using what Jonathan Culler (following Elaine Showalter) calls "the hypothesis of a female reader."[20] Unfortunately, I could find no poem on Exodus 19:15. Most poems in this anthology (by men as well as women) that present female and in some cases feminist perspectives have as their overt subjects female biblical characters. However, I would also include under this rubric some poems, such as Alicia Ostriker's "The Story of Abraham," that are about male characters. As Ostriker reports the event, when God commands Abraham to mark their covenant by circumcision the response of the Patriarch is "I'd like to check/Some of this out with my wife." Abraham is told he can't do this because it's "between us men," and the poem goes on to other matters. But a point has been made by means of midrash.

In some cases, the anthology shows a gap, a modern response yet to be written. For example, there are texts that appear to attract only men. Yehuda Amichai, Léopold Sédar Senghor, and Aleksander Wat have all written long poems on the visit of the Queen of Sheba to King Solomon, and William Butler Yeats has three poems on the visit, two of which are reproduced here. Perhaps it may not seem surprising that the tale of a beautiful queen coming all the way from Sheba to go to bed with Solomon, the extraordinarily wise and wealthy king who was also a great lover, attracted only male poets. But this version of the story is not in the text, which has Sheba come to test Solomon "with hard questions," indicating (apart from intelligence and wit on her part) a meeting of minds.[21]

In the world of literary criticism, midrash has assumed importance in recent years because of its resemblance to deconstruction and related currents in literary theory. Geoffrey H. Hartman and Sanford Budick, in their introduction to *Midrash and Literature*, speaking of the midrashic acknowledgment of the open character of texts, refer to "the resemblances between midrash and highly similar critical phenomena which, for whatever reasons, have acquired central importance in contemporary literature, criticism and theory."

By confronting the undecidability of textual meaning, this species of interpretation does not paralyze itself. Instead its own activity is absorbed into the activity of the text, producing a continuum of intertextual supplements, often in a spirit of high-serious play.[22]

Other critics, however, see the relationship between midrash and recent critical theory as more problematical.[23] Robert Alter emphasizes the literary character of the biblical text itself in understanding the nature of the exegesis it has attracted:

The Bible . . . is artfully contrived . . . to open up a dense swarm of variously compelling possibilities, leading us to ponder the imponderables of individual character, human nature, historical causation, revelation, election, and man's encounters with the divine. If all literary texts are open-ended, the Bible, certainly in its narrative aspect, is willfully, provocatively open-ended: that, indeed, is why there is always room for more commentary.[24]

And more midrash.

The genre of midrash gives readers the pleasure of a necessary and feasible participation by requiring them to know the biblical stories and propositions it plays against. By the same token, modern midrash gives its readers a precise expectation of reward in the form of a surprising and contemporary addition to a permanent foundation—something easily memorable, since it fits into the known, and individual, since it is new. Imaginative works of this nature add to the common culture. Because of this I believe they have potentially larger and more grateful audiences than works of idiosyncratic vision that emphasize our alienation from each other, a point that by now no longer needs to be made.

And even though William Blake was sure there is no competition in the Kingdom of Heaven, I believe one pleasure of midrash is that of a genuine competition, a competition in which all new responses with imaginative point can secure their place in a discussion that has continued over millennia down to the end of the twentieth century. Such competition can be seen throughout this anthology in the groups of poems by different poets on the same text.

Akhmatova and Szymborska on Lot's wife; Borges and Kafka and Seifert and Fried and Milosz and Rilke and Auden on the expulsion from Eden. Perhaps Blake is right. There is no competition. These are conversations in the Kingdom of Heaven.

A NOTE ON SELECTION

The Poems

I have selected poems composed in the twentieth century that seem to me both skillfully written and imaginative, intelligible, and interesting responses to one biblical verse or short passage. To be in the genre, it must be possible to read the entire poem as a response to such a text. The genre includes poems leading up to a denouement that uses the text, but it excludes those with only a passing reference to it. It also excludes poems of general meditation on a biblical character or subject that are not tied to one particular short text. In a few cases the selections do not conform to the rules; some of the reasons for these exceptions are given below, others in notes to the poems.

Most poems in this anthology are so closely tied to a biblical text by their titles and overt subject matter that it is not only possible to "read" the poem as a response to the text but also to be sure that this is something the poet had in mind. Whatever the author's intent, however, knowledge of a specific biblical text is needed to fully appreciate the poems collected here.

None of the poems selected are devotional in the sense of expressing untroubled belief. The scarcity of midrashic poems in existing anthologies of religious poetry forced me to realize how far modern midrash is from conventional notions of the religious.

Over half the poems in the anthology were written in English. Poems in other languages were judged by their qualities in English translation and included only if a good translation was found. A few translations were made for this anthology. In half a dozen cases, published poems contained typographical errors, or errors of translation or reference; these have been silently corrected with the agreement of the authors.

I have tried to represent adequately the midrashic poems of poets who are at ease in the genre and so have selected several poems by, for example, Rainer Maria Rilke, Jorge Luis Borges, and Czeslaw Milosz, many poems from Hebrew and Yiddish, and a much higher proportion of Jewish poets than would be found in a general anthology of twentieth-century poetry. On the other hand, many great poets of the twentieth century did not write any midrashic poems. Others have written in the genre, but not well. The basis for selection was the poem, not the poet.

All anthologies should introduce some poets who will be new to most readers and should also modify to some extent readers' notions of what constitutes an interesting poem and who they regard as important poets. To my mind the poems of Jacob Glatstein, Anna Kamienska, Dan Pagis, Gabriel Preil, Dahlia Ravikovitch, Wislawa Szymborska, and Natan Zach are not as well known in the English-speaking literary world as they should be, and I hope this anthology will prompt readers to seek these poems out. Primo Levi also falls into this category; he is well known, but not as a poet, even though his collected poems are available in English. Paul Celan is a different case; here what was surprising to me (and I presume will be to many others) is the extent of his use of biblical allusions and the way they clarify the meaning of the poems in which they occur.

The long poem always poses a problem for anthologists. Where long poems in the genre consist of a series of separate sections, I have reproduced the complete texts of one or more of these sections. For the others, I chose to excerpt something from the poem so that interested readers could be introduced to it, rather than exclude the poem altogether for fear of destroying its unity.

I have attempted to represent a wide range of poetic and midrashic techniques and to take into account the balance in representation between women and men, various cultural and language groups, and of poems from the early, middle, and late phases of the century. Quite a few of the living poets in the collection are known to me, and some are friends. It would be absurd to pretend that this played no role in my selection, but the role was minimal. I have strained some relationships, as all anthologists of the living must do. No one could be more aware than myself of how many poems in the genre are not here. I could easily have doubled the size of this anthology. But I was trying to illustrate a genre, not be exhaustive. I was also trying to keep the size and cost of the book within reasonable limits.

I made no attempt to cover all books of the Hebrew Bible. The groupings of poems were determined by the attraction of the poets in the collection to specific biblical texts and not by any traditional divisions of the Hebrew Bible. Abishag, for example, gets a section to herself even though only a minor character because she attracted many poets and inspired some wonderful poems. Within sections with more than one poem, I kept in mind complementarities and contrasts when making the final selection. These sections generally start with poems that use the text in a straightforward way and end with those that make only indirect or figurative use of it.

Spirituals such as "Go Down Moses," "Balm in Gilead," "Didn't My Lord Deliver Daniel?", "Ezekiel Saw the Wheel," "Joshua Fit de Battle of Jericho," and "L'il David Play on Your Harp" seem to me important midrashim. But they were composed well before the twentieth century, in some cases in the eighteenth century, and so couldn't be included. In any case, they were composed to be sung, as were twentieth-century gospel songs on Old Testament themes, and lose almost everything when reduced to the words without their music.

There are a few short prose pieces in the anthology; with one exception these are from books of poetry and so were treated by their authors as compositions to be read in a context of poetry. The exception is Kafka; some of his biblically based parables—those on Paradise—were included on the grounds that it felt absurd to leave him out.[25] The same grounds determined the inclusion of excerpts from Robert Frost's two masques.

The Biblical Passages

The passages quoted are the shortest that include both the main biblical references of the poems in the section and whatever additional material seemed needed. My aim was to make the anthology as self-contained as possible. In a few places the sequence of texts is continuous; the anthology contains all of Genesis 1:1–4:16 and the book of Jonah, as well as some shorter continuities.

Both the Jewish and Christian religious traditions consider the Hebrew Bible a sacred text. In the Jewish tradition it is known as the Tanakh, an acronym based on the Hebrew words for its three divisions, the Torah, the Prophets, and the Writings. In the Christian tradition, it is known as the Old Testament since it is considered completed by the New Testament. Apart from the names, however, the texts are almost but not quite the same. Of several textual differences between these traditions only two need to be noted here.[26] First, the sequence of books is different. Someone familiar with the Old Testament will be surprised to find in the Tanakh that Psalms, Job, Ecclesiastes, and the other Writings come after the Prophets and not before them. Second, the numbering of the verses in each psalm is different; the Tanakh numbers the headings, while the Old Testament does not. As a result the verse numbers of psalms in the Old Testament are normally one less than those of the corresponding verses in the Tanakh.

There are many English translations of the Hebrew Bible available. The norm in this anthology is the 1985 translation of the Jewish Publication Society, which of course follows the Jewish tradition in the sequence of books and the numbering of the psalms. However, if a poet or translator utilizes phraseology from another translation, then this is the one quoted opposite the poem; all translations other than

JPS 1985 are cited. Normally biblical phraseology quoted directly by a poet or translator writing in English would be from the King James Version, and where this is the case the Jewish Publication Society translation of 1917, which followed the King James Version very closely, is used except where its departures require the King James text itself. Where poets quoted a biblical text as an epigraph to their poem, no further text is given in a few cases.

Some Hebrew poets, who are naturally thinking of the original text, have written poems that dictate a choice of translations for reasons that have midrashic interest. Yehuda Amichai, for example, in his poem "Ashkelon Beach" asks a question about Samson's death among the Philistines that depends on an ambiguity in the Hebrew:

> Did he embrace the columns as in a final love
> or push them away—
> to be alone in his death?

A biblical translation telling us that he pulled the columns toward him, as some do, destroys the textual ambiguity that is the basis of the poem. For another poem by Amichai, "Like the Streams in the Negev," none of the existing translations of Psalm 126, which the title quotes, seemed to me to reproduce the meaning the poem depended on. In this case, a new biblical translation was made for the anthology.

Finally, a small case study in biblical translation, prompted by the epigraph to Léopold Sédar Senghor's poem "Elegy for the Queen of Sheba." The epigraph is taken from Song of Songs 1:5, and the issue is the connective, which, in a literal translation of the Hebrew, would be "and" but which is often translated by other connectives:

French (Senghor epigraph)	Moi noir et belle
King James Version, 1611	I am black but comely
Revised Standard Version, 1952	I am very dark, but comely
New English Bible, 1970	I am dark but lovely
Jewish Publication Society, 1985	I am dark, but comely
New Revised Std. Version, 1989	I am black and beautiful

NOTES

1. For those interested in reading about the rabbinic Midrash the best place to start is the chapter on Midrash in Barry Holtz, ed., *Back to the Sources* (New York: Summit Books, 1984). The chapter, which is

by the editor, ends with a detailed guide to further reading. Louis Ginzberg, *The Legends of the Jews*, 7 vols. (Philadelphia: Jewish Publication Society, 1909–38), which includes two volumes of notes, is the monumental basic reference work in the field, the place to look for a summary of all legends relating to a biblical figure or passage, citations of all the primary sources, notes on variants, and so on. The article on midrash in the *Encyclopedia Judaica* (Jerusalem: Keter Publishing House Ltd., 1971), Jacob Neusner's *Invitation to Midrash* (New York: Harper & Row, 1973), and Burton L. Visotzky's *Reading the Book* (New York: Doubleday, 1991) are recommended for their virtues of, respectively, comprehensiveness, pedagogical intensity, and accessibility. There are excellent academic essays on the general nature of midrash, as well as on many other related topics, in Geoffrey H. Hartman and Sanford Budick, eds., *Midrash and Literature* (New Haven: Yale University Press, 1986). While not on midrash itself, Robert Alter and Frank Kermode, eds., *The Literary Guide to the Bible* (Cambridge: Harvard University Press, 1987) has authoritative chapters on all books of the Old and New Testaments, and several general essays, including "Midrash and Allegory," by Gerald L. Bruns.

2. *Midrash Rabbah*, 3d ed., 10 vols. (London: Soncino Press, 1983), 3:302–3. The proof-texts have been deleted from this excerpt; see "Implicit Proof-Texts" above for a fuller quotation, with two of the proof-texts in place.

3. The point here, apart from telling us what the manna tasted like, is, in my reading, that nourishment from heaven fulfills the heart's desire; or, with inversion and a touch of anachronism, if you get nourishment that fulfills your heart's desire, consider it a gift from heaven.

4. *Midrash Rabbah*, 1:266. Here and in some subsequent quotations I have slightly altered the English translation by making phraseology and punctuation more contemporary and by translating terms left in Hebrew by the translator.

5. Ginzberg, *Legends of the Jews*, 1:255; see *Pirke de Rabbi Eliezer*, trans. Gerald Friedlander, 4th ed. (New York: Sepher-Hermon Press, 1981), 186, for a primary source in English. A powerful use of the story of Lot's wife as a proof-text occurs in the New Testament, Luke 17:30–33:

> [30]Even thus shall it be in the day when the Son of Man is revealed. [31]In that day he which shall be upon the housetop, and his stuff in the house, let him not come down to take it away: and he that is in the field let him likewise not return

back. [32]Remember Lot's wife. [33]Whosoever shall seek to save his life shall lose it; and whosoever shall lose his life shall preserve it.

6. Ginzberg, *Legends of the Jews*, 1:361; *Midrash Rabbah*, 2:650, gives the full exchange.

7. Ginzberg, *Legends of the Jews*, 1:70. The primary source is Hullin 60b (*The Babylonian Talmud*, Tractate Hullin, trans. Eli Cashdan, 35 vols. [London: Soncino Press, 1948], 1:332).

8. *Midrash Rabbah*, 8:171.

9. Ibid., 9:215.

10. Ibid., 1:269, 250.

11. Ibid., 1:486, contains the full exchange. However, I am following the presentation in Ginzberg, *Legends of the Jews*, 1:274; he has as usual combined several variants.

12. *The Midrash on Psalms*, trans. William G. Braude, 2 vols. (New Haven: Yale University Press, 1959), 1:327.

13. Ginzberg, *Legends of the Jews*, 3:104; see *Mekilta de-Rabbi Ishmael*, trans. Jacob Z. Lauterbach, 3 vols. (Philadelphia: Jewish Publication Society, 1933), 2:262, for a primary source in English. Here the comparison is presented in terms of which commandments were opposite each other on the two tablets Moses brought down from Sinai.

14. See, for example, the description of this type of sermon in David Stern, "Midrash and the Language of Exegesis" in Hartman and Budick, eds., *Midrash and Literature*, 107ff.

15. Ginzberg, *Legends of the Jews*, 3:18; *Midrash Rabbah*, 3:267, gives a full version of the exchange.

16. Some readers may imagine that Moses should have responded, "How could I have read the opening of the Torah when it hasn't been written yet?" Such a question must be dismissed with the same phrase given to me by a professor of physics when, as a sophomore, I asked, "If electrons can move from one quantum level to another, don't they pass through intermediate positions that are not quantum levels?" I was rightly told that I had posed a "forbidden question," namely one that violated the assumptions of the Bohr model we were discussing. Like the Bohr model of the atom, or for that matter any other scientific model, the Midrash is based on a number of hermeneutical assumptions, one of which is that "there is no early or late in Torah" and that all texts can be applied to all others as if they occurred in a world of simultaneity.

17. Needless to say, the relationship of the Old Testament to the New Testament is a complex matter; see Frank Kermode's chapter,

"The Plain Sense of Things," in Hartman and Budick, eds., *Midrash and Literature*, for a literary and midrashic view of some of the issues involved.

18. The writers were not alone in this preoccupation. The philosopher Karl Popper, in an essay entitled "Toward a Rational Theory of Tradition" (*Conjectures and Refutations* [New York: Harper Torchbooks, 1968]), distinguishes between a tradition, such as that of science, which is tolerant of differing views, and traditions that are not tolerant. Later in the same essay, Popper points out that in science "observations are not usually important unless they are related to a theory" and goes on to argue that in nonscientific spheres tradition plays a role analogous to that of theory in science.

19. T. S. Eliot, "Tradition and the Individual Talent," in *The Sacred Wood* (London: Routledge, 1920), 48.

20. Jonathan Culler, *On Deconstruction* (Ithaca, N.Y.: Cornell University Press, 1982), 50–51; the entire section entitled "Reading as a Woman" is pertinent.

21. Ginzberg, *Legends of the Jews*, 4:145–49, gives twenty-two riddles asked by Sheba of Solomon, and his answers. See also *The Midrash on Proverbs*, trans. by Burton L. Visotzky (New Haven: Yale University Press, 1992), 18–19. Even in the rabbinic tradition, however, not all was a meeting of minds. For example, Ginzberg, *Legends of the Jews*, 6:289 n. 41, also supplies information on the chemical composition of the depilatory used by Solomon for Sheba's legs. "The legend concerning the hair on the queen's legs very likely supposes that she was a genii . . . for the bodies of demons are covered with hair." Such legendary material was not exploited by Yeats et al. and awaits its modern use, although Yeats did refer to Sheba as a witch in a poem ("Solomon and the Witch") not included in this anthology.

22. Geoffrey H. Hartman and Sanford Budick, "Introduction," in Hartman and Budick, eds., *Midrash and Literature*, xi.

23. For those interested in the relationship between rabbinic midrash and literary theory, the following books are recommended: Susan A. Handelman, *The Slayers of Moses: The Emergence of Rabbinic Interpretation in Modern Literary Theory* (Albany: State University of New York Press, 1982), and, more recently, Norman Finkelstein, *The Ritual of New Creation: Jewish Tradition and Contemporary Literature* (Albany: State University of New York Press, 1992).

24. Robert Alter, *The World of Biblical Literature* (New York: Basic Books, 1992), 152.

25. The delightful midrashic stories of his fellow countryman, Karel

Čapek, in *Apocryphal Stories* (London: Penguin, 1975), were left out with a feeling of loss but not absurdity.

26. In what follows I am referring to Protestant Bibles such as the King James Version and its successors. There are significant differences among Protestant, Roman Catholic, Greek, and Slavonic Bibles; the latter three canons, for example, contain additional books, such as 1 and 2 Maccabees, that are treated as apocryphal in the Jewish and Protestant traditions. The Roman Catholic numbering of the psalms follows the Vulgate in combining Psalms 9 and 10, resulting for the remaining psalms in a numbering one less than that of the Jewish and Protestant canons.

A ▪ The Creation

GENESIS 1:1–5

In the beginning God created the heaven and the earth. [2]Now the earth was unformed and void, and darkness was upon the face of the deep; and the spirit of God hovered over the face of the waters. [3]And God said: 'Let there be light.' And there was light. [4]And God saw the light, that it was good; and God divided the light from the darkness. [5]And God called the light Day, and the darkness He called Night. And there was evening and there was morning, one day.

Translation: JPS 1917

PRIMO LEVI   □

In the Beginning

Fellow humans, to whom a year is a long time,
A century a venerable goal,
Struggling for your bread,
Tired, fretful, tricked, sick, lost:
Listen, and may it be mockery and consolation.
Twenty billion years before now,
Brilliant, soaring in space and time,
There was a ball of flame, solitary, eternal,
Our common father and our executioner.
It exploded, and every change began.
Even now the thin echo of this one reverse catastrophe
Resounds from the farthest reaches.
From that one spasm everything was born:
The same abyss that enfolds and challenges us,
The same time that spawns and defeats us,
Everything anyone has ever thought,
The eyes of every woman we have loved,
Suns by the thousands
And this hand that writes.

13 August 1970

Translated from the Italian
by Ruth Feldman and Brian Swann

ROBINSON JEFFERS   □

The Great Explosion

The universe expands and contracts like a great heart.[a]
It is expanding, the farthest nebulae
Rush with the speed of light into empty space.
It will contract, the immense navies of stars and galaxies,
    dust-clouds and nebulae
Are recalled home, they crush against each other in one
    harbor, they stick in one lump
And then explode it, nothing can hold them down; there
    is no way to express that explosion; all that exists

[a] See "Notes on the Poems," p. 333

Roars into flame, the tortured fragments rush away from
each other into all the sky, new universes
Jewel the black breast of night; and far off the outer
nebulae like charging spearmen again
Invade emptiness.
No wonder we are so fascinated with
fire-works
And our huge bombs: it is a kind of homesickness per-
haps for the howling fire-blast that we were born
from.

But the whole sum of the energies
That made and contained the giant atom survives. It will
gather again and pile up, the power and the glory—
And no doubt it will burst again; diastole and systole:
the whole universe beats like a heart.
Peace in our time was never one of God's promises; but
back and forth, die and live, burn and be damned,
The great heart beating, pumping into our arteries His
terrible life.

He is beautiful beyond belief.
And we, God's apes—or tragic children—share in the
beauty. We see it above our torment, that's what
life's for.
He is no God of love, no justice of a little city like
Dante's Florence, no anthropoid God
Making commandments: this is the God who does not
care and will never cease. Look at the seas there
Flashing against this rock in the darkness—look at the
tide-stream stars—and the fall of nations—and
dawn
Wandering with wet white feet down the Carmel Valley
to meet the sea. These are real and we see their
beauty.
The great explosion is probably only a metaphor—I know
not—of faceless violence, the root of all things.

EUGENIO MONTALE □

Big Bang or Whatever

I find it strange that the universe
was born of an explosion;
I find it strange that it is due instead
to a swarming stagnation.[b]

Still more incredible that
it issued from the magic wand
of a god with alarmingly
anthropomorphic characteristics.

But how can one think of crediting
such a machination to anyone living?
Though he be the worst kind of thief
and murderer, he is still innocent.

Translated from the Italian
by Ruth Feldman

NATAN ZACH □

When God First Said

When God first said Let there be light
He meant it would not be dark for Him.
In that moment He didn't think about the sky,
but the trees already were filling with water,
the birds receiving air and body.
Then the first wind touched God's eyes
and He saw it in all His glory
and thought It is good. He didn't think then
about people, people in their multitude,
but they already were standing apart from the fig leaves,
unraveling in their hearts
a scheme about pain.
When God first thought of night
He didn't think about sleep.

[b] See "Notes on the Poems," p. 333

So be it, God said, I will be happy.
But they were multitudes.

Translated from the Hebrew
by Peter Everwine and Shulamit Yasny-Starkman

NICANOR PARRA □

Genesis

In the beginning God created slums
and garbage dumps
He looked out from his balcony
                    and saw they were gorgeous
and said:
            Let there be many more

And as if by the arts of magic
other garbage dumps appeared
more dreadful than the former
and an infinite number of new slums
with of course no sanitary facilities
but vast contingents of flies
in contention over the commonweals' shit

This is oh so very amusing
                    God exclaimed

And there was evening and there was morning, one day
                    to be continued.

Translated from the Spanish
by Adriana Valdés and David Curzon

HOWARD NEMEROV □

Creation Myth on a Moebius Band [c]

This world's just mad enough to have been made
By the Being his beings into Being prayed.

[c] See "Notes on the Poems," p. 333

ANNE WINTERS □

The First Verse

Bereshit bara elohim et ha-shamayim v'et ha-eretz.

Genesis 1:1

My black-lettered Hebrew Bible, dense
and doughty as a cobble. The Bible in
    Hebrew—irreducible!
Yet at the first verse, a hair-thin net of cracks
appears, each crack a vast highway, and wildly we
    leap
onto this first, this universal, cobble, BERESHIT.
    "In-the-beginning."
Or maybe, "In-the-beginning-*of*." Of what, you may
    ask—of "making"? No—
and so the slight break ramifies and blooms
into shelf-feet of commentaries, monographs, and now
you must swiftly ransack your Sumerian—
yes, without Enuma Elish there's no understanding the
    matter—
For it seems that that stately cosmogony begins
with just such another hermetic, mind-boggling
    ellipsis,
and so the two master-texts, with archaic courtesy,
    nod
across the millennia. But I forgot to mention
the Crimean War. It seems the war upset the local
Karaites, who saddled up and fled
to St. Petersburg, taking their cherished, oldest dated
scrolls of the Bible, wrapped, for freshness, in
    date-leaves, and left them
in the Public Library. But naturally, the Public
    Library!
And so these sectarians, not even actually, exactly,
Jewish—the rabbis' deep-dyed foes—preserved the
    inerrant Word,
though not without hosts of tiny scribal errors
some day to set shuddering
whole forests of editors, compositors, microfilmers—

BARA. Verb transitive, sacred, used with no Subject
    but
God, translation "made." We'll do well to pause

GENESIS 1:1–5 • 33

for the comment of Rashi, winding forth
from the medieval balconies of Troyes—
"The world is made for Torah." For this very
　　sentence!
(The lovely sentence—the terrible world.) A floating
　　circule
next to *BARA* reminds us to look below
our biblical text with its verse-carets, vowel-points and
　　the jots
that flourish the great text with the summery human
　　voice,
for the medieval mine of the Masora,
coded word-frequencies (frequently upbraiding Bible)
with its own typeface, learned circles, note-makers,
　　exception-takers—
How world upon subworld attests the young Creator
riding the stormwind with earth and moon in his
　　hands,

ELOHIM. The third word in the Bible is
God. Well literally "gods," but by convention—
except in pagan contexts—though Christians, too,
find Trinity adumbrations here, faint rushes
of the Presence-packed Unseen. Yet our verb
is a singular verb; God alone is God; and anyway, *BARA*
is male. —What next, a verb should be male? Yes. For
　　such
is the nature of that mode of being
which is the Bible. God, whether singular
or in himself the very host of Heaven,
is male. —But what about goddess Tiamat? Did you know
　　that in Enuma Elish
her wrestling with God produced our world? Her very
　　name
is cognate to "the deep" *(tehom)* God moves on. Of
　　course,
the Enuma Elish is *not* the Bible. But isn't there something
columnar and stark, and, well, male
about this first verse? (This Tiamat sprouts up
in the Psalms, as well . . .)

ET . . . ET? The fourth word in the Bible,
ET? Yes, and the sixth. Translation: asterisk. Even in
　　Hebrew-

English Interlinear, darkly forbidden to students,
asterisk. (Lexicon adds *Mark of the accus.*)
In fact, this recurrent biblical
—unword, reflects the perception
that verbs, in accusing their nouns, comb them out
from the static of the Indeterminate. Think of the Karaites,
how amidst the grapeshot, the dusty saddlery
and willow baskets, they bore off their Bible. And there it
    lay,
now the Leningrad Codex (L), until the Stuttgart professor
sent for his photographs, and then Kittel proceeded
to make his historic redaction. How leisurely his world
seems from our chaos, a single late-twenties afternoon
of peaceful scholarship. . . . His fanatical accuracy, the fonts
made to his specifications, his strangely intelligible
face, melted down in the carpet-bombing of Leipzig—

HA-SHAMAYIM. The heavens. This word
reminds you of Arabic *sham*, as Allah recalls EL
or *ELOHIM*, God. Not to mention God's own
self name, the Tetragrammaton, supreme
and half-conjugate IS. Never right-printed or uttered
(in English Bible suppressed, in Hebrew misvowelled),
    so that
we students, reciting aloud, approaching again and again
    the great letters
must stammer out LORD, or else NAME. . . .
For so the word is still set up in our time. Even Kittel,
meticulous scholar and (I've never seen this in print)
    root-and-branch
anti-Semite, whose very professorship, it is whispered. . . .
    But wait, isn't *this*
Kittel's Hebrew Bible (the BHK)? No. Look. This is
    now "Hebrew Bible
of Stuttgart" (the BHS)—new preface, Masora, even
    from Leningrad
microfilms new—the K is no more. And why not? You
    know why
not. Ever try to look up
Endlösung, Final Solution, in a modern German-
English dictionary? Well, it's not there. And where a
    word

—isn't, mightn't *anything* be? You could replace
    BERESHIT
with "In the beginning the Word"—and *voilà,* you're in
    Chartres! Why not?
On the right, Jesse's stem, overhead
Heaven's Queen in her rose—this too is the Bible.
    North of the transept
the cult-statue stands, Black Virgin of Chartres,
her apron lost in initialed bronze tablets,
toes curling, planted on her ancient pillar
which lips of brides caress for centuries,
while tourists stream in before the majesty of EL. . . .

Seventh word, last word. HA-ERETZ, the earth. Can it
    really,
this temple-built, mosque-planted, stave-churched and
    belfry'd earth,
be made for Torah? For Rashi is still,
as medieval people love to do, explaining the Bible.
    His argument
weaves on, crochety and scholastic as Romanesque
capitals with their tiny figures from the Apocrypha
where one biblical name, like Tubal-Cain, takes on
a florid history, five wives, and murders with a
    cross-bow;
and the Virgin goes on nursing among the hieratic,
    sympathizing
beasts' faces, angular as those old Hebrew
characters like fishhooks and little horns
(for the biblical characters before us are not *exactly*
Hebrew—Chaldean. Aramaic.) Yet everything's here.
    As in the delicate
midrash where Moses stands weeping
because he is copying down the words
describing his own death hither-side of Jordan. The
    lovely
sentence, the terrible world—the beginning. Inerrant,
perfect, the first verse of the Bible.

GENESIS 1:6–13

⁶God said, "Let there be an expanse in the midst of the water, that it may separate water from water." ⁷God made the expanse, and it separated the water which was below the expanse from the water which was above the expanse. And it was so. ⁸God called the expanse Sky. And there was evening and there was morning, a second day.

⁹God said, "Let the water below the sky be gathered into one area, that the dry land may appear." And it was so. ¹⁰God called the dry land Earth, and the gathering of waters He called Seas. And God saw that this was good. ¹¹And God said, "Let the earth sprout vegetation: seed-bearing plants, fruit trees of every kind on earth that bear fruit with the seed in it." And it was so. ¹²The earth brought forth vegetation: seed-bearing plants of every kind, and trees of every kind bearing fruit with the seed in it. And God saw that this was good. ¹³And there was evening and there was morning, a third day.

LINDA PASTAN ☐

The Imperfect Paradise

If God had stopped work after the third day
With Eden full of vegetables and fruits,
If oak and lilac held exclusive sway
Over a kingdom made of stems and roots,
If landscape were the genius of creation
And neither man nor serpent played a role
And God must look to wind for lamentation
And not to picture postcards of the soul,
Would he have rested on his bank of cloud
With nothing in the universe to lose,
Or would he hunger for a human crowd?
Which would a wise and just creator choose:
The green hosannas of a budding leaf
Or the strict contract between love and grief?

A. D. HOPE ☐

Protest to Fred Hoyle

*The graph shows the absorption spectra of the two types of chlorophyll—
an indication of how well they trap sunlight at different wave lengths.
Above these is the emission spectrum of the Sun, showing how intense its
light is over the same wave length range. Although both chlorophylls
absorb blue and red light well, yellow and green sunlight is hardly
absorbed at all. The green color of leaves shows the light they are
losing; really effective leaves would be black.*

Fred Hoyle, *The Intelligent Universe*, p. 126

You are devilishly clever, Fred, as I have reason to know.
Perhaps angelic wisdom is a little beyond your scope.
I was brought up to think God created the world, and so
May I question one point as you cast its horoscope?

Evidence for the existence of God, Fred Hoyle,
(The last of the Bridgewater Treatises[d] is now on the
    track.
Not that my trust in its logic brings my wits to the boil)
Simply my horror to think all leaves should be black.

[d] See "Notes on the Poems," p. 333

But suppose that poets know things that scientists miss,
Things we know in our bones. How we know none of us
    know
If we trust what we see—though we know how deceptive
    it is.
We accept what science demonstrates, but can it show

There was not a good reason why chlorophyll failed your
    test?
Could whoever made my world, if it was made at all,
By any chance have listened to you protest
And agreed so that everything afterwards went to the wall.

If mind arranged it no man could possibly know
The range and reach of that cosmic consciousness
Yet we could guess from his work that even so
The beauty that marks this world must more or less

Have ranked very high among his priorities.
If you, as I say, had chanced to be standing near
When he came to designing the form of its grass and trees
He'd have smiled at the reasons you gave but I very much
    fear

Would have answered, 'They say that among the blind
You will find that the one-eyed is bound to be king.
But I must keep other and higher values in mind.
Mere efficiency, my friend, is not everything.'

When I look at my garden so radiant and so green,
The trees that mount so varied against the blue,
I think how deadly and dull it would have been
If he who created it had listened to you.

But a god would have set your arguments aside
Since the cleverest men are not able to see very far.
It would not have taken him long to foresee and decide
That green leaves are quite efficient enough as they are.

GENESIS 1:14–19

[14]God said, "Let there be lights in the expanse of the sky to separate day from night; they shall serve as signs for the set times— the days and the years; [15]and they shall serve as lights in the expanse of the sky to shine upon the earth." And it was so. [16]God made the two great lights, the greater light to dominate the day and the lesser light to dominate the night, and the stars. [17]And God set them in the expanse of the sky to shine upon the earth, [18]to dominate the day and the night, and to separate light from darkness. And God saw that this was good. [19]And there was evening and there was morning, a fourth day.

SALVATORE QUASIMODO □

To the New Moon

In the beginning God created the heaven
and the earth, and in due time
set moon and stars in the heavens;
and on the seventh day he rested.

After a thousand ages, man,
made in his image and likeness,
without ever resting, with his
lay intelligence
one October night, without fear,
set in the tranquil heavens
other bodies like those
that had been spinning
since the creation of the world. Amen.

Translated from the Italian
by Jack Bevan

GENESIS 1:20–23

[20]God said, "Let the waters bring forth swarms of living creatures, and birds that fly above the earth across the expanse of the sky." [21]God created the great sea monsters, and all the living creatures of every kind that creep, which the waters brought forth in swarms; and all the winged birds of every kind. And God saw that this was good. [22]God blessed them, saying, "Be fertile and increase, fill the waters in the seas, and let the birds increase on the earth." [23]And there was evening and there was morning, a fifth day.

D. H. LAWRENCE ☐

The Work of Creation

The mystery of creation is the divine urge of creation,
but it is a great, strange urge, it is not a Mind.
Even an artist knows that his work was never in his mind,
he could never have *thought* it before it happened.
A strange ache possessed him, and he entered the struggle,
and out of the struggle with his material, in the spell of the urge
his work took place, it came to pass, it stood up and saluted his mind.

God is a great urge, wonderful, mysterious, magnificent
but he knows nothing before-hand.
His urge takes shape in the flesh, and lo!
it is creation! God looks himself on it in wonder, for the first time.
Lo! there is a creature, formed! How strange!
Let me think about it! Let me form an idea!

GENESIS 1:24–31

24God said, "Let the earth bring forth every kind of living creature: cattle, creeping things, and wild beasts of every kind." And it was so. 25God made wild beasts of every kind and cattle of every kind, and all kinds of creeping things of the earth. And God saw that this was good. 26And God said, "Let us make man in our image, after our likeness. They shall rule the fish of the sea, the birds of the sky, the cattle, the whole earth, and all the creeping things that creep on earth." 27And God created man in His image, in the image of God He created him; male and female He created them. 28God blessed them and God said to them, "Be fertile and increase, fill the earth and master it; and rule the fish of the sea, the birds of the sky, and all the living things that creep on earth."

29God said, "See, I give you every seed-bearing plant that is upon all the earth, and every tree that has seed-bearing fruit; they shall be yours for food. 30And to all the animals on land, to all the birds of the sky, and to everything that creeps on earth, in which there is the breath of life, [I give] all the green plants for food." And it was so. 31And God saw all that He had made, and found it very good. And there was evening and there was morning, the sixth day.

ALAIN BOSQUET □

Poems from "God's Torment"

. . .

God speaks:
"I am not always fond of what I create.
For instance, this man:
I give him two eyes, two arms, two legs . . .
which is very practical . . .
but all of a sudden I'm more stingy:
. . . a single skeleton,
and only one heart—
as if I feared he might sit too straight
or have too much love.
I would do well to begin him again, this man."

. . .

God speaks:
"It was an emergency case.
I wondered of what use
were my strangest creatures:
the dragon, the angel and the unicorn.
I summoned the ones I believed in,
the real, the mighty, the incontestable:
the baobab, the plough horse,
the mountain leaning into the sea.
They held ten conferences
without coming to any agreement.
And so I watched over
the dragon, the angel and the unicorn;
to avoid certain misunderstandings
I thought it proper in any event to make them invisible."

Translated from the French
by Jesse Abbot

YEHUDA AMICHAI ☐

My Son

Because of love and because of making love
and because the pain of the unborn
is greater than the pain of the born,
I said to the woman: "Let us make a man
in our own image." And we did. But he grows
different from us,
day by day.

Furtively he eavesdrops on his parents' talk,
he doesn't understand but he grows on those words
as a plant grows without understanding
oxygen, nitrogen, and other elements.

Later on he stands before the opened
holy arks of legend
and before the lighted display windows
of history, the Maccabean wars, David and Goliath,
the suicides of Masada, the ghetto uprising,
Hannah and her seven sons,
he stands with gaping eyes
and, deep down, he grows a vow like a big flower:
To live, to live, not to die like them.

When he writes, he starts the letters from the bottom.
When he draws two fighting knights
he starts with the swords, then come the hands,
and then the head. And outside the page
and beyond the table—hope and peace.

Once he did something bad in school
and was punished: I saw him,
alone in an empty classroom,
eating with the gestures of a tamed beast.
I told him, fight me
but he fights the school,
law and order.
I told him, pour out your wrath on me
but he caresses me and I caress him.

The first real
big school outing
is the outing from which
they never return.

Translated from the Hebrew
by Barbara and Benjamin Harshav

DAN PAGIS □

Testimony

No no: they definitely were
human beings: uniforms, boots.
How to explain? They were created
in the image.

I was a shade.
A different creator made me.

And he in his mercy left nothing of me that would die.
And I fled to him, floated up weightless, blue,
forgiving—I would even say: apologizing—
smoke to omnipotent smoke
that has no face or image.

Translated from the Hebrew
by Stephen Mitchell

GENESIS 2:1–4a

The heaven and the earth were finished, and all their array. [2]On the seventh day God finished the work which He had been doing, and He ceased* on the seventh day from all the work which He had done. [3]And God blessed the seventh day and declared it holy, because on it God ceased from all the work of creation which He had done. [4]Such is the story of heaven and earth when they were created.

* Or "rested"

JAMES McAULEY □

From "The Seven Days of Creation"

for Leonard French

The Seventh Day

Stillness is highest act,
Therefore be still and know
The pattern in the flow,
The reason in the fact.

Sabbath of the mind:
The beaked implacable
Tearing of the will
Arrested and defined.

Not to need either
To kill or to possess
Is a day's clear weather.

The grinding stops; we untether
The abused beast, and confess
We've heard of happiness.

B ▪ Adam and Eve in Eden

GENESIS 2:4b–7

When the LORD God made earth and heaven—⁵when no shrub of the field was yet on earth and no grasses of the field had yet sprouted, because the LORD God had not sent rain upon the earth and there was no man to till the soil, ⁶but a flow would well up from the ground and water the whole surface of the earth—⁷the LORD God formed man* from the dust of the earth.† He blew into his nostrils the breath of life, and man became a living being.

* Heb. *'adam*
† Heb. *'adamah*

PAUL CELAN □

Psalm

No one kneads us again out of earth and clay,
no one summons our dust.[c]
No one.

Blessed art thou, No One.
In thy sight would
we bloom.
In thy
spite.

A nothing
we were, are now, and ever
shall be, blooming:
the nothing-, the
No-One's-Rose.

With
our pistil soul-bright,
our stamen heaven-waste,
our corona red
from the purpleword we sang
over, oh over
the thorn.

Translated from the German
by John Felstiner

EDMOND JABÈS □

From "Adam, or the Birth of Anxiety"

. . .

And God created Adam.
He created him a man, depriving him of memory.
Man without childhood, without past.
(Without tears, without laughter or smiles.)

---

[c] See "Notes on the Poems," p. 333

Man come out of Nothing, unable even to claim a portion of this Nothing.

Did God consider for a moment that with one stroke He deprived this man of what He would in the future grant all other creatures?

Adam, son of Nothing by the will of God, fruit of wanton benevolence,

fruit ripe before ripening, tree in full leaf before growing, world completed before emerging from nothing, *but only in the Mind of God.*

Man of strange thoughts on which, however, his life depends.

Man chained to the Void, chained to the absence of all absence.

The past reassures us. Man without such security, delivered to whom? to what?

Man without light or shadow, without origin or road, without place, unless part of that place outside time which is indifferent to man.

Things must feel this way. But no doubt even they have their thing-memory, recalling wood or steel, clay or marble. Recalling their slow progress toward the idea, the knowledge of the thing they were to embody.

O emptiness! Nothing to lean against, nothing to rest on, is this anxiety?

Time molds us. Without past there is no present, and the *I* cannot be imagined.

Orphaned in the fullest sense of the term, of father and mother, but also of himself—are we not engendered in that moment of carnal and spiritual experience?—what could seeing and hearing be for him? What could speaking or acting mean? What weight had a word, what reverberations in the future? What could it profit him? What contentment, what soothing could he expect from any gesture?

Discoveries, encounters, surprises, disappointments, wonder? Probably. But in relation to what other approaches, in reply to which inner question, lacking all comparison?

. . .   Translated from the French
                                   by Rosemarie Waldrop

EVA TÓTH □

Genesis

Your hands create my body
your mouth breathes life in me
my face shines in your eyes
you call me by my name

Alone how should I shine?
Alone I am in darkness
Alone unshapely clod of earth
Alone I do not exist

Translated from the Hungarian
by Peter Jay

GENESIS 2:8–17

[8]And the LORD God planted a garden eastward, in Eden; and there He put the man whom He had formed. [9]And out of the ground made the LORD God to grow every tree that is pleasant to the sight, and good for food; the tree of life also in the midst of the garden, and the tree of the knowledge of good and evil. [10]And a river went out of Eden to water the garden; and from thence it was parted, and became four heads. [11]The name of the first is Pishon; that is it which compasseth the whole land of Havilah, where there is gold; [12]and the gold of that land is good; there is no bdellium and the onyx stone. [13]And the name of the second river is Gihon; the same is it that compasseth the whole land of Cush. [14]And the name of the third river is *Tigris; that is it which goeth toward the east of Asshur. And the fourth river is the Euphrates. [15]And the LORD God took the man, and put him into the garden of Eden to dress it and to keep it. [16]And the LORD God commanded the man, saying: "Of every tree of the garden thou mayest freely eat; [17]but of the tree of the knowledge of good and evil, thou shalt not eat of it; for in the day that thou eatest thereof thou shalt surely die."

Translation: JPS 1917

* Heb. *Hiddekel*

YEVGENY VINOKUROV ☐

Adam

On the first day, gazing idly around,
He trampled the grass down and stretched himself
In the shade of the fig tree.

                And placing
His hands behind his head,
                dozed.

Sweetly he slept, untroubled was his sleep
In Eden's quiet, beneath the pale blue sky.
And in his dreams he saw the ovens of Auschwitz
And he saw ditches filled with corpses.

He saw his own children!
                In the bliss
Of paradise, his face lit up.
He slept, understanding nothing,
Not knowing good and evil yet.

Translated from the Russian
by Daniel Weissbort

STANLEY H. BARKAN ☐

As Yet Unborn

Oh to be Adam
again
with all his ribs
yearning for a woman
as yet unborn,
mouth free
of the taste of apples,
ears without
the hiss of snakes,
mindless of
nakedness and shame
in the garden
of gentle creatures
waiting for a name.

GENESIS 2:18–20

[18]The LORD God said, "It is not good for man to be alone; I will make a fitting helper for him." [19]And the LORD God formed out of the earth all the wild beasts and all the birds of the sky, and brought them to the man to see what he would call them; and whatever the man called each living creature, that would be its name. [20]And the man gave names to all the cattle and to the birds of the sky and to all the wild beasts; but for Adam no fitting helper was found.

LOUISE GLÜCK ☐

The Gift

Lord, You may not recognize me
speaking for someone else.
I have a son. He is
so little, so ignorant.
He likes to stand
at the screen door, calling
oggie, oggie, entering
language, and sometimes
a dog will stop and come up
the walk, perhaps
accidentally. May he believe
this is not an accident?
At the screen
welcoming each beast
in love's name, Your emissary.

CZESLAW MILOSZ ☐

Spider

The thread with which he landed stuck to the bottom of the
    bathtub
And he desperately tries to walk on the glossy white
But not one of his thrashing legs gets a hold
On that surface so unlike anything in Nature.
I do not like spiders. Between me and them there is enmity.
I have read a lot about their habits
Which are loathsome to me. In a web
I have seen the quick run, a lethal stabbing
With poison that, in some species,
Is dangerous also for us. Now I take a look
And leave him there. Instead of running water
To end this unpleasantness. For, after all, what can we,
People, do except not to harm?
Not to pour toxic powder on the road of marching ants,
Save stupid moths rushing to the light
By putting a windowpane between them and the kerosene lamp
By which I used to write. Name this at last,

I tell myself: Reluctance to think to the end
Is lifesaving for the living. Could lucid consciousness
Bear everything that in every minute,
Simultaneously, occurs on the earth?
Not to harm. Stop eating fish and meat.
Let oneself be castrated, like Tiny, a cat innocent
Of the drownings of kittens every day in our city.

The Cathari were right: Avoid the sin of conception
(For either you kill your seed and will be tormented by conscience
Or you will be responsible for a life of pain).
My house has two bathrooms. I leave the spider
In an unused tub and go back to my work
Which consists in building diminutive boats
More wieldy and speedy than those in our childhood,
Good for sailing beyond the borderline of time.

Next day I see my spider:
Dead, rolled into a black dot on the glittering white.

I think with envy of the dignity that befell Adam
Before whom creatures of field and forest paraded
To receive names from him. How much he was elevated
Above everything that runs and flies and crawls.

Translated from the Polish
by Czeslaw Milosz and Robert Hass

JOHN HOLLANDER □

Adam's Task

*And Adam gave names to all cattle, and to the fowl of the
air, and to every beast of the field . . .*
Genesis 2:20

Thou, paw-paw-paw; thou, glurd; thou, spotted
   Glurd; thou, whitestap, lurching through
The high-grown brush; thou, pliant-footed,
   Implex; thou, awagabu.

Every burrower, each flier
   Came for the name he had to give:
Gay, first work, ever to be prior,
   Not yet sunk to primitive.

Thou, verdle; thou, McFleery's pomma;
  Thou; thou; thou—three types of grawl;
Thou, flisket; thou, kabasch; thou, comma-
  Eared mashawk; thou, all; thou, all.

Were, in a fire of becoming,
  Laboring to be burned away,
Then work, half-measuring, half-humming,
  Would be as serious as play.

Thou, pambler; thou, rivarn; thou, greater
  Wherret, and thou, lesser one;
Thou, sproal; thou, zant; thou, lily-eater.
  Naming's over. Day is done.

ANTHONY HECHT   □

Naming the Animals

Having commanded Adam to bestow
Names upon all the creatures, God withdrew
To empyrean palaces of blue
That warm and windless morning long ago,
And seemed to take no notice of the vexed
Look on the young man's face as he took thought
Of all the miracles the Lord had wrought,
Now to be labelled, dubbed, yclept, indexed.

Before an addled mind and puddled brow,
The feathered nation and the finny prey
Passed by; there went biped and quadruped.
Adam looked forth with bottomless dismay
Into the tragic eyes of his first cow,
And shyly ventured, "Thou shalt be called 'Fred.' "

SUSAN DONNELLY □

Eve Names the Animals

To me, *lion* was sun on a wing
over the garden. *Dove,*
a burrowing, blind creature.

I swear that man
never knew animals. Words
he lined up according to size,

while elephants slipped flat-eyed
through water

and trout
hurtled from the underbrush, tusked
and ready for battle.

The name he gave me stuck
me to him. He did it to comfort me,
for not being first.

Mornings, while he slept,
I got away. Pickerel
hopped on the branches above me.
Only spider accompanied me,

nosing everywhere,
running up to lick my hand.

Poor finch. I suppose I was
woe to him—

the way he'd come looking for me,
not wanting either of us
to be ever alone.

But to myself I was
palomino
      raven
         fox . . .

I strung words
by their stems and wore them
as garlands on my long walks.

The next day
I'd find them withered.

I liked change.

CZESLAW MILOSZ ☐

Linnaeus

He was born in 1707 at 1:00 A.M. *on May 23rd, when spring was in
beautiful bloom, and cuckoo had just announced the coming of summer.*
from Linnaeus's biography

Green young leaves. A cuckoo. Echo.
To get up at four in the morning, to run to the river
Which steams, smooth under the rising sun.
A gate is open, horses are running,
Swallows dart, fish splash. And did we not begin with an
    overabundance
Of glitterings and calls, pursuits and trills?
We lived every day in hymn, in rapture,
Not finding words, just feeling it is too much.

He was one of us, happy in our childhood.
He would set out with his botanic box
To gather and to name, like Adam in the garden
Who did not finish his task, expelled too early.
Nature has been waiting for names ever since:
On the meadows near Uppsala, white, at dusk
Platanthera is fragrant, he called it *bifolia.*
Turdus sings in a spruce thicket, but is it *musicus?*
That must remain the subject of dispute.
And the botanist laughed at a little perky bird
For ever *Troglodytes troglodytes L.*

He arranged three kingdoms into a system.
Animale. Vegetale. Minerale.
He divided: classes, orders, genuses, species.
"How manifold are Thy works, O Jehovah!"
He would sing with the psalmist. Rank, number, symmetry

Are everywhere, praised with a clavecin
And violin, scanned in Latin hexameter.

We have since had the language of marvel: atlases.
A tulip with its dark, mysterious inside,
Anemones of Lapland, a water lily, an iris
Faithfully portrayed by a scrupulous brush.
And a bird in foliage, russet and dark blue,
Never flies off, retained
On the page with an ornate double inscription.

We were grateful to him. In the evenings at home
We contemplated colors under a kerosene lamp
With a green shade. And what there, on earth,
Was unattainable, over much, passing away, perishing,
Here we could love, safe from loss.

May his household, orangery, the garden
In which he grew plants from overseas
Be blessed with peace and well-being.
To China and Japan, America, Australia,
Sailing-ships carried his disciples;
They would bring back gifts: seeds and drawings.
And I, who in this bitter age deprived of harmony
Am a wanderer and a gatherer of visible forms,
Envying them, bring to him my tribute—
A verse imitating the classical ode.

Translated from the Polish
by Czeslaw Milosz and Robert Hass

GENESIS 2:21–24

[21]So the Lord God cast a deep sleep upon the man; and, while he slept, He took one of his ribs and closed up the flesh at that spot. [22]And the Lord God fashioned the rib that He had taken from the man into a woman; and He brought her to the man. [23]Then the man said,

"This one at last
Is bone of my bones
And flesh of my flesh.
This one shall be called Woman,*
For from man† was she taken."

[24]Hence a man leaves his father and mother and clings to his wife, so that they become one flesh.

* Heb. *'ishshah*
† Heb. *'ish*

ELIZABETH JENNINGS □

One Flesh

Lying apart now, each in a separate bed,
He with a book, keeping the light on late,
She like a girl dreaming of childhood,
All men elsewhere—it is as if they wait
Some new event: the book he holds unread,
Her eyes fixed on the shadows overhead.

Tossed up like flotsam from a former passion,
How cool they lie. They hardly ever touch,
Or if they do it is like a confession
Of having little feeling—or too much.
Chastity faces them, a destination
For which their whole lives were a preparation.

Strangely apart, yet strangely together,
Silence between them like a thread to hold
And not wind in. And time itself's a feather
Touching them gently. Do they know they're old,
These two who are my father and my mother
Whose fire, from which I came, has now grown cold?

LOUISE GLÜCK □

Paradise

I grew up in a village: now
it's almost a city.
People came from the city, wanting
something simple, something
better for the children.
Clean air; nearby
a little stable.
All the streets
named after sweethearts or girl children.

Our house was gray, the sort of place
you buy to raise a family.
My mother's still there, all alone.
When she's lonely, she watches television.

The houses get closer together,
the old trees die or get taken down.

In some ways, my father's
close, too; we call
a stone by his name.
Now, above his head, the grass blinks,
in spring, when the snow has melted.
Then the lilac blooms, heavy, like clusters of grapes.

They always said
I was like my father, the way he showed
contempt for emotion.
They're the emotional ones,
my sister and my mother.

More and more
my sister comes from the city,
weeds, tidies the garden. My mother
lets her take over: she's the one
who cares, the one who does the work.
To her, it looks like country—
the clipped lawns, strips of colored flowers.
She doesn't know what it once was.

But I know. Like Adam,
I was the firstborn.
Believe me, you never heal,
you never forget the ache in your side,
the place where something was taken away
to make another person.

ROBERT FROST □

Never Again Would Birds' Song Be the Same

He would declare and could himself believe
That the birds there in all the garden round
From having heard the daylong voice of Eve
Had added to their own an oversound,
Her tone of meaning but without the words.
Admittedly an eloquence so soft
Could only have had an influence on birds

When call or laughter carried it aloft.
Be that as may be, she was in their song.
Moreover her voice upon their voices crossed
Had now persisted in the woods so long
That probably it never would be lost.
Never again would birds' song be the same.
And to do that to birds was why she came.

GENESIS 2:25–3:7

[25]The two of them were naked,* the man and his wife, yet they felt no shame. **3** [1]Now the serpent was the shrewdest of all the wild beasts that the LORD God had made. He said to the woman, "Did God really say: You shall not eat of any tree of the garden?" [2]The woman replied to the serpent, "We may eat of the fruit of the other trees of the garden. [3]It is only about fruit of the tree in the middle of the garden that God said: You shall not eat of it or touch it, lest you die." [4]And the serpent said to the woman, "You are not going to die, [5]but God knows that as soon as you eat of it your eyes will be opened and you will be like †⁻divine beings who know⁻† good and bad." [6]When the woman saw that the tree was good for eating and a delight to the eyes, and that the tree was desirable as a source of wisdom, she took of its fruit and ate. She also gave some to her husband, and he ate. [7]Then the eyes of both of them were opened and they perceived that they were naked; and they sewed together fig leaves and made themselves loincloths.

---

* Heb. *'arummin*, play on *'arum* "shrewd" in 3:1
†-† Others "God, who knows"

PAUL VALÉRY □

From "Silhouette of a Serpent"

To Henri Ghéon

. . .

O Vanity! Very First Cause!
The Other who reigns in the Heavens,
With the word that was light itself
Opened the spacious universe.
As though bored with the pure theater
Of Self, God broke the barrier
Of his perfect eternity:
He became He who fritters away
His Primal Cause in consequences,
And in stars his Unity.

Skies, his blunder! Time, his undoing!
And the animal abyss agape!
What a collapse into origin,
Glitters in place of total void! . . .
But the first syllable of his Word
Was ME! . . . The proudest of the stars
Uttered by the besotted maker,
I am! . . . Shall be! . . . I illuminate
How divinity was diminished
By all the fires of the Seducer!

Radiant target of my hate
Whom I once desperately loved,
You who had to give dominion
Over Gehenna to this your lover,
See yourself in my mirroring gloom!
Faced with your own funereal image,
Glory of my darkling glass,
So profound was your distress
That when you breathed over the clay
It was a sign of hopelessness!

All in vain You, out of the mud,
Molded these infants, facile toys,
So that Your triumphant deeds
Be lauded day-long by their praise!
No sooner molded and set to breathe

Than Snake applauded with a hiss
The pretty infants You had made!
Hi there, said I, you new arrivals,
You know you are human, and stark naked,
Oh snow-white sanctimonious beasts!

In the likeness of the accursed
You were made, and you I hate
As I hate the Name that creates
All these imperfect prodigies!
I am He who modifies,
I re-touch the incautious heart
With a sure, mysterious finger! . . .
We'll transform these tender products,
These self-effacing little snakes
Into reptiles of pure fury!

My Numberless Intelligence
Finds in the souls of human things
A playable instrument of my vengeance
Put together by your hands!
And though your Paternity,
Veiled aloft in its starry chamber,
May receive nothing but incense,
Still my overpowering charms
Can disturb its almighty designs
With the remotest of alarms!

I come, I go, I glide, I plunge
Vanishing into the pure of heart!
Was there ever a soul so tough
As to leave no lodgment for a dream?
Whoever you be, whatever am I
If not the connivance that begins
In your mind when it pleases itself?
In the depths of that very pleasure
I'm the inimitable flavor
You find that you alone possess!

Eve, long since, I took by surprise
In the depths of her dawning mind,
Her lip just opened to the ideas
Inspired by the rocking roses.
That perfection greeted my gaze,
Her spacious flank overrun with golden

Light, fearless of sun or man;
All exposed to the watching air,
Her soul still stupid, as it were,
Nonplused on the sill of the flesh.

. . .

"Nothing," I prompted, "is more unsure
Than the divine pronouncement, Eve!
A live knowledge will soon burst
The enormity of that ripe fruit.
Don't heed the ancient Puritan
Who laid a curse on the briefest bite.
For if your mouth holds a daydream,
A thirst, musing upon a savor,
That just-about-to-be delight
Is melt-in-the-mouth eternity, Eve!"

She drank in my casual words,
As they built a curious edifice;
Her eye would quit an angel's flight
To turn back towards my bower.
The craftiest of animal kind
Teasing you for being so hard,
Oh traitorous one, big with evils,
Is a bodiless voice in the greenery!
—But solemn she stood, this Eve,
Under the bough, listening hard!

"Soul," I murmured, "tender retreat
Of all prohibited ecstasy,
Can you divine the sinuous love
Which from the Father I've purloined?
That very essence of Heaven
To a purpose sweeter than honey
I have delicately devised. . . .
Try this fruit. . . . Stretch your arm . . . !
To choose and pick whatever you will
Is why you were given that lovely hand!"

. . .

Translated from the French
by David Paul

EAVAN BOLAND ☐

The Serpent in the Garden

How often
in this loneliness,
unlighted
but for the porcelain

brightening
of the bath,
have I done this.
Again and again this.

This time,
in the shadowy
and woody light
between the bath and blind,

between the day and night,
the same blue
eyeshadow
rouge and blusher

will mesh with
my fingers
to a weaving
pulse.

In a ringed
coiling,
a convulsion,
I will heave

to a sinuous
and final
shining off
of skin:

look at the hood
I have made
for my eyes,
my head

and how quickly,
over my lips,
slicked and cold,
my tongue flickers.

GENESIS 3:8–19

[8]They heard the sound of the LORD God moving about in the garden at the breezy time of day; and the man and his wife hid from the LORD God among the trees of the garden. [9]The LORD God called out to the man and said to him, "Where are you?" [10]He replied, "I heard the sound of You in the garden, and I was afraid because I was naked, so I hid." [11]Then He asked, "Who told you that you were naked? Did you eat of the tree from which I had forbidden you to eat?" [12]The man said, "The woman You put at my side—she gave me of the tree, and I ate." [13]And the LORD God said to the woman, "What is this you have done!" The Woman replied, "The serpent duped me, and I ate." [14]Then the LORD God said to the serpent,

"Because you did this,
More cursed shall you be
Than all cattle
And all the wild beasts:
On your belly shall you crawl
And dirt shall you eat
All the days of your life.
[15]I will put enmity
Between you and the woman,
And between your offspring and hers;
They shall strike at your head,
And you shall strike at their heel."
[16]And to the woman He said,
"I will make most severe
Your pangs in childbearing;
In pain shall you bear children.
Yet your urge shall be for your husband,
And he shall rule over you."
[17]To Adam He said, "Because you did as your wife said and ate of the tree about which I commanded you, 'You shall not eat of it,'
Cursed be the ground because of you;
By toil shall you eat of it

All the days of your life:
[18]Thorns and thistles shall it sprout for you.
But your food shall be the grasses of the field;
[19]By the sweat of your brow
Shall you get bread to eat,
Until you return to the ground—
For from it you were taken.
For dust you are,
And to dust you shall return."

STEVIE SMITH □

How Cruel Is the Story of Eve

How cruel is the story of Eve
What responsibility
It has in history
For cruelty.

Touch, where the feeling is most vulnerable,
Unblameworthy—ah reckless—desiring children,
Touch there with a touch of pain?
Abominable.

Ah what cruelty,
In history
What misery.

Put up to barter
The tender feelings
Buy her a husband to rule her
Fool her to marry a master
She must or rue it
The Lord said it.

And man, poor man,
Is he fit to rule,
Pushed to it?
How can he carry it, the governance,
And not suffer for it
Insuffisance?
He must make woman lower then
So he can be higher then.

Oh what cruelty,
In history what misery.

Soon woman grows cunning
Masks her wisdom,
How otherwise will he
Bring food and shelter, kill enemies?
If he did not feel superior
It would be worse for her
And for the tender children
Worse for them.

Oh what cruelty,
In history what misery
Of falsity.

It is only a legend
You say? But what
Is the meaning of the legend
If not
To give blame to women most
And most punishment?

This is the meaning of a legend that colours
All human thought; it is not found among animals.

How cruel is the story of Eve,
What responsibility it has
In history
For misery.

Yet there is this to be said still:
Life would be over long ago
If men and women had not loved each other
Naturally, naturally,
Forgetting their mythology
They would have died of it else
Long ago, long ago,
And all would be emptiness now
And silence.

Oh dread Nature, for your purpose,
To have made them love so.

WILLIAM BUTLER YEATS □
Adam's Curse

We sat together at one summer's end,
That beautiful mild woman, your close friend,
And you and I, and talked of poetry.
I said, "A line will take us hours maybe;
Yet if it does not seem a moment's thought,
Our stitching and unstitching has been naught.
Better go down upon your marrow-bones
And scrub a kitchen pavement, or break stones
Like an old pauper, in all kinds of weather;
For to articulate sweet sounds together
Is to work harder than all these, and yet
Be thought an idler by the noisy set
Of bankers, schoolmasters, and clergymen
The martyrs call the world."

     And thereupon
That beautiful mild woman for whose sake
There's many a one shall find out all heartache
On finding that her voice is sweet and low
Replied, "To be born woman is to know—
Although they do not talk of it at school—
That we must labour to be beautiful."

I said, "It's certain there is no fine thing
Since Adam's fall but needs much labouring.
There have been lovers who thought love should be
So much compounded of high courtesy
That they would sigh and quote with learned looks
Precedents out of beautiful old books;
Yet now it seems an idle trade enough."

We sat grown quiet at the name of love;
We saw the last embers of daylight die,
And in the trembling blue-green of the sky
A moon, worn as if it had been a shell
Washed by time's waters as they rose and fell
About the stars and broke in days and years.

I had a thought for no one's but your ears:
That you were beautiful, and that I strove
To love you in the old high way of love;
That it had all seemed happy, and yet we'd grown
As weary-hearted as that hollow moon.

C · The Expulsion from Eden

GENESIS 3:20–24

²⁰The man named his wife Eve,* because she was the mother of all the living.† ²¹And the LORD God made garments of skins for Adam and his wife, and clothed them.

²²And the LORD God said, "Now that the man has become like one of us, knowing good and bad, what if he should stretch out his hand and take also from the tree of life and eat, and live forever!" ²³So the LORD God banished him from the garden of Eden, to till the soil from which he was taken. ²⁴He drove the man out, and stationed east of the garden of Eden the cherubim and the fiery ever-turning sword, to guard the way to the tree of life.

* Heb. *hawwah*
† Heb. *hay*

JORGE LUIS BORGES □

Adam Cast Forth

The Garden—was it real or was it dream?
Slow in the hazy light, I have been asking,
Almost as a comfort, if the past
Belonging to this now unhappy Adam
Was nothing but a magic fantasy
Of that God I dreamed. Now it is imprecise
In memory, that lucid paradise,
But I know it exists and will persist
Though not for me. The unforgiving earth
Is my affliction, and the incestuous wars
Of Cains and Abels and their progeny.
Nevertheless, it means much to have loved,
To have been happy, to have touched upon
The living Garden, even for one day.

> Translated from the Spanish
> by Alastair Reid

CZESLAW MILOSZ □

After Paradise

Don't run anymore. Quiet. How softly it rains
On the roofs of the city. How perfect
All things are. Now, for the two of you
Waking up in a royal bed by a garret window.
For a man and a woman. For one plant divided
Into masculine and feminine which longed for each other.
Yes, this is my gift to you. Above ashes
On a bitter, bitter earth. Above the subterranean
Echo of clamorings and vows. So that now at dawn
You must be attentive: the tilt of a head,
A hand with a comb, two faces in a mirror
Are only forever once, even if unremembered,
So that you watch what is, though it fades away,
And are grateful every moment for your being.
Let that little park with greenish marble busts
In the pearl-gray light, under a summer drizzle,

Remain as it was when you opened the gate.
And the street of tall peeling porticoes
Which this love of yours suddenly transformed.

Translated from the Polish
by Czeslaw Milosz and Robert Hass

ERICH FRIED □

Paradise Lost

When I had lost
my first country
and when in my second country
and in my place of refuge
and in my third country
and in my second place of refuge
I had lost everything
then I set out

to look for a land
that was not poisoned
by any memories
of irreplaceable losses

So I came to Paradise
there I found peace
Everything was whole and good
I lacked for nothing

Then a sentry
with a flaming sword
said: 'Get away
Here you have lost nothing'

Translated from the German
by Stuart Hood

FRANZ KAFKA □

Paradise

The expulsion from Paradise is in its main significance eternal: Consequently the expulsion from Paradise is final, and life in this world irrevocable, but the eternal nature of the occurrence (or, temporally expressed, the eternal recapitulation of the occurrence) makes it nevertheless possible that not only could we live continuously in Paradise, but that we are continuously there in actual fact, no matter whether we know it here or not.

Why do we lament over the fall of man? We were not driven out of Paradise because of it, but because of the Tree of Life, that we might not eat of it.

We are sinful not merely because we have eaten of the Tree of Knowledge, but also because we have not yet eaten of the Tree of Life. The state in which we find ourselves is sinful, quite independent of guilt.

We were fashioned to live in Paradise, and Paradise was destined to serve us. Our destiny has been altered; that this has also happened with the destiny of Paradise is not stated.

We were expelled from Paradise, but Paradise was not destroyed. In a sense our expulsion from Paradise was a stroke of luck, for had we not been expelled, Paradise would have had to be destroyed.

God said that Adam would have to die on the day he ate of the Tree of Knowledge. According to God, the instantaneous result of eating of the Tree of Knowledge would be death; according to the serpent (at least it can be understood so), it would be equality with God. Both were wrong in similar ways. Men did not die, but became mortal; they did not become like God, but received the indispensable capacity to become so. Both were right in similar ways. Man did not die, but the paradisiacal man did; men did not become God, but divine knowledge.

He is a free and secure citizen of the world, for he is fettered to a chain which is long enough to give him the freedom of all earthly space, and yet only so long that nothing can drag him past the frontiers of the world. But simultaneously he is a free and secure citizen of Heaven as well, for he is also fettered by a similarly designed heavenly chain. So that if he heads, say, for the earth, his heavenly collar throttles him, and if he heads for Heaven, his earthly one does the same. And yet all the possibilities are his, and he feels it; more, he actually refuses to account for the deadlock by an error in the original fettering.

Since the Fall we have been essentially equal in our capacity to recognize good and evil; nonetheless it is just here that we seek to show our individual superiority. But the real differences begin beyond that knowledge. The opposite illusion may be explained thus: nobody can remain content with the mere knowledge of good and evil in itself, but must endeavor as well to act in accordance with it. The strength to do so, however, is not likewise given him, consequently he must destroy himself trying to do so, at the risk of not achieving the necessary strength even then; yet there remains nothing for him but this final attempt. (That is moreover the meaning of the threat of death attached to eating of the Tree of Knowledge; perhaps too it was the original meaning of natural death.) Now, faced with this attempt, man is filled with fear; he prefers to annul his knowledge of good and evil (the term, "the fall of man," may be traced back to that fear); yet the accomplished cannot be annulled, but only confused. It was for this purpose that our rationalizations were created. The whole world is full of them, indeed the whole visible world is perhaps nothing more than the rationalization of a man who wants to find peace for a moment. An attempt to falsify the actuality of knowledge, to regard knowledge as a goal still to be reached.

Translated from the German
by Willa and Edwin Muir

JAROSLAV SEIFERT □

Lost Paradise

The Old Jewish Cemetery
is one great bouquet of grey stone
on which time has trodden.
I was drifting among the graves,
thinking of my mother.
She used to read the Bible.

The letters in two columns
welled up before her eyes
like blood from a wound.
The lamp was guttering and smoking
and Mother put on her glasses.
At times she had to blow it out
and with her hairpin straighten
the glowing wick.

But when she closed her tired eyes
she dreamed of Paradise,
before God had garrisoned it

with armed cherubim . . .
Often she fell asleep over the Book
which slipped from her lap.

I was still young
when I discovered in the Old Testament
those fascinating verses about love
and eagerly searched for
the passages on incest . . .
That time I did not yet suspect
how much tenderness is hidden in the names
of Old Testament women.

Adah is Ornament and Orpah[f]
is a Hind,
Naamah is the Pleasant
and Nikol is the Little Brook.
Abigail is the Fount of Exultation.

But if I recall how helplessly I watched
as they dragged off the Jews,
even the crying children,
I still shudder with horror
and a chill runs down my spine.

Jemima is the Dove and Tamar
a Palm Tree.
Tirzah is Pleasantness
and Zilpah a Raindrop.
My God, how beautiful this is.

We were living in hell
yet no one dared to strike the weapon
from the murderers' hands.
As if within our hearts we did not have
a spark of humanity!

The name Jecholiah means
The Lord is Mighty.
And yet their frowning God
gazed over the barbed wire
and did not move a finger—

Delilah is the Delicate, Rachel
the Ewe Lamb,

[f] See "Notes on the Poems," p. 333

Deborah the Bee
and Esther the Bright Star.

I'd just returned from the cemetery
when the June evening with its scents
leaned against the windows.
But from the silent distance now and then came thunder
of a future war.
There is no time without murder.

I almost forgot:
Rhoda is the Rose.
And this flower perhaps is the only thing
that's left us on earth
from ancient Paradise.

Translated from the Czech
by Ewald Osers

RAINER MARIA RILKE □

Adam

Dazed, he stands at the cathedral's steep
Upsurge, where the window-rose is,
As if scared by the apotheosis
Which had grown and by a sudden leap

Placed him over many a so-and-so.
And he looms there, glad of his firm presence,
Artless his resolve, as is the peasant's
Who had made a start and did not know

How to find, from lush and finished Eden,
A descent into the virgin earth.
God took a tremendous deal of wheedling,

And, so far from granting, he would cry,
Over and again, that he would die.
But the man held out: she would give birth.

Translated from the German
by Walter Arndt

RAINER MARIA RILKE ☐

Eve

Plain, she stands by the cathedral's tall
Exaltation near the window-rose,
Apple in the apple-proffering pose,
Guiltlessly to blame once and for all

For the growing life she founded here
Since for love she left the unison
Of eternities to struggle on
Through the soil as does the youthful year.

Not that she would not have liked to stay
Somewhat longer in that grove, attending
To the beasts' astute and peaceful way;

But she found the man's resolve was set,
And she sought with him the lethal ending,
Having barely known the Lord as yet.

Translated from the German
by Walter Arndt

JUDITH WRIGHT ☐

Eve to Her Daughters

It was not I who began it.
Turned out into draughty caves,
hungry so often, having to work for our bread,
hearing the children whining,
I was nevertheless not unhappy.
Where Adam went I was fairly contented to go.
I adapted myself to the punishment: it was my life.

But Adam, you know . . . !
He kept on brooding over the insult,
over the trick They had played on us, over the scolding.
He had discovered a flaw in himself
and he had to make up for it.

Outside Eden the earth was imperfect,
the seasons changed, the game was fleet-footed,
he had to work for our living, and he didn't like it.
He even complained of my cooking
(it was hard to compete with Heaven).

So he set to work.
The earth must be made a new Eden
with central heating, domesticated animals,
mechanical harvesters, combustion engines,
escalators, refrigerators,
and modern means of communication
and multiplied opportunities for safe investment
and higher education for Abel and Cain
and the rest of the family.
You can see how his pride had been hurt.

In the process he had to unravel everything,
because he believed that mechanism
was the whole secret—he was always mechanical-minded.
He got to the very inside of the whole machine
exclaiming as he went, So this is how it works!

And now that I know how it works, why, I must have invented it.
As for God and the Other, they cannot be demonstrated,
and what cannot be demonstrated
doesn't exist.
You see, he had always been jealous.

Yes, he got to the centre
where nothing at all can be demonstrated.
And clearly he doesn't exist; but he refuses
to accept the conclusion.
You see, he was always an egotist.

It was warmer than this in the cave;
there was none of this fall-out.
I would suggest, for the sake of the children,
that it's time you took over.

But you are my daughters, you inherit my own faults of
    character;
you are submissive, following Adam
even beyond existence.
Faults of character have their own logic

and it always works out.
I observed this with Abel and Cain.

Perhaps the whole elaborate fable
right from the beginning
is meant to demonstrate this; perhaps it's the whole secret.
Perhaps nothing exists but our faults?
At least they can be demonstrated.

But it's useless to make
such a suggestion to Adam.
He has turned himself into God,
who is faultless, and doesn't exist.

CZESLAW MILOSZ □

Theodicy

No, it won't do, my sweet theologians.
Desire will not save the morality of God.
If he created beings able to choose between good and evil,
And they chose, and the world lies in iniquity,
Nevertheless, there is pain, and the undeserved torture of creatures,
Which would find its explanation only by assuming
The existence of an archetypal Paradise
And a pre-human downfall so grave
That the world of matter received its shape from diabolic power.

Translated from the Polish
by Czeslaw Milosz and Robert Hass

JORGE LUIS BORGES □

Possession of Yesterday

I know the things I've lost are so many that I could not begin
    to count them
and that those losses
now, are all I have.
I know that I've lost the yellow and the black and I think
of those unreachable colors

as those that are not blind can not.
My father is dead, and always stands beside me.
When I try to scan Swinburne's verses, I am told, I speak with my
    father's voice.
Only those who have died are ours, only what we have lost is ours.
Ilium vanished, yet Ilium lives in Homer's verses.
Israel was Israel when it became an ancient nostalgia.
Every poem, in time, becomes an elegy.
The women who have left us are ours, free as we now are from
    misgivings,
from anguish, from the disquiet and dread of hope.
There are no paradises other than lost paradises.

Translated from the Spanish
by Nicomedes Suarez Arauz

W. H. AUDEN □

From "Horae Canonicae"

Prime

Simultaneously, as soundlessly,
    Spontaneously, suddenly
As, at the vaunt of the dawn, the kind
    Gates of the body fly open
To its world beyond, the gates of the mind,
    The horn gate and the ivory gate
Swing to, swing shut, instantaneously
    Quell the nocturnal rummage
Of its rebellious fronde, ill-favoured,
    Ill-natured and second-rate,
Disenfranchised, widowed and orphaned
    By an historical mistake:
Recalled from the shades to be a seeing being,
    From absence to be on display,
Without a name or history I wake
    Between my body and the day.

Holy this moment, wholly in the right,
    As, in complete obedience
To the light's laconic outcry, next
    As a sheet, near as a wall,

Out there as a mountain's poise of stone,
    The world is present, about,
And I know that I am, here, not alone
    But with a world and rejoice
Unvexed, for the will has still to claim
    This adjacent arm as my own,
The memory to name me, resume
    Its routine of praise and blame,
And smiling to me is this instant while
    Still the day is intact, and I
The Adam sinless in our beginning,
    Adam still previous to any act.

I draw breath; that is of course to wish
    No matter what, to be wise,
To be different, to die and the cost,
    No matter how, is Paradise
Lost of course and myself owing a death:
    The eager ridge, the steady sea,
The flat roofs of the fishing village
    Still asleep in its bunny,
Though as fresh and sunny still are not friends
    But things to hand, this ready flesh
No honest equal, but my accomplice now,
    My assassin to be, and my name
Stands for my historical share of care
    For a lying self-made city,
Afraid of our living task, the dying
    Which the coming day will ask.

D · Cain and Abel

GENESIS 4:1–16

Now the man knew* his wife Eve, and she conceived and bore Cain, saying, "I have gained† a male child with the help of the LORD." ²She then bore his brother Abel. Abel became a keeper of sheep, and Cain became a tiller of the soil. ³In the course of time, Cain brought an offering to the LORD from the fruit of the soil; ⁴and Abel, for his part, brought the choicest of the firstlings of his flock. The LORD paid heed to Abel and his offering, ⁵but to Cain and his offering He paid no heed. Cain was much distressed and his face fell. ⁶And the LORD said to Cain,

"Why are you distressed,
And why is your face fallen?
⁷‡Surely, if you do right,
There is uplift.
But if you do not do right
Sin couches at the door;
Its urge is toward you,
Yet you can be its master."

⁸Cain said to his brother Abel . . . § and when they were in the field, Cain set upon his brother Abel and killed him. ⁹The LORD said to Cain, "Where is your brother Abel?" And he said, "I do not know. Am I my brother's keeper?" ¹⁰Then He said, "What have you done? Hark, your brother's blood cries out to Me from the ground! ¹¹Therefore, you shall be more cursed than the ground,‖ which opened its mouth to receive your brother's blood from your hand. ¹²If you till the soil, it shall no longer yield its strength to you. You shall become a ceaseless wanderer on earth."

¹³Cain said to the LORD, "My punishment is too great to bear!

---

* Heb. *yada'* often in the sense of "experienced"
† Heb. *qanithi*, connected with "Cain"
‡ Heb. verse obscure
§ Ancient versions, including the Targum, read "Come, let us go out into the field"
‖ See 3:17

¹⁴Since You have banished me this day from the soil, and I must avoid Your presence and become a restless wanderer on earth—anyone who meets me may kill me!" ¹⁵The LORD said to him, "I promise, if anyone kills Cain, sevenfold vengeance shall be taken on him." And the LORD put a mark on Cain, lest anyone who met him should kill him. ¹⁶Cain left the presence of the LORD and settled in the land of Nod, east of Eden.

DAN PAGIS □

Autobiography

I died with the first blow and was buried
among the rocks of the field.
The raven taught my parents
what to do with me.

If my family is famous,
not a little of the credit goes to me.
My brother invented murder,
my parents invented grief,
I invented silence.

Afterwards the well-known events took place.
Our inventions were perfected. One thing led to another,
orders were given. There were those who murdered in their
    own way,
grieved in their own way.

I won't mention names
out of consideration for the reader,
since at first the details horrify
though finally they're a bore:

you can die once, twice, even seven times,
but you can't die a thousand times.
I can.
My underground cells reach everywhere.

When Cain began to multiply on the face of the earth,
I began to multiply in the belly of the earth,

and my strength has long been greater than his.
His legions desert him and go over to me,
and even this is only half a revenge.

Translated from the Hebrew
by Stephen Mitchell

JORGE LUIS BORGES □

Legend

Abel and Cain met again after Abel's death. They were walking in the desert and knew each other from a distance, for both men were very tall. The brothers sat on the ground, made a fire, and ate. For a while, they were untalkative, the way tired men can be after a long day's work. In the sky, some still unnamed star appeared. By the firelight, Cain made out the mark of the stone on Abel's forehead, dropped the food he was about to put into his mouth, and asked to be forgiven for his crime.

"I no longer remember—did you kill me or was it I who killed you?" Abel answered. "Here we are together again, just as we used to be."

"Now I know for sure you've forgiven me," said Cain, "because to forget is to have forgiven. I'll try my best to forget, too."

"Yes," said Abel, speaking slowly, "you're right. As long as there's remorse, there's guilt."

Translated from the Spanish
by Norman Thomas di Giovanni

DAN PAGIS □

Scrawled in Pencil in a Sealed Railway Car

here in this transport
i eve
and abel my son
if you should see my older son
cain son of man
tell him that i

Translated from the Hebrew
by Robert Friend

E · Noah

GENESIS 6:9–7:5

⁹This is the line of Noah.—Noah was a righteous man; he was blameless in his age; Noah walked with God.—¹⁰Noah begot three sons: Shem, Ham, and Japheth.

¹¹The earth became corrupt before God; the earth was filled with lawlessness. ¹²When God saw how corrupt the earth was, for all flesh had corrupted its ways on earth, ¹³God said to Noah, "I have decided to put an end to all flesh, for the earth is filled with lawlessness because of them: I am about to destroy them with the earth. ¹⁴Make yourself an ark of gopher wood; make it an ark with compartments, and cover it inside and out with pitch. ¹⁵This is how you shall make it: the length of the ark shall be three hundred cubits, its width fifty cubits, and its height thirty cubits. ¹⁶Make an opening for daylight in the ark, and *⁻terminate it within a cubit of the top.⁻* Put the entrance to the ark in its side; make it with bottom, second, and third decks.

7 Then the LORD said to Noah, "Go into the ark, with all your household, for you alone have I found righteous before Me in this generation. ²Of every clean animal you shall take seven pairs, males and their mates, and of every animal which is not clean, two, a male and its mate; ³of the birds of the sky also, seven pairs, male and female, to keep seed alive upon all the earth. ⁴For in seven days' time I will make it rain upon the earth, forty days and forty nights, and I will blot out from the earth all existence that I created." ⁵And Noah did just as the LORD commanded him.

⁻ Meaning of Heb. uncertain

CHRIS WALLACE-CRABBE □

Noah

Hammering away
Day after sunny day
Noah can hear what they say:

"That poor old siren, Progress,
Lost every rag of her dress:
Things are always a mess."

Caulking chinks in the hull,
Noah can feel the pull
Of a life less dull

Than professional carpentry;
The strains of tragedy
Stretch in his mind like the sea.

The easiest way out
Would be to drink and shout,
Join the complaining rout

And not burden his wife
With hammer and putty-knife,
With his prickly belief in life.

Red sunset runs away.
He laid five planks today;
"I must sharpen the plane and oil the stone,"
Is all he finds to say.

ROBERT GRAVES □

The Ark

Beasts of the field, fowls likewise of the air,
Came trooping, seven by seven or pair by pair;
And though from Hell the arch-fiend Samael[g]
Bawled out "Escapist!" Noah did not care.

---

[g] See "Notes on the Poems," p. 333

JAY MACPHERSON □

The Ark

Ark to Noah

I wait, with those that rest
In darkness till you come,
Though they are murmuring flesh
And I a block and dumb.

Yet when you come, be pleased
To shine here, be shown
Inward as all the creatures
Drawn through my bone.

Ark Articulate

Shaped new to your measure
From a mourning grove,
I am your sensing creature
And may speak for love.

If you repent again
And turn and unmade, me,
How shall I rock my pain
In the arms of a tree?

Ark Anatomical

Set me to sound for you
The world unmade
As he who rears the head
In light arrayed,

That its vision may quicken
Every wanting part
Hangs deep in the dark body
A divining heart.

Ark Artefact

Between me and the wood
I grew in, you stand
Firm as when first I woke
Alive in your hand.

How could you know your love,
If not defined in me,

From the grief of the always wounded,
Always closing sea?

Ark Apprehensive

I am a sleeping body
Hulling down the night,
And you the dream I ferry
To shores of light.

I sleep that you may wake,
That the black sea
May not gape sheer under you
As he does for me.

Ark Astonished

Why did your spirit
Strive so long with me?
Will you wring love from deserts,
Comfort from the sea?

Your dove and raven speed,
The carrion and the kind.
Man, I know your need,
But not your mind.

Ark Overwhelmed

When the four quarters shall
Turn in and make one whole,
Then I who wall your body,
Which is to me a soul,

Shall swim circled by you
And cradled on your tide,
Who was not even, not ever,
Taken from your side.

Ark Parting

You dreamed it. From my ground
You raised that flood, these fears.
The creatures all but drowned
Fled your well of tears.

Outward the fresh shores gleam
Clear in new-washed eyes.
Fare well. From your dream
I only shall not rise.

JANE SHORE □

The Ark

On the avenue below, they file past—
Two and two, two and two,

And are recorded. Men and women
Climb the ramp and enter my body

To be welcomed; as Eve welcomed
Adam, who bore her, and broke him

Uninjured by her departure.
And the children, each with his small grief,

And the animals, each with his complaint,
Issue from the planet that would keep

Its strict count. Male and female
He made them, beasts unlinked by gender;

Monstrous or innocent, they fill me,
Who will carry them to safety.

And the dove now circling the tree,
Once circled this wilderness inside me:

An instrument meant to receive life
And not to judge it.

WISLAWA SZYMBORSKA □

Into the Ark

An endless rain is just beginning.
Into the ark, for where else can you go:
you poems for a single voice,
private exultations,

unnecessary talents,
surplus curiosity,
short-range sorrows and fears,
eagerness to see things from all six sides.

Rivers are swelling and bursting their banks.
Into the ark: all you chiaroscuros and halftones,
you details, ornaments, and whims,
silly exceptions,
forgotten signs,
countless shades of the color gray,
play for play's sake,
and tears of mirth.

As far as the eye can see, there's water and a hazy horizon.
Into the ark: plans for the distant future,
joy in difference,
admiration for the better man,
choice not narrowed down to one of two,
outworn scruples,
time to think it over,
and the belief that all of this
will still come in handy some day.

For the sake of the children
that we still are,
fairy tales have happy endings.
That's the only finale that will do here, too.
The rain will stop,
the waves will subside,
the clouds will part
in the cleared-up sky,
and they'll be once more
what clouds overhead ought to be:
lofty and rather lighthearted
in their likeness to things
drying in the sun—
isles of bliss,
lambs,
cauliflowers,
diapers.

Translated from the Polish
by Stanislaw Baranczak and Claire Cavanagh

EUGENIO MONTALE □

The Ark

The umbrella of the willow tree
turns upside-down in the spring storm;
in April's whirlwind
the golden fleece hiding my dead ones,
my faithful dogs, my old servants,
becomes entangled in the garden—how many of them since then
(when the willow was golden and I would break
its fingers with my sling-shot) have fallen,
still living, into the trap. Surely the storm
will bring them together under
that earlier roof, but far away, farther away
than this lightning-sliced earth
where lime and blood seethe in the imprint
of the human foot. The soup-ladle smokes
in the kitchen, its round, reflecting lens
focusing the lean faces, the pointed muzzles,
and will protect them under the magnolia tree
if a gust of wind blows them there. The spring storm
stirs my ark like the yelp of a faithful dog,
O memories lost in me.

Translated from the Italian
by Charles Wright

GENESIS 8:13–22

[13]In the six hundred and first year, in the first month, on the first of the month, the waters began to dry from the earth; and when Noah removed the covering of the ark, he saw that the surface of the ground was drying. [14]And in the second month, on the twenty-seventh day of the month, the earth was dry.

[15]God spoke to Noah, saying, [16]"Come out of the ark, together with your wife, your sons, and your sons' wives. [17]Bring out with you every living thing of all flesh that is with you: birds, animals, and everything that creeps on earth; and let them swarm on the earth and be fertile and increase on earth." [18]So Noah came out, together with his sons, his wife, and his sons' wives. [19]Every animal, every creeping thing, and every bird, everything that stirs on earth came out of the ark by families.

[20]Then Noah built an altar to the LORD and, taking of every clean animal and of every clean bird, he offered burnt offerings on the altar. [21]The LORD smelled the pleasing odor, and the LORD said to Himself: "Never again will I doom the earth because of man, since the devisings of man's mind are evil from his youth; nor will I ever again destroy every living being, as I have done.

[22]So long as the earth endures,
Seedtime and harvest,
Cold and heat,
Summer and winter,
Day and night
Shall not cease."

DAN PAGIS □

Ararat

While all the ark's survivors lurched onto land
and in joyful disarray
chattered and roared and shouted for prey
and howled for procreation
and overhead came the rainbow and said
no such end would happen again—the end did come
for the carefree fish that had lived
off the mishap like smooth speculators.
Now, on stiffening soil,
they were caught, their fins disheveled,
and with mouths gaping wide,
they died, drowning in air.

Translated from the Hebrew
by Warren Bargad and Stanley F. Chyet

F ▪ The Tower of Babel

GENESIS 11:1–9

All the earth had the same language and the same words. [2]And as men migrated from the east, they came upon a valley in the land of Shinar and settled there. [3]They said to one another, "Come, let us make bricks and burn them hard."—Brick served them as stone, and bitumen served them as mortar.—[4]And they said, "Come, let us build us a city, and a tower with its top in the sky, to make a name for ourselves; else we shall be scattered all over the world." [5]The LORD came down to look at the city and tower which man had built, [6]and the LORD said, "If, as one people with one language for all, this is how they have begun to act, then nothing that they may propose to do will be out of their reach. [7]Let us, then, go down and confound their speech there, so that they shall not understand one another's speech." [8]Thus the LORD scattered them from there over the face of the whole earth; and they stopped building the city. [9]That is why it was called Babel,* because there the LORD confounded[†] the speech of the whole earth; and from there the LORD scattered them over the face of the whole earth.

---

* I.e., "Babylon"
[†] Heb. *balal* "confound," play on "Babel"

WISLAWA SZYMBORSKA ☐

In the Tower of Babel

*—What time is it?—*Yes, I am happy.
All I lack is a little bell at my throat
that would ring above you when you are sleeping.
—So you didn't hear the storm? Wind hit walls,
the tower yawned like a lion, its huge gate
*on squeaking hinges.—*How come, did you forget?
I was wearing a simple grey dress
fastened on the side.*—And at once*
the sky broke in a bolt of blinding lightning. How
could I go out, you were not alone.*—Suddenly, I saw*
*colors I could never see.—*It's a pity
you cannot promise me.*—You are right,*
*obviously it was a dream.—*Why are you lying,
why do you call me by her name,
do you still love her?*—Oh yes, I would like*
*for you to stay with me.—*I don't bear a grudge,
only I should have guessed it.
*—You still think of him?—*But I am not crying!
*—And that's it, that's all?—*No, nobody like you.
—At least you are honest.— Don't worry,
*I'll leave this city.—*Don't worry,
*I'll go away.—*You have such beautiful hands.
—That's an old story, the blade went through
without touching the bone. Don't thank me,
dear, don't thank me.*—I don't know*
and don't want to know what time it is.

Translated from the Polish
by Grażyna Drabik and Sharon Olds

G ▪ The Covenant with Abraham

GENESIS 12:1–9

The LORD said to Abram, "Go forth from your native land and from your father's house to the land that I will show you.
²I will make of you a great nation,
And I will bless you;
I will make your name great,
And you shall be a blessing*
³I will bless those who bless you
And curse him that curses you;
And all the families of the earth
Shall bless themselves by you."
⁴Abram went forth as the LORD had commanded him, and Lot went with him. Abram was seventy-five years old when he left Haran. ⁵Abram took his wife Sarai and his brother's son Lot, and all the wealth that they had amassed, and the persons that they had acquired in Haran; and they set out for the land of Canaan. When they arrived in the land of Canaan, ⁶Abram passed through the land as far as the site of Shechem, at the terebinth of Moreh. The Canaanites were then in the land.

⁷The LORD appeared to Abram and said, "I will give this land to your offspring." And he built an altar there to the LORD who had appeared to him. ⁸From there he moved on to the hill country east of Bethel and pitched his tent, with Bethel on the west and Ai on the east; and he built there an altar to the LORD and invoked the LORD by name. ⁹Then Abram journeyed by stages toward the Negeb.

* I.e., a standard by which blessing is invoked; cf. v. 3 end

JACOB GLATSTEIN □

Genesis

Why don't we start all over again
with a small people,
out of the cradle and little?
The two of us, wanderers over the nations.
Tillers of the soil will bow before You.
You'll live on burnt offerings of grain.
I'll go around preaching folk wisdom;
it won't reach past our borders,
but the least little child will greet me
good morning.

Why don't we both go home and start over,
from the very beginning,
out of our littleness?

Almighty Yahweh, who hast waxed great
over the seven firmaments and continents,
swollen steel-strong in vast churches
and synagogues, God of the Universe!
You've deserted field and barn;
I, the close love of my people.
We've both turned universal.
Come back, dear God, to a land no bigger than a speck.
Dwindle down to only ours.
I'll go around with homely sayings
suitable for chewing over in small places.
We'll both be provincial,
God and His poet.
Maybe it will go sweeter for us.

You'll begin with a scrap of truth,
not promising seventh heaven,
mindful of human flesh, bone, failings;
wine that gladdens the heart of man;
the body's pleasures.
You'll cherish us for those moments of belief
when out of our depths we invoke You.
You'll keep far from blood, blade, killing.
You'll choose to be the approachable God
of a prayerful huddle
rather than an omnipotent God of Prey.

You'll come near.
We'll begin to spin
merciful laws binding on You and on us.

Out of the cradle and little,
why don't we start all over again,
growing up bordered by a hallowed land?
Children will laugh all around in delight.
We'll be poor and full of truth.
Your holy blessing will just suffice
for a people peaceable and good.
My own word will be the warm pride
of a family.
Your nostrils will savor
the pure meal-offering of a nation
nurturing its God with everything good.
And me they'll feed and fondle like a child.
I'll be rocked in cozy fame.
No one beyond our borders will hear my name,
or Yours.

Shouldn't the two of us go home?
Why don't we both, beaten, go home?

Thou hast chosen us.
We were both cried up for grandeur
so that they could bring us to dust
and scatter us and stamp us out.

They tricked You out in stars over a whole universe.
How is it that great nations flock to You?
You are quiet and content with your own.
You are one of us,
completely.
Why did You abandon your closet-ark,
your little tent,
going far away to be converted
into the Lord of the Universe?
Therefore we became Your errant children,
agitators of pillars, world incendiaries.
You lapsed into the Jewish International
before we did.

We followed You into Your wide world
and sickened there.

Save Yourself, return
with Your pilgrims who go up
to a little land. Come back,
be our Jewish God again.

Translated from the Yiddish
by Cynthia Ozick

ALICIA OSTRIKER □

The Story of Abraham

I started by reading the banner headline
The way you read the big print at the eye doctor's.
It said I AM THE LORD GOD
ALMIGHTY AND I LOVE YOU
ESPECIALLY. No problem. Very good.
One line down it said PACK UP,
I'M SENDING YOU OVERSEAS. It said
YOU WILL HAVE AS MANY CHILDREN
AS THERE ARE SANDS IN THE SEA
AND STARS IN THE SKY.
THEY WILL POSSESS THE LAND AND
I AM PERSONALLY GOING TO BLESS THEM.
The smaller print said: I am going
To bless them as long as they obey me.
Otherwise there may be
Certain repercussions. The even smaller
Print explained how we needed
A memorable logo for our organization
And he had just the ticket, a mark of absolute
Distinction, it would only hurt for a minute.
The print kept getting smaller and blurrier,
The instructions more bizarre.
Hold on, I interrupted. I'd like to check
Some of this out with my wife.
NO WAY. THIS IS BETWEEN US MEN.
AND IF YOU HAPPEN TO BE THINKING
ABOUT LOOPHOLES
FORGET IT. It said they preferred

Not to use strongarm techniques. It said
BEAR IN MIND, FRIEND,
YOU'VE ALREADY SIGNED ON.

AMIR OR   ☐

Go Forth

Go forth from your land, my Lord,
Go forth, come to me,
travel my skin with your lips.
Come dark, come night,
touch all of me, touch,
leave no soundness.
Rise in omens within me, grant
an everlasting inheritance, a multitude
of seed, my Lord,
because I grant it to you
I will increase
your hire.

Go forth from your body, my Lord,
go forth, come to me,
wound my heart, smooth of teeth.
Touch my face, touch my eyes,
truly kill, leave nothing.
Rise within me to the fingers of tears, rise
to the man, until before you
I
shall end.

Go forth from yourself, my Lord,
go forth, come to me,
travel my length, my width,
travel my horizon
I
will burn before you, not consumed.
See my spirit
but some face to your void, see
here I am
no more.

Translated from the Hebrew
by the author

GENESIS 15:1–6

Some time later, the word of the LORD came to Abram in a vision, saying,

"Fear not, Abram,
I am a shield to you;
Your reward shall be very great."

[2]But Abram said, "O Lord GOD, what can You give me, seeing that I shall die childless, *⁻and the one in charge of my household is Dammesek Eliezer!"⁻* [3]Abram said further, "Since You have granted me no offspring, my steward will be my heir." [4]The word of the LORD came to him in reply, "That one shall not be your heir; none but your very own issue shall be your heir." [5]He took him outside and said, "Look toward heaven and count the stars, if you are able to count them." And He added, "So shall your offspring be." [6]And because he put his trust in the LORD, He reckoned it to his merit.

⁻ Heb. obscure

YEHUDA AMICHAI ☐

The Onus of Mercy

Count them.
You can count them. They're
not like sand on the seashore. They're
not like stars without number. They're
like separate people.
On the corner and in the street.

Count them. Look at them
watching the sky through ruins.
Leave the rubble and come back. Where can you
come back to? But count them, for they
soothe their days with dreams
and walk about freely, and their unbandaged hopes
are agape, and that's how they'll die.

Count them.
They learned too soon to read the terrible
writing on the wall. To read and to write on
other walls. And the feast goes on in silence.

Count them. Be there, for they've
used up all the blood and still need more.
Like major surgery, when you're weary
and sorely wounded. For who's to judge and what is judgment
unless it's the full import of night
and the full onus of mercy.

Translated from the Hebrew
by Warren Bargad and Stanley F. Chyet

GENESIS 17:9–14

[9]God further said to Abraham, "As for you, you and your offspring to come throughout the ages shall keep My covenant. [10]Such shall be the covenant between Me and you and your offspring to follow which you shall keep: every male among you shall be circumcised. [11]You shall circumcise the flesh of your foreskin, and that shall be the sign of the covenant between Me and you. [12]And throughout the generations, every male among you shall be circumcised at the age of eight days. As for the homeborn slave and the one bought from an outsider who is not of your offspring, [13]they must be circumcised, homeborn and purchased alike. Thus shall My covenant be marked in your flesh as an everlasting pact. [14]And if any male who is uncircumcised fails to circumcise the flesh of his foreskin, that person shall be cut off from his kin; he has broken My covenant."

ALLEN AFTERMAN □

Covenant

Son, half-gentile child
I circumcised you—
forced you. I made you bleed.
The *mohel*[h] uttered words
I neither understood nor believed.
That primitive hour with sweet wine we toasted.

I was afraid to love you,
afraid you would turn against me—
your heart gentile,
impregnable.
The son created,
we entered the ancient covenant of Fathers,

not to leave your body perfect.

[h] See "Notes on the Poems," p. 333

H • Lot and His Family

GENESIS 19:1–11

The two angels arrived in Sodom in the evening, as Lot was sitting in the gate of Sodom. When Lot saw them, he rose to greet them and, bowing low with his face to the ground, [2]he said, "Please, my lords, turn aside to your servant's house to spend the night, and bathe your feet; then you may be on your way early." But they said, "No, we will spend the night in the square." [3]But he urged them strongly, so they turned his way and entered his house. He prepared a feast for them and baked unleavened bread, and they ate.

[4]They had not yet lain down, when the townspeople, the men of Sodom, young and old—all the people to the last man—gathered about the house. [5]And they shouted to Lot and said to him, "Where are the men who came to you tonight? Bring them out to us, that we may be intimate with them" [6]So Lot went out to them to the entrance, shut the door behind him, [7]and said, "I beg you, my friends, do not commit such a wrong. [8]Look, I have two daughters who have not known a man. Let me bring them out to you, and you may do to them as you please; but do not do anything to these men, since they have come under the shelter of my roof." [9]But they said, "Stand back! The fellow," they said, "came here as an alien, and already he acts the ruler! Now we will deal worse with you than with them." And they pressed hard against the person of Lot, and moved forward to break the door. [10]But the men stretched out their hands and pulled Lot into the house with them, and shut the door. [11]And the people who were at the entrance of the house, young and old, they struck with blinding light, so that they were helpless to find the entrance.

DARYL HINE □

The Destruction of Sodom

One would never suspect there were so many vices.
It is, I think, a tribute to the imagination
Of those who in these eminently destructible cities
Have made an exact science of perversion
That they, like us, limited by their bodies,
Could put those bodies to such various uses.

Before now men have been punished for their uses
Contrary to nature, though some, indulging phantom vices
Secretly in the brothels of the imagination,
Have escaped so far a condemnation like these cities'
Which were rebuked for innocent perversion
Through the spirit's envy of too simple bodies.

Do not suppose that I intend to praise their bodies,
Though I admit that bodies have their uses,
Nor is my purpose to defend their vices.
Simply as a pervert of the imagination
I pronounce the funeral oration of two cities
Famous for acts of unimaginable perversion.

All love deserves the epitaph "Perversion,"
Being unnaturally concerned, like physics, with foreign
    bodies,
Inseparable from their uses and abuses.
To those who care for nothing but their vices
Love is the faculty of the imagination.
Fantasy, I say, debauches cities.

Discreetly, Lord, show mercy to these cities,
Not for the sake of their, but your, perversion
That contradicts its own created bodies.
These are precisely the instruments grace uses,
Alchemically reforming virtues of their vices,
To raise a heaven from the imagination.

O, where is that heaven of the imagination,
The first and least accessible of cities,
If not in the impossible kingdom of perversion?
Its angels have no sexes and no bodies,
Its speech, no words, its instruments, no uses.
None enter there but those who know their vices.

Number your vices in imagination:
Would they teach whole cities of perversion?
Forgive us our bodies, forgive our bodies' uses.

CHRISTINE HOLBO   □

Gomorrah

Also, in Gomorrah, there were plays,
a life of the mind;
there were the schools
and the quiet temples; Sodom
and "the new theatre"
were conveniently located,
just an hour's ride away. There
the wife of Lot held her
gatherings, "my *petites
soirées*," for the priests
and the politicians
and the intellectual élite.

> *And in the hills the wild dogs cried*
> *And the sand shifted on the desert stones.*

But Gomorrah was mostly as you will have heard:
litigious, polyglot, city of worlds; a scene
from a favorite story frequently told.
There was the traffic, the market banter—
merchants crying catalogues of marvels: uncut
rubies, silver mirrors, porcelain,
parrots, olives at discount, clocks and
sea salt, carbuncles, pearls—the streets
full of crowds, the dirty gypsies,
the quick brown-ankled girls,
the old men smoking on the temple
stoop, the smells of hashish and tanneries,
the bellowing herds.

> *And in the hills the wild dogs cried*
> *And the desert gods shifted sand across the stones.*

The wife of Lot
was not *so* young anymore.
She didn't laugh like
the brown-ankled girls;
the wife of Lot wore a veil in public,
and held her tongue.
And she kept the books
in the family establishment,
was quick with an abacus
or a bon mot or advice about money;
knew how to cook
wild duck with rice, how to
pack a camel—and the best caterers
in town "just like old friends,"
and most of the city councilmen.
The wife of Lot
did what she thought
fitting and appropriate
for the wife of a public figure
and a pillar of the community.

> *And the gods ran along the desert*
> *And a voice echoed across the stones.*

Also, the forenamed woman kept
the books from "my schoolgirl days"
at the Temple. She remembered
learning how to pray,
and the philosophers, taught
by an old and frightening priest
at the gilded knees of an idol.
"Someday I'll get back to
them," she would say.

The wife of Lot
had two pretty daughters,
"the very image of their mother";
they were sent, like the mother,
to the Temple school, the very best,

and were taught French
and the philosophers, and could
quite intelligently discuss
"the name of God" or, alternatively,
"the common good."

They were only young girls,
of course; they liked best to laugh
and they were beautifully dressed
and were like all girls silly.

She asked, "Who am I
thus to be blessed?"

And a spirit cried, "Atone, atone,"
And the wind ran along the desert stone.

Once in a generation or so,
a war or an epiphany occurs,
or a transformation, or a revolution,
or a waiting God stirs; a name
comes into a city, a word
is passed down—an Idea seeks
ten righteous men to save,
the rest, the evidently lost, to reap;
to separate those who have kept
their faith from the too far gone,
and from those who have lost
what they'd sought to keep.
Once in a generation
a warning is heard—

Flee, flee to the hills, flee to the valleys,
The cities. Abandon. Atone.

Lot consulted his in-laws,
And the two daughters wept,
And the wife of Lot packed, asking
herself, "How much should we keep?
How much can be kept?"

They made
the abandoning leap—
but you know the rest: how
Lot and his daughters fled

from that place, how they passed
the test. And how
a moment's recollection,
a sudden grief, a backward
glance revealed what she
had quietly foreseen: a pocky
and astringent silent thing.

GENESIS 19:12–22

[12]Then the men said to Lot, "Whom else have you here? Sons-in-law, your sons and daughters, or anyone else that you have in the city—bring them out of the place. [13]For we are about to destroy this place; because the outcry against them before the LORD has become so great that the LORD has sent us to destroy it." [14]So Lot went out and spoke to his sons-in-law, who had married his daughters, and said, "Up, get out of this place, for the LORD is about to destroy the city." But he seemed to his sons-in-law as one who jests.

[15]As dawn broke, the angels urged Lot on, saying, "Up, take your wife and your two remaining daughters, lest you be swept away because of the iniquity of the city." [16]Still he delayed. So the men seized his hand, and the hands of his wife and his two daughters—in the LORD's mercy on him—and brought him out and left him outside the city. [17]When they had brought them outside, one said, "Flee for your life! Do not look behind you, nor stop anywhere in the Plain; flee to the hills, lest you be swept away." [18]But Lot said to them, "Oh no, my lord! [19]You have been so gracious to your servant, and have already shown me so much kindness in order to save my life; but I cannot flee to the hills, lest the disaster overtake me and I die. [20]Look, that town there is near enough to flee to; it is such a little place! Let me flee there—it is such a little place—and let my life be saved." [21]He replied, "Very well, I will grant you this favor too, and I will not annihilate the town of which you have spoken. [22]Hurry, flee there, for I cannot do anything until you arrive there." Hence the town came to be called Zoar.*

---

* Connected with *mis'ar* "a little place," v. 20

HOWARD NEMEROV □

From "Lot Later"

Vaudeville for George Finckel

I

. . .

So one young man opens his mouth, he says,
"You've got till sunrise, take the wife and kids
And the kids' husbands, and go. Go up to the hills."
The other says, "The Lord hath sent us to
Destroy this place" and so forth and so forth.
You can imagine how I felt. I said,
"Now look, now after all . . . " and my wife said,
"Give me a few days till I pack our things,"
And one of them looked at his watch and said,
"It's orders, lady, sorry, you've got till dawn."
I said, "Respectfully, gentlemen, but who
Lives in the hills? I've got to go, so why
Shouldn't I go to Zoar, which is a nice
Town with a country club which doesn't exclude
Jews? "So go to Zoar if you want," they said.
"Whatever you do, you shouldn't look back here."
We argued all night long. First this, then that.
My son-in-laws got into the act: "You're kidding,
Things of this nature simply do not happen
To people like us." I said, "These here are angels,
But suit yourselves." The pair of them said, "We'll stay,
Only deed us the house and furniture."
"I wouldn't deed you a dead fish," I said,
"Besides, I'm going to take the girls along."
"So take," they said, "they weren't such a bargain."

. . .

GENESIS 19:23–26

[23]As the sun rose upon the earth and Lot entered Zoar, [24]the LORD rained upon Sodom and Gomorrah sulfurous fire from the LORD out of heaven. [25]He annihilated those cities and the entire Plain, and all the inhabitants of the cities and the vegetation of the ground. [26]Lot's* wife looked back,[†] and she thereupon turned into a pillar of salt.

* Lit. "His"
† Lit. "behind him"

ANNA AKHMATOVA ☐

Lot's Wife

And the just man trailed God's shining agent,
over a black mountain, in his giant track,
while a restless voice kept harrying his woman:
"It's not too late, you can still look back

at the red towers of your native Sodom,
the square where once you sang, the spinning-shed,
at the empty windows set in the tall house
where sons and daughters blessed your marriage-bed."

A single glance: a sudden dart of pain
stitching her eyes before she made a sound . . .
Her body flaked into transparent salt,
and her swift legs rooted to the ground.

Who will grieve for this woman? Does she not seem
too insignificant for our concern?
Yet in my heart I never will deny her,
who suffered death because she chose to turn.

1922–24

Translated from the Russian
by Stanley Kunitz and Max Hayward

WISLAWA SZYMBORSKA ☐

Lot's Wife

I looked back, they say, out of curiosity.
But there might have been other reasons.
I looked back because I missed my silver bowl.
By mistake, tying my sandal thong.
Not to look any more at the righteous nape
of my husband, Lot.
Suddenly sure that if I died,
he wouldn't even stop.
From the disobedience of the meek.
Listening for the chase.
Touched by silence, hoping God had changed his mind.

Our two daughters were disappearing behind a hill.
I felt old. Distant.
Drowsy. I thought of the futility of wandering.
I looked back because I didn't know where to step.
In my path appeared snakes,
spiders, field mice, young vultures.
Neither good nor bad—simply all that lived
and crept and jumped in mass panic.
I looked back in loneliness.
Ashamed that I ran so furtively.
From the wish to scream, to return.
Or merely when the wind rose,
loosened my hair and whipped my dress up.
I felt they saw it from the walls of Sodom
and burst into loud laughter, again and again.
I looked back because I was angry.
To feast on their grand undoing.
I looked back for all those reasons.
I looked back unwillingly.
It was only a boulder that turned, growling under me.
It was a crevice that abruptly cut off my road.
On the bank a hamster tottered on two feet.
And then we both looked back.
No. No. I was running farther,
I crawled and flew upwards
until darkness tumbled down from the heavens,
and with it hot gravel and dead birds.
Breathless I spun around many times.
Someone watching might have thought I was dancing.
Maybe my eyes were open.
It's possible that I fell with my face turned towards the city.

Translated from the Polish
by Grażyna Drabik and Austin Flint

JAMES SIMMONS □

Lot's Wife

Uneasiness confirmed his words were right:
there was a rottenness in all she knew.
She could not see where she was going to
but love for him felt stronger than her fright.

Yet as she travelled on she was bereft
of every landmark but her husband's eyes:
her whole life echoed in her friends' goodbyes.
How could he take the place of all she left?

For him or them, but not for heaven's sake,
she made decisions: these two were opposed.
He led her on his way, her eyes were closed.
At every step she felt her heart would break.

At last Lot drew his wagon to a halt;
dog-tired but glad, he groped his way inside,
looking for pleasure in his sleeping bride,
kissed her, and on her cold cheek tasted salt.

GENESIS 19:30–38

[30]Lot went up from Zoar and settled in the hill country with his two daughters, for he was afraid to dwell in Zoar; and he and his two daughters lived in a cave. [31]And the older one said to the younger, "Our father is old, and there is not a man on earth to consort with us in the way of all the world. [32]Come, let us make our father drink wine, and let us lie with him, that we may maintain life through our father." [33]That night they made their father drink wine, and the older one went in and lay with her father; he did not know when she lay down or when she rose. [34]The next day the older one said to the younger, "See, I lay with Father last night; let us make him drink wine tonight also, and you go and lie with him, that we may maintain life through our father." [35]That night also they made their father drink wine, and the younger one went and lay with him; he did not know when she lay down or when she rose.

[36]Thus the two daughters of Lot came to be with child by their father. [37]The older one bore a son and named him Moab*; he is the father of the Moabites of today. [38]And the younger also bore a son, and she called him Ben-Ammi[†1]; he is the father of the Ammonites of today.

* As though *me-'ab*, "from (my) father"
[†] As though "son of my (paternal) kindred"

A. D. HOPE □

From "Lot and His Daughters"

II

The sun above the hills raged in the height.
Within Lot's cave, his vine-stock's living screen
Filtered the noon-day glare to a dim green
And hung the fat grapes bunched against the light.

The rascal patriarch, the bad old man,
Naked and rollicking on his heap of straw,
Scratching his hairy cods—one drunken paw
Spilled the red liquor from its silver can.

His beard, white as a blossoming branch, gaped wide.
Out flew a laugh: "By God, the wine is out!
More wine!"
    The cavern rumbled to his shout.
Brown fingers pushed the leafy screen aside.

And, padding broadly with their barefoot tread,
Calm-eyed, big-bellied, purposeful and slow,
Lot's delicate daughters, in the bloom and glow
Of their fulfilment stood beside his bed.

Crafty from fear, reckless with joy and greed,
The old man held them in his crapulous eye:
Mountains of promise bulging in his sky;
Ark of his race; God's covenant to his seed.

They stooped to take his cup, tilted and poured;
The must rose mantling to the glittering rim;
And, as the heart of Lot grew bold in him,
It boasted and exulted in the Lord.

"The one Just Man from Sodom saved alive!
Did not His finger point me to this cave?
Behold His hand once more stretched out to save!
For Jahweh too is just. My seed shall thrive.

"Shall not the Judge of all the earth do right?
Why did his angels take me by the hand?
My tribe shall yet be numbered with the sand
Upon the shore and with the stars of night.

"With me it shall be as with Abraham.
Dark are His ways, but sure and swift to bless—
How should my ewes breed in the wilderness?
And lo, the Lord himself provides a ram!"

But Lot's resourceful daughters, side by side,
Smiled back, inscrutable, patient and content;
Their slender bodies, ripe and eloquent,
Swayed like the standing corn at harvest-tide.

And, conscious of what trouble stirred below
His words and flickered in his shrewd old eyes,
They placed the cup that kept their father wise
In that best wisdom, which is not to know.

ENID DAME ☐

From "Lot's Daughter"

2.

Yesterday
a man arrived
with camera and tape recorder
from another century.

He asked me
for my opinion
about the Destruction.

I said
it wasn't a matter
of lovers, or love,
or whom people slept with.

Pa bellowed
into the mike:
"Those sinners
deserved what they got!"

Sister smiled to herself.

STANLEY MOSS □

Lot's Son[i]

Three in his arms we sleep. Lot lies awake
All night, he does not let me lie awake,
Or cut my own meat. All night
Through my ribs, I feel his body's heat.
He will not let me drink from a bright cup
(Unless he wash it), or climb high up.
His game: he points his finger at my eye
Saying, "You are crying," until I cry,
To make me a man. Rope, he holds me taut,
He knots, undoes the knots, I am caught
Round myself. A knot ties mother to son
Not father to daughter; all rope, but Lot,
Lot who tied us together is undone.

[i] See "Notes on the Poems," p. 334

I ▪ Hagar

GENESIS 21:1–14

The LORD took note of Sarah as He had promised, and the LORD did for Sarah as He had spoken. [2]Sarah conceived and bore a son to Abraham in his old age, at the set time of which God had spoken. [3]Abraham gave his new-born son, whom Sarah had borne him, the name of Isaac. [4]And when his son Isaac was eight days old, Abraham circumcised him, as God had commanded him. [5]Now Abraham was a hundred years old when his son Isaac was born to him. [6]Sarah said, "God has brought me laughter; everyone who hears will laugh with[*] me." [7]And she added,

"Who would have said to Abraham
That Sarah would suckle children!
Yet I have borne a son in his old age."

[8]The child grew up and was weaned, and Abraham held a great feast on the day that Isaac was weaned.

[9]Sarah saw the son, whom Hagar the Egyptian had borne to Abraham, playing. [10]She said to Abraham, "Cast out that slave-woman and her son, for the son of that slave shall not share in the inheritance with my son Isaac." [11]The matter distressed Abraham greatly, for it concerned a son of his. [12]But God said to Abraham, "Do not be distressed over the boy or your slave; whatever Sarah tells you, do as she says, for it is through Isaac that offspring shall be continued[†] for you. [13]As for the son of the slave-woman, I will make a nation of him, too, for he is your seed."

[14]Early next morning Abraham took some bread and a skin of water, and gave them to Hagar. He placed them over her shoulder, together with the child, and sent her away.

* Lit. "for"
† Lit. "called"

EDNA APHEK ☐

Sarah

1
Sarah
was a woman
soft and pliant
like a furrowed field
and he with
Hagar.

2
Sarah was
soft and pliant
quiet and kind
a woman
and he with
Hagar.

3
Sarah was
a woman
quiet and kind
crushed and cruel
and he with
Hagar.

4
Sarah was
crushed and cruel
a woman
when her womb
was soft with son
call her the
laughing one.

> Translated from the Hebrew
> by Yishai Tobin

ITSIK MANGER □

Hagar's Last Night in Abraham's House

Hagar, the servant, sits in the kitchen,
A smoking oil lamp spills
The shapes of shadowy cats and dogs
To flicker on the walls.

She weeps because her master
Fired her today.
"Beat it, you bitch," he told her;
"Can't you let me be?"

It was Sarah who egged him on—
That proper deaconess,
Saying, "Either get rid of the girl
Or give me a divorce."

Hagar takes out of her trunk
A summer hat of straw;
She takes her green silk apron
And her blood-red beads of coral.

These were the gifts he gave her
Once upon a day
When they strolled the meadow
By the railroad right-of-way.

"How like the smoke of a chimney,
How like the smoke of a train
Is the love of a man, dear mother,
The love of any man.

God knows where we shall run to,
Myself and his bastard child,
Unless in some alien kitchen
We are allowed to hide."

She takes the kitchen broom,
She sweeps the kitchen floor.
Under her blouse something still says
She loves him—and sweeps some more.

Again, she does the dishes,
And scours the copper pan.
"How like the smoke from a chimney
Is the love of any man."

Translated from the Yiddish
by Leonard Wolf

J · The Binding of Isaac

GENESIS 22:1–14

And it came to pass after these things, that God did prove Abraham, and said unto him: "Abraham"; and he said: "Here am I." [2]And He said: "Take now thy son, thine only son, whom thou lovest, even Isaac, and get thee into the land of Moriah; and offer him there for a burnt-offering upon one of the mountains which I will tell thee of." [3]And Abraham rose early in the morning, and saddled his ass, and took two of his young men with him, and Isaac his son; and he cleaved the wood for the burnt-offering, and rose up, and went unto the place of which God had told him. [4]On the third day Abraham lifted up his eyes, and saw the place afar off. [5]And Abraham said unto his young men: "Abide ye here with the ass, and I and the lad will go yonder; and we will worship, and come back to you." [6]And Abraham took the wood of the burnt-offering, and laid it upon Isaac his son; and he took in his hand the fire and the knife; and they went both of them together. [7]And Isaac spoke unto Abraham his father, and said: "My father." And he said: "Here am I, my son." And he said: "Behold the fire and the wood; but where is the lamb for a burnt-offering?" [8]And Abraham said: "God will provide Himself* the lamb for a burnt-offering, my son." So they went both of them together. [9]And they came to the place which God had told him of; and Abraham built the altar there, and laid the wood in order, and bound Isaac his son, and laid him on the altar, upon the wood. [10]And Abraham stretched forth his hand, and took the knife to slay his son. [11]And the angel of the LORD called unto him out of heaven, and said: "Abraham, Abraham." And he said: "Here am I." [12]And he said: "Lay not thy hand upon the lad, neither do thou any thing unto him; for now I know that thou art a God-fearing man, seeing thou hast not withheld thy son, thine only son, from Me." [13]And Abraham lifted up his eyes, and looked, and behold behind him a ram caught in the thicket by his horns. And

---

* Heb. *jireh;* that is, "see for Himself"

Abraham went and took the ram, and offered him up for a burnt-offering in the stead of his son. [14]And Abraham called the name of that place Adonai-jireh;* as it is said to this day: "In the mount where the LORD is seen."

Translation: JPS 1917

H. LEIVICK □

Sacrifice

Bound hand and foot he lies
on the hard altar stone
and waits.

Eyes half shut, he looks
on his father standing there
and waits.

His father sees his eyes
and strokes his son's brow
and waits.

With old and trembling hands
the father picks up the knife
and waits.

A Voice from above cries, "Stop!"
The hand freezes in air
and waits.

The veined throat suddenly throbs
with the miracle of the test
and waits.

The father gathers up the son.
The altar is bare
and waits.

Ensnared in thorns a lamb
looks at the hand with a knife
and waits.

Translated from the Yiddish
by Robert Friend

* That is, "The LORD seeth"

LINDA ZISQUIT □

After Years of Feasting and No Sacrifice

I can see how Abraham answered.
Even the prodding walk up a mountain,
that slow-motion-holding-back
of a soul anxious to see
what luminous understanding awaits it.
After these things,
how could I not have suffered
hot oil behind my eyes,
the smack across my face to wake me?

WILFRED OWEN □

The Parable of the Old Man and the Young

So Abram rose, and clave the wood, and went,
And took the fire with him, and a knife.
And as they sojourned both of them together,
Isaac the first-born spake and said, My Father,
Behold the preparations, fire and iron,
But where the lamb for this burnt-offering?
Then Abram bound the youth with belts and straps,
And builded parapets and trenches there,
And stretchèd forth the knife to slay his son.
When lo! an angel called him out of heaven,
Saying, Lay not thy hand upon the lad,
Neither do anything to him. Behold,
A ram, caught in a thicket by its horns;
Offer the Ram of Pride instead of him.
But the old man would not so, but slew his son,
And half the seed of Europe, one by one.

1917

ALIZA SHENHAR □

The Akedah

The loudspeaker screamed
"Take your only one
the one you love."
And the altar is destroyed.
Wood of the burnt offering is scattered.
The youths roll balls of love
on the grass of their youth.
Their tongues are hot.
The knife is shining in the wadi
in the light of the moon
of mid-border.
The white angel, the one
who always cries
"Please don't lay a hand"
is on leave.

Translated from the Hebrew
by Linda Zisquit

ZBIGNIEW HERBERT □

Photograph

This boy motionless as an arrow of Eleata
a boy amidst high grass has nothing in common with me
except a date of birth the papillary line

my father took this picture before the second Persian war
from the clouds and foliage I conclude it was August
the birds the crickets rang the smell of corn smell of a full moon

below the river called Hipanis on Roman maps
a watershed and nearby thunder advising them to take shelter with the
     Greeks
their colonies on the sea weren't too far

the boy smiles trustingly the only shadow he knows
is the shadow of a straw hat shadow of a pine tree shadow of the house
and if there is a glow it is the glow of sunset

little one my Isaac bend your head
it is only an instant of pain then you will be
whatever you want—a swallow lily of the field

so I must shed your blood my little one
for you to remain innocent in the summer lightning
safe for ever like an insect in amber
beautiful as a cathedral of fern preserved in coal

Translated from the Polish
by John Carpenter and Bogdana Carpenter

CHANA BLOCH ☐

The Sacrifice

1
The patriarch in black takes
candle and knife
like cutlery,
rehearsing under his breath
the Benediction
on the Death of an Only Son.

Isaac stoops under the raw wood,
carries his father on his back,
candle, velvet and all.

2
On the woodpile
Isaac's body waits
as women wait,
fever trilling under his skin.

He will remember the blade's
white silence,
the waiting
under his father's eyes.

AMIR GILBOA   □

Isaac

Early in the morning the sun took a walk in the woods
with me and my father
my right hand in his left.

A knife flashed between the trees like lightning.
And I'm so scared of the fear in my eyes facing blood
                                    on the leaves.
Father father come quick and save Isaac
so no one will be missing at lunchtime.

It's I who am butchered, my son,
my blood's already on the leaves.
And father's voice was choked.
And his face pale.

I wanted to cry out, struggling not to believe,
I tore my eyes open
and woke.

And my right hand was drained of blood

Translated from the Hebrew
by Shirley Kaufman

JACOB GLATSTEIN   □

My Father Isaac

As Isaac in his old age was led to the sacrifice,
he lifted his clouded eyes to heaven
and said in a tired voice:
"I know I'll be your choice."
No good angel came flying;
the flames burned more brightly and higher.
"The blade has been sharpened for my throat."
Isaac, old, was not deceived
as when he'd been that lad from Genesis;
he knew that there would be no lamb.

And as they bound him to the altar,
and as he smelled the searing fumes,
he spoke his mind thus:
"God will not interrupt this slaughter!"
He called out in a tired voice:
"Here I am—prepared to be your ram."

Translated from the Yiddish
by Etta Blum

K • Jacob, Rachel, and Leah

GENESIS 25:19-34

¹⁹This is the story of Isaac, son of Abraham. Abraham begot Isaac. ²⁰Isaac was forty years old when he took to wife Rebekah, daughter of Bethuel the Aramean of Paddan-aram, sister of Laban the Aramean. ²¹Isaac pleaded with the LORD on behalf of his wife, because she was barren; and the LORD responded to his plea, and his wife Rebekah conceived. ²²But the children struggled in her womb, and she said, "If so, why do I exist?"* She went to inquire of the LORD, ²³and the LORD answered her,

"Two nations are in your womb,
Two separate peoples shall issue from your body;
One people shall be mightier than the other,
And the older shall serve the younger."

²⁴When her time to give birth was at hand, there were twins in her womb. ²⁵The first one emerged red, like a hairy mantle all over; so they named him Esau.† ²⁶Then his brother emerged, holding on to the heel of Esau; so they named him Jacob.‡ Isaac was sixty years old when they were born.

²⁷When the boys grew up, Esau became a skillful hunter, a man of the outdoors; but Jacob was a mild man, who stayed in camp. ²⁸Isaac favored Esau because §-he had a taste for game-§; but Rebekah favored Jacob. ²⁹Once when Jacob was cooking a stew, Esau came in from the open, famished. ³⁰And Esau said to Jacob, "Give me some of that red stuff to gulp down, for I am famished"—which is why he was named Edom.‖ ³¹Jacob said, "First sell me your birthright." ³²And Esau said,

---

* Meaning of Heb. uncertain
† Synonym of *"Seir,"* play on Heb. *se'ar* "hair"
‡ Play on Heb. *'aqeb* "heel"
§-§ Lit. "game was in his mouth"
‖ Play on Heb *'adom* "red"

"I am at the point of death, so of what use is my birthright to me?" [33]But Jacob said, "Swear to me first." So he swore to him, and sold his birthright to Jacob. [34]Jacob then gave Esau bread and lentil stew; he ate and drank, and he rose and went away. Thus did Esau spurn the birthright.

AHARON AMIR   □

Esau's Letter

Thus Esau despised his birthright
                    Genesis 25:34

He calls himself a simple tent-dweller,
no? The crook, the heel! So be it.
Happy is she who bore him. I've nothing to gain griping
against him. After all, don't I know the double-talker
inside-out, like the young of my goats.
I'm familiar with his simple resourcefulness in public relations,
I know his type of mythomaniacs' compulsive
fretting over their place in the Book and Chronicles. I know
and even take a momentary pleasure (why not)
in my own way. Coolheadedly.

I don't mean to sound stuck up, but at least *my* voice
and hands match. I'm your average man, perhaps, who doesn't presume
to struggle with angels, who hasn't any time to chase Gods
and erect new-fangled altars—who's at peace, I believe,
with his own nature and fate, and whose conscience is clear
(if there is such a thing) and more precious than pearls.
My word! I don't envy him. Didn't he show me his mettle.
He can have what's his, birthright and blessing.
I felt their worth in my own flesh and haven't the slightest desire
for them—no thank you. He, his sons, the whole sickening
utopian family can rejoice. His father can rejoice in him
all he wants—he doesn't know his left from his right,
and may his righteous slick-as-olive-oil mother rejoice too.
As for me, I like it here in the fields of Edom,
on this good mountain, Mt. Seir, with my quarry,
my hunters, and with the shepherds of my flock—
My women, the daughters of Ishmael, the Hivite and Hittite,

are better to me than the daughters of Laban the Aramaean
and his maidservants—
and I love the lentil stew
they stuff me with
at all times—
oh, the red,
the red, red
stew—

Translated from the Hebrew
by Gabriel Levin

GENESIS 29:14b–31

When he had stayed with him a month's time, [15]Laban said to Jacob, "Just because you are my kinsman, should you serve me for nothing? Tell me, what shall your wages be?" [16]Now Laban had two daughters; the name of the older one was Leah, and the name of the younger was Rachel. [17]Leah had weak eyes; Rachel was shapely and beautiful. [18]Jacob loved Rachel; so he answered, "I will serve you seven years for your younger daughter Rachel." [19]Laban said, "Better that I give her to you than that I should give her to an outsider. Stay with me." [20]So Jacob served seven years for Rachel and they seemed to him but a few days because of his love for her.

[21]Then Jacob said to Laban, "Give me my wife, for my time is fulfilled, that I may consort with her." [22]And Laban gathered all the people of the place and made a feast. [23]When evening came, he took his daughter Leah and brought her to him; and he cohabited with her.—[24]Laban had given his maidservant Zilpah to his daughter Leah as her maid.—[25]When morning came, there was Leah! So he said to Laban, "What is this you have done to me? I was in your service for Rachel! Why did you deceive me?" [26]Laban said, "It is not the practice in our place to marry off the younger before the older. [27]Wait until the bridal week of this one is over and we will give you that one too, provided you serve me another seven years." [28]Jacob did so: he waited out the bridal week of the one, and then he gave him his daughter Rachel as wife.—[29]Laban had given his maidservant Bilhah to his daughter Rachel as her maid.—[30]And Jacob cohabited with Rachel also; indeed, he loved Rachel more than Leah. And he served him another seven years.

[31]The LORD saw that Leah was unloved and he opened her womb; but Rachel was barren.

RIVKA MIRIAM □

The Tune to Jacob Who Removed the Stone from the Mouth of the Well

He didn't know I was Leah
and I—I was Leah.
Rachel, he said, Rachel, like a lamb
the grass becomes part of, stems are part of you.
Flocks of sheep hummed between our blankets,
tent-flies were pulled to the wind.
Rachel, he said, Rachel—
and my eyes, they were weak
the bottom of a dark swamp.
The whites of his eyes melted
to the whites of my eyes.
The cords of his tent held fast to the ground
while the wind was blowing from the palms of my hands.

And he didn't know I was Leah
and flocks of sons broke through my womb to his hands.

Translated from the Hebrew
by Linda Zisquit

SHIRLEY KAUFMAN □

Leah

> *. . . but Rachel was beautiful . . .*
> —Genesis 29:17

I do what I have to
like an obedient daughter
or a dog. Not for your fingers
in my flesh. I watch you
every day as you watch her.
Since I'm the ugly one,
the one pushed into your bed
at night when you can't
tell the difference.

I've got another
son inside me, and still
you watch her. She doesn't
sag as I do after each birth
until you fill me again.

Why can't you look at me
in daylight, or take
my hand and press it
against your mouth?
I'm not a stone, a shell
your foot rolls over
in the sand. The life
gone out of it.
Maybe I am.
Your sons have sucked me
empty and dull.

I leave your tent at dawn
and walk to the river where I
throw my clothes off,
and the water shows me
my body floating
on the surface. It shivers
when I touch the blue dome
of your unborn child.
I touch my unwanted self
where the smooth skin
stretches over my breasts,
the silver veins. I'm cold.

I enter the water
as you enter me. Quick.
Like insects doing it while
they fly. The shock of it
lifts me,
and I swim raging
against the stream.

GENESIS 32:23–33

[23]And he rose up that night, and took his two wives, and his two handmaids, and his eleven children, and passed over the ford of the Jabbok. [24]And he took them, and sent them over the stream, and sent over that which he had. [25]And Jacob was left alone; and there wrestled a man with him until the breaking of the day. [26]And when he saw that he prevailed not against him, he touched the hollow of his thigh; and the hollow of Jacob's thigh was strained, as he wrestled with him. [27]And he said: "Let me go, for the day breaketh." And he said: "I will not let thee go, except thou bless me." [28]And he said unto him: "What is thy name?" And he said: "Jacob." [29]And he said: "Thy name shall be called no more Jacob, but Israel;* for thou hast striven with God and with men, and hast prevailed." [30]And Jacob asked him, and said: "Tell me, I pray thee, thy name." And he said: "Wherefore is it that thou dost ask after my name?" And he blessed him there. [31]And Jacob called the name of the place Peniel:† "for I have seen God face to face, and my life is preserved." [32]And the sun rose upon him as he passed over Peniel,‡ and he limped upon his thigh. [33]Therefore the children of Israel eat not the sinew of the thigh-vein which is upon the hollow of the thigh, unto this day; because he touched the hollow of Jacob's thigh, even in the sinew of the thigh-vein.

Translation: JPS 1917

* That is, "He who striveth with God"
† That is, "The face of God"
‡ Heb. *Penuel*

YITZHAK LAMDAN □

Israel

And he said: No longer Jacob shall your name be called
but Israel for you have contended with gods
and men and you have prevailed.

Genesis 32:28–29

And so night after night, God, you come to me,
Not to favor me do you come, but my strength to try,
And as I prevail against you until morning—again I am alone,
A poor strange wayfarer, limping upon my thigh.

"You have contended with gods and with men and you have prevailed"—
Is this all the blessing you apportioned me, mysterious one?
Woe is me, I know, against all of you I have prevailed, over everything,
But over one I could not, over myself alone—

Your blessings weigh heavily upon me, I cannot carry them,
Limping and alone over all the highways I go,
Vanquish me once, oh You, and let me rest at morn
The rest that all the vanquished know!

Again it is night. I am alone. Again God descends.
"Israel!"—Here I am, God, here I am!
Oh, why do you come down each night to wrestle with me,
And as dawn rises you forsake me limping again?—

Translated from the Hebrew
by Ruth Finer Mintz

KEVIN HART □

Peniel

Someone is whispering my name tonight.
Not here, although a radio sings the Blues
so softly you could almost hear a breath;

not here, where moonlight chills the lemon tree
and makes a warmth out of the simplest touch.
My mother is dead: I have no name, and so

she quietly sings to me all day all night,
a name I never heard till now, a name
she whispered months before I was born.

My name is quiet as a fingerprint—
it makes no trouble, it tells me who I am,
I've seen it often. And yet, I don't know why,

these past few months I brood on Genesis,
those stories like a rainbow at evening,
and find them all too true. At thirty-five,

all those I love have passed by Peniel,
and everyone longs to take another name,
and everyone knows a blessing is a wound,

and yet, what help is that? I do not know;
those stories tell me nothing but themselves:
at three a.m. I find myself asleep

beside some tales I hardly half-believe,
and doze again, as hearing my name sung,
a name no one has ever called me by,

half me and half a child I never was—
my mother's child.
                    I wake sometime round four
and find the moonlight sleeping on my cheek.

YEHUDA AMICHAI □

Jacob and the Angel

Just before dawn she sighed and held him
that way, and defeated him.
And he held her that way, and defeated her,
and both of them knew that a hold
brings death.
They agreed to do without names.

But in the first light
he saw her body,
which remained white in the places
the swimsuit had covered, yesterday.

Then someone called her suddenly from above,
twice.
The way you call a little girl from playing
in the yard.
And he knew her name; and let her go.

Translated from the Hebrew
by Stephen Mitchell

SHARON OLDS □

Last Words

Three days ago, my suitcases
were hunched there in his hospital room,
in the corner, I had to pick them up
by the scruff of their necks, and leave him. I kept
putting them down, and going back
to kiss him again although he was exhausted,
shining like tarnished silver, and yet
I could not seem to pick up those bags
and walk out the door the last time. I kept
going back to the mouth he would lift, his
forehead glittering with effort, his eyes
slewing back, shying, until
finally he cried out *Last kiss!*
and I kissed him and left. This morning his wife
called to tell me he has ceased to speak,
so those are his last words to me,
the ones he is leaving me with—and it is ending with a *kiss*—
a command for mercy, the offer of his cracked
creator lips. To plead that I leave,
my father asked me for a kiss! I would not
leave till he had done so, I will not let thee go except thou
     beg for it.

GENESIS 35:16–21

[16]They set out from Bethel; but when they were still some distance short of Ephrath, Rachel was in childbirth, and she had hard labor. [17]When her labor was at its hardest, the midwife said to her, "Have no fear, for it is another boy for you." [18]But as she breathed her last— for she was dying—she named him Ben-oni*; but his father called him Benjamin.† [19]Thus Rachel died. She was buried on the road to Ephrath—now Bethlehem. [20]Over her grave Jacob set up a pillar; it is the pillar at Rachel's grave to this day. [21]Israel journeyed on, and pitched his tent beyond Migdal-eder.

---

* Understood as "son of my suffering (or, strength)"
† I.e., "son of the right hand," or "son of the south"

DAHLIA RAVIKOVITCH   ☐

Like Rachel

To die like Rachel
when the soul shivers like a bird,
wants to escape.
Behind the tent, Jacob and Joseph
speak about her, trembling.
Her life turns head over heels inside her
like that infant
ready to be born.

How hard it is.
Jacob's love ate away at her
greedily.
Now she's dying,
she has no use for any of that.

Suddenly the infant's cry—
Jacob comes into the tent, but Rachel
doesn't even notice him.
Pleasure bathes her face,
washes over her head.

A great ease descends on her.
Her breath won't stir a feather now.
They laid her to rest among mountain stones
and did not mourn her.

To die
like Rachel.

Translated from the Hebrew
by Chana Bloch and Ariel Bloch

L ▪ Moses

EXODUS 3:1–15

Now Moses, tending the flock of his father-in-law Jethro, the priest of Midian, drove the flock into the wilderness, and came to Horeb, the mountain of God. ²An angel of the LORD appeared to him in a blazing fire out of a bush. He gazed, and there was a bush all aflame, yet the bush was not consumed. ³Moses said, "I must turn aside to look at this marvelous sight; why doesn't the bush burn up?" ⁴When the LORD saw that he had turned aside to look, God called to him out of the bush: "Moses! Moses!" He answered, "Here I am." ⁵And He said, "Do not come closer. Remove your sandals from your feet, for the place on which you stand is holy ground. ⁶I am," He said, "the God of your father, the God of Abraham, the God of Isaac, and the God of Jacob." And Moses hid his face, for he was afraid to look at God.
. . .

¹³Moses said to God, "When I come to the Israelites and say to them 'The God of your fathers has sent me to you,' and they ask me, 'What is His name?' what shall I say to them?" ¹⁴And God said to Moses, "Ehyeh-Asher-Ehyeh.*" He continued, "Thus shall you say to the Israelites, 'Ehyeh† sent me to you.' " ¹⁵And God said further to Moses, "Thus shall you speak to the Israelites: The LORD,‡ the God of your fathers, the God of Abraham, the God of Isaac, and the God of Jacob, has sent me to you:
This shall be My name forever,
This My appellation for all eternity."

* Meaning of Heb. uncertain; variously translated: "I Am That I Am"; "I Am Who I Am"; "I Will Be What I Will Be"; etc.
† Others, "I Am" or "I Will Be"
‡ The name YHWH (traditionally read Adonai "the LORD") is here associated with the root *hayah* "to be"

160

MELECH RAVITCH □

Twelve Lines about the Burning Bush

What's going to be the end for both of us—God?
Are you really going to let me die like this
and really not tell me the big secret?

Must I really become dust, gray dust, and ash, black ash,
while the secret, which is closer than my shirt, than my skin,
still remains secret, though it's deeper in me than my own heart?

And was it really in vain that I hoped by day and waited by night?
And will you, until the very last moment, remain godlike-cruel and
    hard?
Your face deaf like dumb stone, like cement, blind-stubborn?

Not for nothing is one of your thousand names—thorn,[j] you thorn in
    my spirit and flesh and bone,
piercing me—I can't tear you out; burning me—I can't stamp you
    out,
moment I can't forget, eternity I can't comprehend.

Translated from the Yiddish
by Ruth Whitman

[j] See "Notes on the Poems," p. 334

EXODUS 13:18b–22

Now the Israelites went up armed* out of the land of Egypt. [19]And Moses took with him the bones of Joseph, who had exacted an oath from the children of Israel, saying, "God will be sure to take notice of you: then you shall carry up my bones from here with you."

[20]They set out from Succoth and encamped at Etham, at the edge of the wilderness. [21]The LORD went before them in a pillar of cloud by day, to guide them along the way, and in a pillar of fire by night, to give them light, that they might travel day and night. [22]The pillar of cloud by day and the pillar of fire by night did not depart from before the people.

* Meaning of Heb. *hamushim* uncertain

HARVEY SHAPIRO ☐

Exodus

When they escaped
They carried a pack of bones
In a mummy-coffin like an ark.
Of course they had the pillar
Of clouds by day and fire by night,
But those were like dreams
Or something painted on the sky.
God was in the bones
Because Joseph had said,
God will remember you
If you take me hence.
This was before the miracle
By the sea or the thundering mountain,
Before the time of thrones
And cherubim. They were
Only now drawn forth
To eat the history feast
And begin the journey.
Why then should they carry history
Like an ark, and the remembering
Already begun?

EXODUS 19:1–19

On the third new moon after the Israelites had gone forth from the land of Egypt, on that very day, they entered the wilderness of Sinai. [2]Having journeyed from Rephidim, they entered the wilderness of Sinai and encamped in the wilderness. Israel encamped there in front of the mountain, [3]and Moses went up to God. The LORD called to him from the mountain, saying, "Thus shall you say to the house of Jacob and declare to the children of Israel :[4]"You have seen what I did to the Egyptians, how I bore you on eagles' wings and brought you to Me. [5]Now then, if you will obey Me faithfully and keep My covenant, you shall be My treasured possession among all the peoples. Indeed, all the earth is Mine, [6]but you shall be to Me a kingdom of priests and a holy nation.' These are the words that you shall speak to the children of Israel."

[7]Moses came and summoned the elders of the people and put before them all the words that the LORD had commanded him. [8]All the people answered as one, saying, "All that the LORD has spoken we will do!"

. . .

[16]On the third day, as morning dawned, there was thunder, and lightning, and a dense cloud upon the mountain, and a very loud blast of the horn; and all the people who were in the camp trembled. [17]Moses led the people out of the camp toward God, and they took their places at the foot of the mountain.

[18]Now Mount Sinai was all in smoke, for the LORD had come down upon it in fire; the smoke rose like the smoke of a kiln, and the whole mountain* trembled violently. [19]The blare of the horn grew louder and louder. As Moses spoke, God answered him in thunder.

---

* Some Hebrew manuscripts and the Greek read, "all the people"; cf. v. 16

JACOB GLATSTEIN □

Dead Men Don't Praise God[k]

We received the Torah on Sinai
and in Lublin we gave it back.
Dead men don't praise God,
the Torah was given to the living.
And just as we all stood together
at the giving of the Torah,
so did we all die together at Lublin.

I'll translate the tousled head, the pure eyes,
the tremulous mouth of a Jewish child
into this frightful fairy tale.
I'll fill the sky with stars
and I'll tell him:
our people is a fiery sun
from beginning to beginning to beginning.
Learn this, my little one,
from beginning to beginning to beginning.

Our whole imagined people
stood at Mount Sinai
and received the Torah.
The dead, the living, the unborn,
every soul among us answered:
we will obey and hear.
You, the saddest boy of all generations,
you also stood on Mount Sinai.
Your nostrils caught the raisin-almond fragrance of each
        word of the Torah.
It was Shavuoth, the green holiday.
You sang with them like a songbird:
I will hear and obey, obey and hear
from beginning to beginning to beginning.

Little one, your life is carved
in the constellations of our sky,
you were never absent,
you could never be missing.
When we were, you were.

[k] See "Notes on the Poems," p. 334

And when we vanished,
you vanished with us.

And just as we all stood together
at the giving of the Torah,
so did we all die together in Lublin.
From all sides the souls came flocking,
The souls of those who had lived out their lives, of those
       who had died young,
of those who were tortured, tested in every fire,
of those who were not yet born,
and of all the dead Jews from great grandfather Abraham
      down,
they all came to Lublin for the great slaughter.
All those who stood at Mount Sinai
and received the Torah
took these holy deaths upon themselves.
"We want to perish with our whole people,
we want to be dead again,"
the ancient souls cried out.
Mama Sara, Mother Rachel,
Miriam and Deborah the prophetess
went down singing prayers and songs,
and even Moses, who so much didn't want to die
when his time came,
now died again.
And his brother, Aaron,
and King David
and the Rambam, the Vilna Gaon,
and Mahram and Marshal
the Seer and Abraham Eiger.
And with every holy soul
that perished in torture
hundreds of souls
of Jews long dead died with them.

And you, beloved boy, you too were there.
You, carved against the constellated sky,
you were there, and you died there.
Sweet as a dove you stretched out your neck
and sang together with the fathers and mothers.
From beginning to beginning to beginning.

Shut your eyes, Jewish child,
and remember how the Baal Shem rocked you
in his arms
when your whole imagined people
vanished in the gas chambers of Lublin.

And above the gas chambers
and the holy dead souls,
a forsaken abandoned Mount Sinai veiled itself in smoke.
Little boy with the tousled head, pure eyes, tremulous mouth,
that was you, then,—the quiet, tiny, forlorn
given-back Torah.
You stood on top of Mount Sinai and cried,
you cried your cry to a dead world.
From beginning to beginning to beginning.

And this was your cry:
we received the Torah on Sinai
and in Lublin we gave it back.
Dead men don't praise God.
The Torah was given to the living.

Translated from the Yiddish
by Ruth Whitman

KADYA MOLODOVSKY □

God of Mercy

O God of Mercy
Choose—
another people.
We are tired of death, tired of corpses,
We have no more prayers.
Choose—
another people.
We have run out of blood
For victims,
Our houses have been turned into desert,
The earth lacks space for tombstones,
There are no more lamentations
Nor songs of woe
In the ancient texts.

God of Mercy
Sanctify another land,
Another Sinai.
We have covered every field and stone
With ashes and holiness.
With our crones
With our young
With our infants
We have paid for each letter in your Commandments.

God of Mercy
Lift up your fiery brow,
Look on the peoples of the world,
Let them have the prophecies and Holy Days
Who mumble your words in every tongue.
Teach them the Deeds
And the ways of temptation.

God of Mercy
To us give rough clothing
Of shepherds who tend sheep
Of blacksmiths at the hammer
Of washerwomen, cattle slaughterers
And lower still.
And O God of Mercy
Grant us one more blessing—
Take back the divine glory of our genius.

1945

Translated from the Yiddish
by Irving Howe

NUMBERS 20:1–11

The Israelites arrived in a body at the wilderness of Zin on the first new moon,* and the people stayed at Kadesh. Miriam died there and was buried there.

²The community was without water, and they joined against Moses and Aaron. ³The people quarreled with Moses, saying, "If only we had perished when our brothers perished at the instance of the LORD! ⁴Why have you brought the LORD's congregation into this wilderness for us and our beasts to die there? ⁵Why did you make us leave Egypt to bring us to this wretched place, a place with no grain or figs or vines or pomegranates? There is not even water to drink!"

⁶Moses and Aaron came away from the congregation to the entrance of the Tent of Meeting, and fell on their faces. The Presence of the LORD appeared to them, ⁷and the LORD spoke to Moses, saying, ⁸"You and your brother Aaron take the rod and assemble the community, and before their very eyes order the rock to yield its water. Thus you shall produce water for them from the rock and provide drink for the congregation and their beasts."

⁹Moses took the rod from before the LORD, as He had commanded him. ¹⁰Moses and Aaron assembled the congregation in front of the rock; and he said to them, "Listen, you rebels, shall we get water for you out of this rock?" ¹¹And Moses raised his hand and struck the rock twice with his rod. Out came copious water, and the community and their beasts drank.

* Of the fortieth year; cf. Num. 33:36–38

GABRIEL PREIL ☐

Biographical Note

It has been many years
since I was imprisoned
in the hothouse.
My bread is sour
and in my bones there grows
the rust of time.
Every desire turns to snow.

But when I beat my head
against the rock
of a poem
the fountain that springs forth
is sweet.

Had it not been for this
I could have been a knight
flickering and dying
in a forest of loves,
or one whose wrath
sets cities and villages
on fire.

Praise to the rock.

Translated from the Hebrew
by Howard Schwartz

LEVITICUS 1:1–5

The LORD called to Moses and spoke to him from the Tent of Meeting, saying: ²Speak to the Israelite people, and say to them:

When any of you presents an offering of cattle to the LORD, *⁻he shall choose his⁻* offering from the herd, or from the flock.

³If his offering is a burnt offering from the herd, he shall make his offering a male without blemish. He shall bring it to the entrance of the Tent of Meeting, for acceptance in his behalf before the LORD. ⁴He shall lay his hand upon the head of the burnt offering, that it may be acceptable in his behalf, in expiation for him. ⁵The bull shall be slaughtered before the LORD; and Aaron's sons, the priests, shall offer the blood, dashing the blood against all sides of the altar which is at the entrance of the Tent of Meeting.

⁻ Lit. "you shall offer your"

D. H. LAWRENCE □

The Old Idea of Sacrifice[1]

The old idea of sacrifice was this:
that blood of the lower life must be shed
for the feeding and strengthening of the handsome, fuller life.

O when the old world sacrificed a ram
it was to the gods who make us splendid
and it was for a feast, a feast of meat, for men and maids
on a day of splendour, for the further splendour of being men.

It was the eating up of little lives,
even doves, even small birds
into the dance and splendour of a bigger life.

There is no such thing as sin.
There is only life and anti-life.

And sacrifice is the law of life which enacts
that little lives must be eaten up into the dance and splendour
of bigger lives, with due reverence and acknowledgement.

[1] See "Notes on the Poems," p. 334

DEUTERONOMY 8:1–3

All the commandment which I command thee this day shall ye observe to do, that ye may live, and multiply, and go in and possess the land which the LORD swore unto your fathers. [2]And thou shalt remember all the way which the LORD thy God hath led thee these forty years in the wilderness, that He might afflict thee, to prove thee, to know what was in thy heart, whether thou wouldest keep His commandments, or no. [3]And He afflicted thee, and suffered thee to hunger, and fed thee with manna, which thou knewest not, neither did thy fathers know; that He might make thee know that man doth not live by bread only,[m] but by every thing that proceedeth out of the mouth of the LORD doth man live.

Translation: JPS 1917

[m] See "Notes on the Poems," p. 334

SAMUEL MENASHE ☐

Manna

Open your mouth
To feed that flesh
Your teeth have bled
Tongue us out
Bone by bone
Do not allow
Man to be fed
By bread alone

DEUTERONOMY 25:17–19

[17]Remember what Amalek did to you on your journey, after you left Egypt—[18]how, undeterred by fear of God, he surprised you on the march, when you were famished and weary, and cut down all the stragglers in your rear. [19]Therefore, when the LORD your God grants you safety from all your enemies around you, in the land that the LORD your God is giving you as a hereditary portion, you shall blot out the memory of Amalek from under heaven. Do not forget!

FRIEDRICH TORBERG   ☐

Amalek

Deuteronomy 25:17–18

Thus spoke the Lord to Israel:
Because you are my chosen people,
you shall not hate the ones I did not choose,
nor shall you fall into the sin of pride.

Reserve your rancor if they do you harm,
do not turn bitter if they show their scorn,
neither Babylon nor Edom shall you hate,
not the Assyrian nor the Edomite.

And even he who boasted with a hardened heart
that he would snuff you out of life and breath,
he who paid the price with man and horse—
even the Egyptian you shall forgive.

But he who slew you from behind,
once you escaped from Pharaoh's ruthless men
and made your way towards the Promised Land,
open to every hope and all deceit,

He who struck your old and weak,
who would not let you go your way—
Amalek, the enemy of Israel—
him, said the Lord, him you shall hate.

Translated from the German
by Erna Baber Rosenfeld

DEUTERONOMY 34:1–8

Moses went up from the steppes of Moab to Mount Nebo, to the summit of Pisgah, opposite Jericho, and the LORD showed him the whole land: Gilead as far as Dan; [2]all Naphtali; the land of Ephraim and Manasseh; the whole land of Judah as far as the Western* Sea; [3]the Negeb; and the Plain—the valley of Jericho, the city of palm trees—as far as Zoar. [4]And the LORD said to him, "This is the land of which I swore to Abraham, Isaac, and Jacob, 'I will give it to your offspring.' I have let you see it with your own eyes, but you shall not cross there."

[5]So Moses the servant of the LORD died there, in the land of Moab, at the command of the LORD. [6]He buried him in the valley in the land of Moab, near Beth-peor; and no one knows his burial place to this day. [7]Moses was a hundred and twenty years old when he died; his eyes were undimmed and his vigor unabated. [8]And the Israelites bewailed Moses in the steppes of Moab for thirty days.

* I.e., Mediterranean

RAINER MARIA RILKE □

The Death of Moses[n]

None of them were willing, just the dark
defeated angel; choosing a weapon, he cruelly approached
the commanded one. But even he
went clanging backward, upward,
and screamed into the heavens: I can't!

For through the thicket of his brow, Moses
had patiently noticed him and gone on writing:
words of blessing and the infinite Name. And his eyes
were clear right to the bottom of his powers.

So the Lord, dragging half of the heaven behind him,
came hurling down in person and made up a bed from the mountain;
laid the old man out. From its orderly dwelling
he summoned the soul; and spoke of much they had shared
in the course of an immeasurable friendship.

But finally the soul was satisfied. Admitted
enough had been done, it was finished. Then the old
God slowly lowered down over the old
man his ancient face. Drew him out with a kiss

and into his own older age. And with the hands of creation
he closed the mountain again. So it would be like one,
one created all over again among the mountains of earth,
hidden to us.

Translated from the German
by Franz Wright

[n] See "Notes on the Poems," p. 334

M ▪ Joshua

ALICIA OSTRIKER □

The Story of Joshua

And Joshua said, Hereby ye shall know that the
living God is among you, and that he will
without fail drive out from before you the
Canaanites, and the Hittites, and the Hivites,
and the Perizzites, and the Girgashites, and
the Amorites, and the Jebusites.
                    Joshua 3:10

The New Englanders are a people of God settled
in those which were once the devil's territories.
                    Cotton Mather,
                    The Wonders of the Invisible World, 1692

We reach the promised land
Forty years later
The original ones who were slaves
Have died
The young are seasoned soldiers
There is wealth enough for everyone and God
Here at our side, the people
Are mad with excitement.
Here is what to do, to take
This land away from the inhabitants:
Burn their villages and cities
Kill their men
Kill their women
Consume the people utterly.
God says: is that clear?
I give you the land, but
You must murder for it.
You will be a nation
Like other nations,

Your hands are going to be stained like theirs
Your innocence annihilated.
Keep listening, Joshua.
Only to you among the nations
Do I also give knowledge
The secret
Knowledge that you are doing evil
Only to you the commandment:
Love ye therefore the stranger, for you were
Strangers in the land of Egypt,° a pillar
Of fire to light your passage
Through the blank desert of history forever.
This is the agreement.
Is it entirely
Clear, Joshua,
Said the Lord.
I said it was. He then commanded me
To destroy Jericho.

° See "Notes on the Poems," p. 335

JOSHUA 24:1–13

Joshua assembled all the tribes of Israel at Schechem. He summoned Israel's elders and commanders, magistrates and officers; and they presented themselves before God. ²Then Joshua said to all the people, "Thus said the LORD, the God of Israel: In olden times, your forefathers—Terah, father of Abraham and father of Nahor—lived beyond the Euphrates and worshiped other gods. ³But I took your father Abraham from beyond the Euphrates and led him through the whole land of Canaan and multiplied his offspring. I gave him Isaac, ⁴and to Isaac I gave Jacob and Esau. I gave Esau the hill country of Seir as his possession, while Jacob and his children went down to Egypt.

⁵"Then I sent Moses and Aaron, and I plagued Egypt with [the wonders] that I wrought in their midst, after which I freed you—⁶I freed your fathers—from Egypt, and you came to the Sea. But the Egyptians pursued your fathers to the Sea of Reeds with chariots and horsemen. ⁷They cried out to the LORD, and He put darkness between you and the Egyptians; then He brought the Sea upon them, and it covered them. Your own eyes saw what I did to the Egyptians.

. . .

¹¹"Then you crossed the Jordan and you came to Jericho. The citizens of Jericho and the Amorites, Perizzites, Canaanites, Hittites, Girgashites, Hivites, and Jebusites fought you, but I delivered them into your hands. ¹²I sent a plague ahead of you, and it drove them out before you—[just like] the two Amorite kings—not by your sword or by your bow. ¹³I have given you a land for which you did not labor and towns which you did not build, and you have settled in them; you are enjoying vineyards and olive groves which you did not plant.

CHARLES REZNIKOFF □

Joshua at Shechem

Joshua XXIV:13

You Hebrews are too snug in Ur,
said God; wander about waste places,
north and south leave your dead;
let kings fight against you,
and the heavens rain fire and brimstone
on you. And it was so.
And God looked again and saw
the Hebrews with their sons and daughters
rich in flocks and herds,
with jewels of silver
and jewels of gold.
And God said, Be slaves
to Pharaoh. And it was so.
And God looked again and saw
the Hebrews at the fleshpots,
with fish to eat,
cucumbers and melons.
And God said, Be gone
into the wilderness by the Red Sea
and the wilderness of Shur and the wilderness
of Shin; let Amalek come upon you,
and fiery serpents bite you. And it was so.
And God looked again and saw in a land of brooks and
        springs and fountains,
wheat and barley,
the Hebrews, in a land on which they did not labor,
in cities which they did not build,
eating of vineyards and olive trees which they did not plant.
And God scattered them—
through the cities of the Medes, beside the waters of Babylon;
they fled before Him into Egypt and went down to the sea in ships;
the whales swallowed them,
the birds brought word of them to the king;
the young men met them with weapons of war,
the old men with proverbs—
and God looked and saw the Hebrews
citizens of the great cities,
talking Hebrew in every language under the sun.

N • Judges

JUDGES 4:1–10

The Israelites again did what was offensive to the LORD—Ehud now being dead. [2]And the LORD surrendered them to King Jabin of Canaan, who reigned in Hazor. His army commander was Sisera, whose base was Harosheth-goiim. [3]The Israelites cried out to the LORD; for he had nine hundred iron chariots, and he had oppressed Israel ruthlessly for twenty years.

[4]Deborah, wife of Lappidoth, was a prophetess; she led Israel at that time. [5]She used to sit under the Palm of Deborah, between Ramah and Bethel in the hill country of Ephraim, and the Israelites would come to her for decisions.

[6]She summoned Barak son of Abinoam, of Kedesh in Naphtali, and said to him, "The LORD, the God of Israel, has commanded: Go, march up to Mount Tabor, and take with you ten thousand men of Naphtali and Zebulun. [7]And I will draw Sisera, Jabin's army commander, with his chariots and his troops, toward you up to the Wadi Kishon; and I will deliver him into your hands." [8]But Barak said to her, "If you will go with me, I will go; if not, I will not go." [9]"Very well, I will go with you," she answered. "However, there will be no glory for you in the course you are taking, for then the LORD will deliver Sisera into the hands of a woman." So Deborah went with Barak to Kedesh. [10]Barak then mustered Zebulun and Naphtali at Kedesh; ten thousand men marched up *ᐨafter him;ᐨ* and Deborah also went up with him.

ᐨ Lit. "at his feet"

JANET RUTH HELLER   □

Devorah

It is not recorded of Devorah
That she settled down with Barak,
Raised a tribe of children,
And left off judging Israel.

JUDGES 5:1, 5:24–31

On that day Deborah and Barak son of Abinoam sang:

. . .

24Most blessed of women be Jael,
Wife of Heber the Kenite,
Most blessed of women in tents.
25He asked for water, she offered milk;
In a princely bowl she brought him curds.
26Her [left] hand reached for the tent pin,
Her right for the workmen's hammer.
She struck Sisera, crushed his head,
Smashed and pierced his temple.
27At her feet he sank, lay outstretched,
At her feet he sank, lay still;
Where he sank, there he lay—destroyed.

28Through the window peered Sisera's mother,
Behind the lattice she whined:*
"Why is his chariot so long in coming?
Why so late the clatter of his wheels?"
29The wisest of her ladies give answer;
She, too, replies to herself:
30"They must be dividing the spoil they have found:
A damsel or two for each man,
Spoil of dyed cloth for Sisera,
Spoil of embroidered cloths,
A couple of embroidered cloths
Round every neck as spoil."

31So may all Your enemies perish, O Lord!
But may His friends be as the sun rising in might!

And the land was tranquil forty years.

* Or "gazed"; meaning of Heb. uncertain

HAIM GOURI   ☐

His Mother

It was years ago, at the end of Deborah's Song,
I heard the silence of Sisera's chariot so long in coming,

I watch Sisera's mother peer out the window,
A woman with a silver streak in her hair.

This is what the maidens saw: A spoil of multi-hued embroidery,
Multi-hued embroideries two for the throat of each despoiler.
That very hour he lay in the tent as one asleep
His hands quite empty.
On his chin traces of milk, butter, blood.

The silence was not broken by horses and chariots.
Even the maidens fell silent one after another.
My silence reached out to theirs.
After a while sunset.
After a while the afterglow is gone.

Forty years the land knew peace. Forty years
No horses galloped, no dead horsemen stared glassily.
But her death came soon after her son's.

Translated from the Hebrew
by Warren Bargad and Stanley F. Chyet

JUDGES 16:23–30

[23]And the lords of the Philistines gathered them together to offer a great sacrifice unto Dagon their god, and to rejoice; for they said: "Our god hath delivered Samson our enemy into our hand." [24]And when the people saw him, they praised their god; for they said: "Our god hath delivered into our hand our enemy, and the destroyer of our country, who hath slain many of us." [25]And it came to pass, when their hearts were merry, that they said: "Call for Samson, that he may make us sport." And they called for Samson out of the prison-house; and he made sport before them; and they set him between the pillars. [26]And Samson said unto the lad that held him by the hand: "Suffer me that I may feel the pillars whereupon the house resteth, that I may lean upon them." [27]Now the house was full of men and women; and all the lords of the Philistines were there; and there were upon the roof about three thousand men and women, that beheld while Samson made sport. [28]And Samson called unto the LORD, and said: "O Lord God, remember me, I pray Thee, and strengthen me, I pray Thee, only this once, O God, that I may be this once avenged of the Philistines for my two eyes." [29]And Samson took fast hold of the two middle pillars upon which the house rested, and leaned up on them, the one with his right hand, and the other with his left. [30]And Samson said: "Let me die with the Philistines." And he bent with all his might; and the house fell upon the lords, and upon all the people that were therein.

Translation: JPS 1917

YEHUDA AMICHAI ☐

Ashkelon Beach

Here on Ashkelon beach we arrive at the end of memory
like rivers that come to the sea.
The recent past sets into the distant past
and the past rises from its depths to the near.
Peace, peace—to near and far.

Here, among the ruins of statues and columns,
I ask—how did Samson raze the temple
in which, blind, he stood and said:
"Let me perish with the Philistines!"

Did he embrace the columns as in a final love
or push them away—
to be alone in his death?

Translated from the Hebrew
by Karen Alkalay-Gut

O • Kings: Saul and David

1 SAMUEL 17:1–11

The Philistines assembled their forces for battle; they massed at Socoh of Judah, and encamped at Ephes-dammim, between Socoh and Azekah. ²Saul and the men of Israel massed and encamped in the valley of Elah. They drew up their line of battle against the Philistines, ³with the Philistines stationed on one hill and Israel stationed on the opposite hill, the ravine was between them. ⁴A champion* of the Philistine forces stepped forward; his name was Goliath of Gath, and he was six cubits and a span tall. ⁵He had a bronze helmet on his head, and wore a breastplate of scale armor, a bronze breastplate weighing five thousand shekels. ⁶He had bronze greaves on his legs, and a bronze javelin [slung] from his shoulders. ⁷The shaft of his spear was like a weaver's bar, and the iron head of his spear weighed six hundred shekels; and the shield-bearer marched in front of him.

⁸He stopped and called out to the ranks of Israel and he said to them, "Why should you come out to engage in battle? I am the Philistine [champion], and you are Saul's servants. Choose† one of your men and let him come down against me. ⁹If he bests me in combat and kills me, we will become your slaves; but if I best him and kill him, you shall be our slaves and serve us." ¹⁰And the Philistine ended, "I herewith defy the ranks of Israel. Give me a man and let's fight it out!" ¹¹When Saul and all Israel heard these words of the Philistine, they were dismayed and terror stricken.

* Lit. "the man of the space between," i.e., between the armies
† Meaning of Heb. uncertain

JOSEPHINE MILES □

David

Goliath stood up clear in the assumption of status,
Strong and unquestioning of himself and others,
Fully determined by the limits of his experience.
I have seen such a one among surgeons, sergeants,
Deans, and giants, the power implicit.

Then there was David, who made few assumptions,
Had little experience, but for more was ready,
Testing and trying this pebble or that pebble,
This giant or that giant.
He is not infrequent.

How could Goliath guess, with his many assumptions,
The force of the slung shot of the pure-hearted?
How could David fear, with his few hypotheses,
The power of status which is but two-footed?
So he shot, and shouted!

1 SAMUEL 17:38–40

³⁸Saul clothed David in his own garment; he placed a bronze helmet on his head and fastened *-a breastplate on him.-* ³⁹David girded his sword over his garment. Then he [†]-tried to walk; but-[†] he was not used to it. And David said to Saul, "I cannot walk in these, for I am not used to them." So David took them off. ⁴⁰He took his stick, picked a few[‡] smooth stones from the wadi, put them in the pocket[§] of his shepherd's bag and, sling in hand, he went toward the Philistine.

- Heb. "clothed him in a breastplate" (cf. v. 5), because a breastplate was combined with a leather jerkin
^{†-†} Septuagint reads "was unable to walk, for . . . "
[‡] Lit. "five"
[§] Meaning of Heb. uncertain.

CHARLES REZNIKOFF □

From "Autobiography, New York"

X

I do not believe that David killed Goliath.
It must have been—
you will find the name in the list of David's captains.
But, whoever it was, he was no fool
when he took off the helmet
and put down the sword and the spear and the shield
and said, The weapons you have given me are good,
but they are not mine:
I will fight in my own way
with a couple of pebbles and a sling.

1 SAMUEL 17:41–51a

⁴¹The Philistine, meanwhile, was coming closer to David, preceded by his shield-bearer. ⁴²When the Philistine caught sight of David, he scorned him, for he was but a boy, ruddy and handsome. ⁴³And the Philistine called out to David, "Am I a dog that you come against me with sticks?" The Philistine cursed David by his gods; ⁴⁴and the Philistine said to David, "Come here, and I will give your flesh to the birds of the sky and the beasts of the field."

⁴⁵David replied to the Philistine, "You come against me with sword and spear and javelin; but I come against you in the name of the LORD of Hosts, the God of the ranks of Israel, whom you have defied. ⁴⁶This very day the LORD will deliver you into my hands. I will kill you and cut off your head; and I will give *⁻the carcasses⁻* of the Philistine camp to the birds of the sky and the beasts of the earth. All the earth shall know that there is a God in† Israel. ⁴⁷And this whole assembly shall know that the LORD can give victory without sword or spear. For the battle is the LORD's, and He will deliver you into our hands."

⁴⁸When the Philistine began to advance toward him again, David quickly ran up to the battle line to face the Philistine. ⁴⁹David put his hand into the bag; he took out a stone and slung it. It struck the Philistine in the forehead; the stone sank into his forehead, and he fell face down on the ground. ⁵⁰Thus David bested the Philistine with sling and stone; he struck him down and killed him. David had no sword; ⁵¹so David ran and stood over the Philistine, grasped his sword and pulled it from its sheath; and with it he dispatched him and cut off his head.

⁻ Septuagint reads "your carcass and the carcasses"
† So many Heb. mss. and ancient versions; other mss. and the editions read "to"

RICHARD HOWARD ☐

The Giant on Giant-Killing

HOMAGE TO THE BRONZE *DAVID* OF DONATELLO, 1430

I am from Gath where my name
in Assyrian means *destroyer*, a household word
by now, and deservedly. Every household needs
a word for destroyer—nothing secret in the fact,
nothing disgraceful about a universal need—
    and my name is a good word.
Try the syllables on your own tongue, say *Goliath*.
It sounds right, doesn't it—powerful and Philistine
and destructive, somehow. It always sounded like that
to me. *Goliath!* I shouted, and the sun would break
    in pieces on my armor.
The world, as far as I could see, was the sun breaking
on things, making them break. So I was hardly surprised
when the world came to an end because the sun broke *through:*
no pieces, unbroken, whole—no longer flash but flesh.
    The end came as a body.
You see, I am past the end, or I could not know it:
look at my face under his left foot and you *will* see,
look at my mouth—is that the mouth of a man surprised
by the end of the world? Notice the way my moustache turns
    over his triumphant toe
(a kind of caress, and not the only one), notice
my full lips softened into a little smile. You see:
the triumph is mine, whatever the tale. And the scene
on my helmet tells the true story: a chariot,
    eight naked boys, wingèd ones,
and the wine, the mirror, the parasol—my triumph
inherits me. He holds my sword. He is what I see,
that is why you see him: the naked boy without wings.
There is a wing, but it happens to be my helmet's
    and inches up the inside
of his right thigh stiffening to allow the feathers
an overture, covertly spread, to that focus where
nothing resembles a hollow so much as a swelling.
That focus?—those. Find one place on his fertile torso
    where your fingers cannot feed,
one interval to which all the others fail to pay
their respects, even as they take the light, the shadows.

It is why the sun broke through me that morning—no stone
could lay Goliath low. See it still in the boy's hand?
       No need for a stone! My eyes
were my only enemy, my only weapon too,
and fell upon David like a sword. The body is
what is eternal; the rest—boots, hat ribboned and wreathed,
even the coarse, boy's hair that has not once been cut—
       a brevity, accidents,
though it is no accident when it is all you have.
Almost I think his face too is an accident, dim
under the long pointed brim. Call it an absence then,
an absence where life is refreshed and comforted
       while the body has its way:
a presence, a proof emptied of past and future, drained
of obligations pending. Climb across the belly,
up the insolent haunches from which the buttocks are
slung (there, that is the boy's sling), scan the rhyming
       landscape of the waist between
the simple nipples arched by his simpler, supple arms—
even the vulnerable shoulderblades, the vain wrists
are present but not the face, not David's mouth that is
the curved weapon used to kill a smile. And the carved eyes,
       what are they seeing? Only
the body sees, the eyes look neither down at me nor
out at you. They look away, for they cannot acquit
what is there: the eyes know what the body will become.
It is why they are absent, not blind like mine, not blank
       as iridescent agates.
They see the white colossus which in eighty years will come,
unwelcome: marble assertion of a will to wound
against which no man or music can survive. It is
what giant-killers must become. Michelangelo . . .
       They become giants: no head
of Goliath kisses those unsolicited feet,
no one is there . . . Yes, I go, I have gone already.
I would rather mourn my going than mourn my David.
I am the man Goliath, and my name in Israel
       is also a household word,
every household needs the word—perhaps there *is* a shame
in that, a secret about such universal need—
but it is a good word, my name; try it on your own
tongue, savor the hard syllables, say *Goliath*
       which in Hebrew means *exile*.

1 SAMUEL 18:1–9

When [David] finished speaking with Saul, Jonathan's soul became bound up with the soul of David; Jonathan loved David as himself. ²Saul took him [into his service] that day and would not let him return to his father's house.—³Jonathan and David made a pact, because [Jonathan] loved him as himself. ⁴Jonathan took off the cloak and tunic he was wearing and gave them to David, together with his sword, bow, and belt. ⁵David went out [with the troops], and he was successful in every mission on which Saul sent him, and Saul put him in command of all the soldiers; this pleased all the troops and Saul's courtiers as well. ⁶When the [troops] came home [and] David returned from killing the Philistine, *⁻the women of all the towns of Israel came out singing and dancing to greet King Saul⁻* with timbrels, shouting, and sistrums.† ⁷The women sang as they danced, and they chanted:

Saul has slain his thousands;

David, his tens of thousands!

⁸Saul was much distressed and greatly vexed about the matter. For he said, "To David they have given tens of thousands, and to me they have given thousands. All that he lacks is the kingship!" ⁹From that day on Saul kept a jealous eye on David.

⁻ Meaning of Heb. uncertain; Septuagint reads "the dancing women came out to meet David from all the towns of Israel"

† Meaning of Heb. uncertain

THOMAS W. SHAPCOTT □

From "Portrait of Saul"

Jonathan and David

Yes, but to remember them for their love
is to remember them for their youth: laughter,
not a covert whispering; the noisy clatter
of playingfield and bodies so alike they move
in a teamwork: do not suppose that what they give
each other is theirs to hold or withhold. Bitter
and old I watch how they embrace each other
free with the one gift I no longer have.

The strings of David's harp are bars of a cage,
a sour taste corrodes through his sweet song.
I am afraid. The desires of a King
are comfortless: my Palace holds me hostage.
And, if I had him, what then could I, Saul,
do but mortify, condemn, despoil?

1 SAMUEL 18:10–16

¹⁰The next day an evil spirit of God gripped Saul and he began to rave in the house, while David was playing [the lyre], as he did daily. Saul had a spear in his hand, ¹¹and Saul threw* the spear, thinking to pin David to the wall. But David eluded him twice. ¹²Saul was afraid of David, for the LORD was with him and had turned away from Saul. ¹³So Saul removed him from his presence and appointed him chief of a thousand, [†]-to march at the head of the troops.^{-†} ¹⁴David was successful in all his undertakings, for the LORD was with him; ¹⁵and when Saul saw that he was successful, he dreaded him. ¹⁶All Israel and Judah loved David, for he marched at their head.

---

* Change of vocalization yields "raised"
^{†-†} Lit. "and he went out and came in before the troops"

NATAN ZACH □

And Perhaps Only Music

And perhaps only music. Since the emotion
is obscure, call it what you wish.
Only music, perhaps. Here it is
of an evening, hesitant
in the absence of strong feeling,
uncertain. So David, in his day,
must have played. But Saul didn't suspect.
Manly and confident he hurled his spear
as if in David's song there stood forth
matters final and clear-cut
like the severed head of Goliath.

> Translated from the Hebrew
> by Peter Everwine and Shulamit Yasny-Starkman

1 SAMUEL 18:17–29

[17]Saul said to David, "Here is my older daughter Merab, I will give her to you in marriage; in return, you be my warrior and fight the battles of the LORD." Saul thought: "Let not my hand strike him; let the hand of the Philistines strike him." [18]David replied to Saul, "Who am I and *-what is my life-*—my father's family in Israel—that I should become Your Majesty's son-in-law?" [19]But at the time that Merab, daughter of Saul, should have been given to David, she was given in marriage to Adriel the Meholathite. [20]Now Michal daughter of Saul had fallen in love with David; and when this was reported to Saul, he was pleased. [21]Saul thought: "I will give her to him, and she can serve as a snare for him, so that the Philistines may kill him." So Saul said to David, †-"You can become my son-in-law even now through the second one."-† [22]And Saul instructed his courtiers to say to David privately, "The king is fond of you and all his courtiers like you. So why not become the king's son-in-law?" [23]When the king's courtiers repeated these words to David, David replied, "Do you think that becoming the son-in-law of a king is a small matter, when I am but a poor man of no consequence?" [24]Saul's courtiers reported to him, "This is what David answered." [25]And Saul said, "Say this to David: 'The king desires no other bride price than the foreskins of a hundred Philistines, as vengeance on the king's enemies.' "—Saul intended to bring about David's death at the hands of the Philistines.—[26]When his courtiers told this to David, David was pleased with the idea of becoming the king's son-in-law. †-Before the time had expired,-† [27]David went out with his men and killed two hundred‡ Philistines; David brought their foreskins and †-they were counted out-† for the king, that he might become the king's son-in-law. Saul then gave him his daughter Michal in marriage. [28]When Saul realized that the LORD was with David §-and that Michal daughter of Saul loved him,-§ [29]Saul grew still more afraid of David; and Saul was David's enemy ever after.

- Meaning of Heb. uncertain. Change of vocalization yields "who are my kin"
†-† Meaning of Heb. uncertain
‡ Septuagint reads "one hundred," and cf. 2 Sam. 3:14
§-§ Septuagint reads "and that all Israel loved him"

ANNA AKHMATOVA □

Michal

But David was loved . . . by the daughter of
Saul, Michal. Saul thought: I will give her to
him, and she will be a snare for him.

First Book of Kings
[Slavonic Bible]

And the youth plays for the mad king,
And annihilates the merciless night,
And loudly summons triumphant dawn
And smothers the specters of fright.
And the king speaks kindly to him:
"In you, young man, burns a marvelous flame,
And for such a medicine
I will give you my daughter and my kingdom."
And the king's daughter stares at the singer,
She needs neither songs nor the marriage crown;
Her soul is full of grief and resentment,
Nevertheless, Michal wants David.
She is paler than death; her mouth is compressed,

*

In her green eyes, frenzy;
Her garments gleam and with each motion
Her bracelets ring harmoniously.
Like a mystery, like a dream, like the first mother, Lilith . . .
She speaks without volition:
"Surely they have given me drink with poison
And my spirit is clouded.
My shamelessness! My humiliation!
A vagabond! A brigand! A shepherd!
Why do none of the king's courtiers,
Alas, resemble him?
But the sun's rays . . . and the stars at night . . .
And this cold trembling . . . "

1959–61

Translated from the Russian
by Judith Hemschemeyer

2 SAMUEL 6:16–23

[16]As the Ark of the LORD entered the City of David, Michal daughter of Saul looked out of the window and saw King David leaping and whirling before the LORD; and she despised him for it.

[17]They brought in the Ark of the LORD and set it up in its place inside the tent which David had pitched for it, and David sacrificed burnt offerings and offerings of well-being before the LORD. [18]When David finished sacrificing the burnt offerings and the offerings of well-being, he blessed the people in the name of the LORD of Hosts. [19]And he distributed among all the people—the entire multitude of Israel, man and woman alike—to each a loaf of bread, *⁻a cake made in a pan, and a raisin cake.⁻* Then all the people left for their homes.

[20]David went home to greet his household. And Michal daughter of Saul came out to meet David and said, "Didn't the king of Israel do himself honor today—exposing himself today in the sight of the slavegirls of his subjects, as one of the riffraff might expose himself!" [21]David answered Michal, "It was before the LORD who chose me instead of your father and all his family and appointed me ruler over the LORD's people Israel! I will dance before the LORD [22]and dishonor myself even more, and be low in †⁻my own⁻† esteem; but among the slavegirls that you speak of I will be honored." [23]So to her dying day Michal daughter of Saul had no children.

⁻ Meaning of Heb. uncertain
†⁻† Septuagint reads "your"

RACHEL □

Michal

And Michal Saul's daughter loved David—
and she despised him in her heart.

Michal, distant sister, time's thread has not been
    severed,
time's thorns in your sad vineyard have not prevailed.
Still in my ear I hear the tinkling of your gold
    anklet,
The stripes in your silk garment have not paled.

Often have I seen you standing by your small window,
pride and tenderness mingling in your eyes.
Like you I am sad, O Michal, distant sister,
and like you doomed to love a man whom I despise.

Translated by Robert Friend
with Shimon Sandbank

2 SAMUEL 11:2-27

²Late one afternoon, David rose from his couch and strolled on the roof of the royal palace; and from the roof he saw a woman bathing. The woman was very beautiful, ³and the king sent someone to make inquiries about the woman. He reported, "She is Bathsheba daughter of Eliam [and] wife of Uriah the Hittite." ⁴David sent messengers to fetch her; she came to him and he lay with her—she had just purified herself after her period—and she went back home. ⁵The woman conceived, and she sent word to David, "I am pregnant." ⁶Thereupon David sent a message to Joab, "Send Uriah the Hittite to me"; and Joab sent Uriah to David.

. . .

¹⁴In the morning, David wrote a letter to Joab, which he sent with Uriah. ¹⁵He wrote in the letter as follows: "Place Uriah in the front line where the fighting is fiercest; then fall back so that he may be killed." ¹⁶So when Joab was besieging the city, he stationed Uriah at the point where he knew that there were able warriors. ¹⁷The men of the city sallied out and attacked Joab, and some of David's officers among the troops fell; Uriah the Hittite was among those who died.

. . .

²³The messenger said to David, "First the men prevailed against us and sallied out against us into the open; then we drove them back up to the entrance to the gate. ²⁴But the archers shot at your men from the wall and some of Your Majesty's men fell; your servant Uriah the Hittite also fell." ²⁵Whereupon David said to the messenger, "Give Joab this message: 'Do not be distressed about the matter. The sword *⁻always takes its toll.⁻* Press your attack on the city and destroy it!' Encourage him!"

²⁶When Uriah's wife heard that her husband Uriah was dead, she lamented over her husband. ²⁷After the period of mourning was over, David sent and had her brought into his palace; she became his wife and she bore him a son.

- Lit. "consumes the like and the like"

SIEGFRIED SASSOON ☐

Devotion to Duty

I was near the King that day. I saw him snatch
And briskly scan the G.H.Q. dispatch.
Thick-voiced, he read it out. (His face was grave.)
"This officer advanced with the first wave,

And when our first objective had been gained,
(Though wounded twice), reorganized the line:
The spirit of the troops was by his fine
Example most effectively sustained."

He gripped his beard; then closed his eyes and said,
"Bathsheba must be warned that he is dead.
Send for her. I will be the first to tell
This wife how her heroic husband fell."

February 1919

P • Abishag

1 KINGS 1:1–4

King David was now old, advanced in years; and though they covered him with bedclothes, he never felt warm. [2]His courtiers said to him, "Let a young virgin be sought for my lord the king, to wait upon Your Majesty and be his attendant;* and let her lie in your bosom, and my lord the king will be warm." [3]So they looked for a beautiful girl throughout the territory of Israel. They found Abishag the Shunammite and brought her to the king. [4]The girl was exceedingly beautiful. She became the king's attendant* and waited upon him; but the king was not intimate with her.

* Meaning of Heb. uncertain

RAINER MARIA RILKE □

Abishag

I

She lay. And her childlike arms were bound
by servants around the withering king,
on whom she lay throughout the sweet long hours,
a little frightened of his many years.

And now and then she turned her face
in his beard, whenever an owl cried;
and all that was night came and flocked
around her with fear and longing.

The stars trembled just as she did,
a scent went searching through the sleeping room,
the curtain stirred and made a sign,
and her gaze went softly after it—.

But she kept clinging to the dark old man
and, not reached by what the nights call forth,
lay on his potent slumber's deepening chill
with virgin lightness, like a buoyant soul.

II

The king sat thinking through the empty day
of deeds accomplished, of unfelt pleasures,
and of his favorite dog, on whom he doted.
But in the evening Abishag arched
over him. His tangled life lay
abandoned like an ill-famed coast
beneath the constellation of her silent breasts.

And now and then, as one adept in women,
he recognized through his eyebrows
the unmoved, kissless mouth;
and saw: her feeling's green divining rod
did not point downward to his depths.
A chill went through him. He hearkened like a hound
and sought himself in his last blood.

Translated from the German
by Edward Snow

JACOB GLATSTEIN □

Abishag

Abishag. Small, young, warm Abishag.
Shout in the streets—King David isn't dead yet.
All King David wants is some sleep, but they won't let him alone.
Adonijah and his gang shout the crown from my gray head.
The fat Bathsheba blesses me with eternal life and watches over my
    last words with a sly smile.

Sleep, my king. The night is still. We are all your slaves.

Abishag. Small, country-girl Abishag.
Throw my crown into the street—up for grabs.
Dead might whimpers in each of my fingers.
Only you now are ruled by this sovereign, this repugnant old man.
David—the King—and all his servants gone. Only one left.

Sleep a while, my king. The night is dead. We are all your slaves.

Abishag. Small, sad Abishag.
A tiny kitten thrown in the cage of the old toothless lion.
It figures my old age would peter out in the lap of your
    fretful young years.
The great battles I won—only pools of blood in my memory.
How long it has been since girls sang and praised me.

Rest, my king. The night is still. We are all your slaves.

Abishag. Small, dear Abishag.
Fear scrambles through all my limbs.
Can you really stumble onto the ways of God through pools of blood?
At this crossroad, will the soft songs from my pious days
    be any help?
Abishag, there must be songs steeped in more truth than my sins.

Dream, my king. The night is dead. We are all your slaves.

Abishag, small, young, warm Abishag.
Shout in the streets—King David isn't dead yet.
King David just wants to die.
Throw away my crown—up for grabs.
Adonijah or Solomon over the people, and me over you
    these last days of my disgusting old age.

Go to sleep, my king, it's almost dawn. We are all your slaves.

Translated from the Yiddish
by Richard J. Fein

SHIRLEY KAUFMAN □

Abishag

*. . . and let her lie in thy bosom that the lord my
king may get heat.*

1 Kings 1:2

That's what they ordered
for the old man
to dangle around his neck,
send currents of fever
through his phlegmatic nerves, something
like rabbit fur, silky,
or maybe a goat-hair blanket
to tickle his chin.

He can do nothing else
but wear her, pluck at her body
like a lost bird
pecking in winter.
He spreads her out
like a road-map, trying
to find his way from one point
to another, unable.

She thinks if she pinches
his hand it will turn to powder.
She feels his thin claws, his wings
spread over her like arms, not bones
but feathers ready to fall.
She suffers the jerk
of his feeble legs. Take it easy,
she tells him, cruelly

submissive in her bright flesh.
He's cold from the fear
of death, the sorrow
of failure, night after night
he shivers with her breasts
against him like an accusation,
her mouth slightly open,
her hair spilling everywhere.

ITSIK MANGER □

Abishag Writes a Letter Home

Abishag sits in her room
and writes a letter home:
Greetings to the calves and sheep—
she writes, sighing deeply.

Greetings to her old mother
and the old linden tree;
she sees both old folk
in her dreams frequently.

Greet the handsome miller
who works in the mill—
and the shepherd Oizer, whose
piping she cherishes still.

King David is old and pious
and she herself is, "oh, well"—
She's the king's hotwater bottle
against the bedroom chill.

She thought—but who cares what
a village girl may think . . .
more than once at night
she softly mourned her fate.

True, wise people say
she's being charitable.
They even promise her
a line in the Bible.

A line for her young flesh,
the years of her youth.
A line of ink on parchment
for the whole long truth.

Abishag puts down her pen,
her heart is strangely bitter,
a tear drips from her eyes
and falls on the letter.

The tear erases "mother"
and erases "linden tree"
while girlish in a corner
a dream sobs tenderly.

Translated from the Yiddish
by Ruth Whitman

ROBERT LOWELL ☐

King David Old

Two or three times a night, and for a month,
we wrang the night-sweat from his shirt and sheets;
on the fortieth day, we brought him Abishag,
and he recovered, and he knew her not—
cool through the hottest summer day, and moist;
a rankness more savage than all the flowers,
as if her urine caused the vegetation,
Jerusalem leaping from the golden dew;
but later, the Monarch's well-beloved shaft
lay quaking in place; men thought the world was flat,
yet half the world was hanging on each breast,
as two spent swimmers that did cling together—
Sion had come to Israel, if they had held. . . .
This clinch is quickly broken, they were glad to break.

ROBERT FROST ☐

Provide, Provide

The witch that came (the withered hag)
To wash the steps with pail and rag
Was once the beauty Abishag,

The picture pride of Hollywood.
Too many fall from great and good
For you to doubt the likelihood.

Die early and avoid the fate.
Or if predestined to die late,
Make up your mind to die in state.

Make the whole stock exchange your own!
If need be occupy a throne,
Where nobody can call *you* crone.

Some have relied on what they knew,
Others on being simply true.
What worked for them might work for you.

No memory of having starred
Atones for later disregard
Or keeps the end from being hard.

Better to go down dignified
With boughten friendship at your side
Than none at all. Provide, provide!

Q · Solomon, and Sheba

1 KINGS 3:5–15

⁵At Gibeon the LORD appeared to Solomon in a dream by night; and God said, "Ask, what shall I grant you?" ⁶Solomon said, "You dealt most graciously with Your servant my father David, because he walked before You in faithfulness and righteousness and in integrity of heart. You have continued this great kindness to him by giving him a son to occupy his throne, as is now the case. ⁷And now, O LORD my God, You have made Your servant king in place of my father David; but I am a young lad, *⁻with no experience in leadership.⁻* ⁸Your servant finds himself in the midst of the people You have chosen, a people too numerous to be numbered or counted. ⁹Grant, then, Your servant an understanding mind to judge Your people, to distinguish between good and bad; for who can judge this vast people of Yours?"

¹⁰The LORD was pleased that Solomon had asked for this. ¹¹And God said to him, "Because you asked for this—you did not ask for long life, you did not ask for riches, you did not ask for the life of your enemies, but you asked for discernment in dispensing justice— ¹²I now do as you have spoken. I grant you a wise and discerning mind; there has never been anyone like you before, nor will anyone like you arise again. ¹³And I also grant you what you did not ask for—both riches and glory all your life—the like of which no king has ever had. ¹⁴And I will further grant you long life, if you will walk in My ways and observe My laws and commandments, as did your father David."

¹⁵Then Solomon awoke: it was a dream! He went to Jerusalem, stood before the Ark of the Covenant of the LORD, and sacrificed burnt offerings and presented offerings of well-being; and he made a banquet for all his courtiers.

⁻ Lit. "I do not know to go out and come in"; cf. Num. 27:17

MARIANNE MOORE ☐

O to Be a Dragon

If I, like Solomon, . . .
could have my wish—

my wish . . . O to be a dragon,
a symbol of the power of Heaven—of silkworm
size or immense; at times invisible.
Felicitous phenomenon!

1 KINGS 10:1–13

The queen of Sheba heard of Solomon's fame, *⁻through the name of the LORD,⁻* and she came to test him with hard questions. ²She arrived in Jerusalem with a very large retinue, with camels bearing spices, a great quantity of gold, and precious stones. When she came to Solomon, she asked him all that she had in mind. ³Solomon had answers for all her questions; there was nothing that the king did not know, [nothing] to which he could not give her an answer. ⁴When the queen of Sheba observed all of Solomon's wisdom, and the palace he had built, ⁵the fare of his table, the seating of his courtiers, the service and attire of his attendants, and his wine service, †⁻and the burnt offerings which he offered at⁻† the House of the LORD, she was left breathless.

⁶She said to the king, "The report I heard in my own land about you and your wisdom was true. ⁷But I did not believe the reports until I came and saw with my own eyes that not even the half had been told me; your wisdom and wealth surpass the reports that I heard. ⁸How fortunate are your men and how fortunate are these your courtiers, who are always in attendance on you and can hear your wisdom! ⁹Praised be the LORD your God, who delighted in you and set you on the throne of Israel. It is because of the LORD's everlasting love for Israel that He made you king to administer justice and righteousness."

¹⁰She presented the king with one hundred and twenty talents of gold, and a large quantity of spices, and precious stones. Never again did such a vast quantity of spices arrive as that which the queen of Sheba gave to King Solomon.—¹¹Moreover, Hiram's fleet, which carried gold from Ophir, brought in from Ophir a huge quantity of *almug* wood‡ and precious stones. ¹²The King used the *almug* wood for decorations in the House of the LORD and in the royal palace, and for

---

- The force of the phrase is uncertain
†-† 2 Chron. 9:4 reads " . . . and the procession with which he went up to . . . "
‡ Others "sandalwood"

harps and lyres for the musicians. Such a quantity of *almug* wood has never arrived or been seen to this day.—[13]King Solomon, in turn, gave the queen of Sheba everything she wanted and asked for, in addition to what King Solomon gave her out of his royal bounty. Then she and her attendants left and returned to her own land.

WILLIAM BUTLER YEATS ☐

Solomon to Sheba

Sang Solomon to Sheba,
And kissed her dusky face,
'All day long from mid-day
We have talked in the one place,
All day long from shadowless noon
We have gone round and round
In the narrow theme of love
Like an old horse in a pound.'

To Solomon sang Sheba,
Planted on his knees,
'If you have broached a matter
That might the learned please,
You had before the sun had thrown
Our shadows on the ground
Discovered that my thoughts, not it,
Are but a narrow pound.'

Said Solomon to Sheba,
And kissed her Arab eyes,
'There's not a man or woman
Born under the skies
Dare match in learning with us two,
And all day long we have found
There's not a thing but love can make
The world a narrow pound.'

YEHUDA AMICHAI ☐

From "The Visit of the Queen of Sheba"

1. Preparations for the Journey

Not resting but
moving her lovely butt,
the Queen of Sheba,
having decided to leave, a-
rose from her lair
among dark spells, tossed her hair,
clapped her hands,
the servants fainted, and
already she drew in the sand
with her big toe:
King Solomon, as though
he were a rubber ball, an
apocalyptic, bearded herring, an
imperial walking-stick, an
amalgam, half chicken
and half Solomon.

The minister of protocol
went too far, with all
those peacocks and ivory boxes.
Later on,
she began to yawn
deliciously, she stretched like a cat
so that
he would be able to sniff
her odif-
erous heart. They spared no expense,
they brought feathers, to tickle
his ears, to make his last defense
prickle.
She had been brought
a vague report
about circumcision,
she wanted to know everything, with absolute precision,
her curiosity
blossomed like leprosy,
the disheveled sisters of her corpuscles

screamed through their loudspeaker into all her muscles.
the sky undid
its buttons, she made herself up and slid
into a vast commotion,
felt her head
spin, all the brothels of her emotions
were lit up in red.
In the factory
of her blood, they worked frantically
till night came: a dark night, like an old table,
a night as eternal
as a jungle.

Translated from the Hebrew
by Stephen Mitchell

ALEKSANDER WAT □

A Turtle from Oxford

TO K. JELENSKI

And when the queen of Sheba heard of the fame of Solomon concerning the name
of the Lord, she came to prove him with hard questions.

1 Kings 10:1

On the eastern sidewalk of Magdalen College a small
turtle reflected a long time before he answered
my question, he moved his jaws like a meccano: "That,
even I cannot remember: I am hardly
two hundred and ninety-three. But in our family
a record has been preserved how our ancestor, of blessed memory,
assisted at the lovemaking of the queen of Sheba with
                              your great-grandfather.
As to the riddles she presumably asked him to solve, our tradition
is silent. What is known: it occurred in a wine-colored chamber
where, instead of lamps, gold was shining, from Tyre, no doubt.
My ancestor was not a learned turtle, but a respectable one,
to be sure. . . . "

With short steps we shuffled after him, I, my beautiful
wife and Adriana, our charming guide.

We listened to the turtle solemnly. When he lost his breath
my wife with a kind stroke of her finger
animated his little snout. After all, that's why I wander!
In strange lands! In my old age!
I write, that is to say, my autobiography and gather data
for the genealogy of our ancient stock. An English duke
in a waterfront dive in Naples brought the turtle to my attention,
in return for a bowl of spaghetti and a glass
of wine ("My great-great-grandfather, an admiral,
took that turtle to Oxford all the way from Abyssinia").
Thus all three of us listened to the turtle with the solemnity due
to a dignified university person. But now
the pause was irritatingly long, when all of a sudden,
from behind an island, young laughter was heard
and a boat passed, carrying a couple away.
Neither of them graceful. But my wife was delighted
to hear laughter of lovers. There is no need to add
that, tiptoeing after the turtle and straining to hear
what he might deign to tell us, we were bent so low
that one might say we were on all fours.
Were they laughing at this? At their love?
At love in general? It does not matter.

       "So, hardly had
he turned over on his back when he asked: 'And *now*
tell me, baby, what do they think of me in your country?'
The queen, still in ecstasies: 'That you love wisdom,'
she faltered, 'and women.' 'Wisdom?' he replied, 'I don't deny,
But women? Hardly. I love femininity.' "

Again there was a pause. This time not laughter but crying
and that of an infant, indeed, more bizarre here
than, for instance, a drunkard's railing in a cathedral.

       "And he was right,"
the turtle added at last. "He was wrong!" exclaimed
charming Adriana, blushing all over. She never interrupted
her elders, since she was well-bred. "He was right,"
the turtle repeated, as though he had not heard. "A great lord
should love only universals: grassiness, not grass,
not humans, humanity, and arsiness, not . . . "
       Whether he finished or not
I don't know, for Adriana again interjected, it is true, somewhat
abashed: "He who never loved someone, doesn't know love
at all." The turtle fell silent, for good; now he had taken

offense: nobody here had dared to contradict him.
We had no flies or anything else to smooth over the incident.
But my wife, who has a way with animals
and children, gently massaged his jowls.
So he spoke again, this time even garrulously:

"When King Solomon rolled off the queen for the third time,
he asked: 'Now, what counsel do your people ask for?
What do they want from me?' 'A toenail,' answered
the queen of Sheba, 'from the little toe of your foot.'
'I'll give it to them,' agreed the king, and himself
handed her a pair of nail scissors. She pulled out a golden cup
artfully engraved by the hand of Hiram-Abi,
which the king after their first intercourse had presented to her.
It had a tight-fitting lid, on it was carved the grim face of
     Ashtoreth.
A short cry, blood spurted into the cup, the lid clicks shut. . . .
What happened next, our ancestor did not relate.
Perhaps the whole thing so tired him, the strain upon his eyes,
upon his attention, that he suddenly fell asleep.
He was not learned. Who, after all, in those times,
was learned?"

                              "But what happened to the cup?
The cup?" I asked hollowly. For just then
a thought disturbed me, that perhaps
if I drink the blood of my ancestor,
youth, eternal, wisdom, forever, will be restored to me!

                              "Oh yes," the turtle replied impassively,
"we know. The ship carrying the queen back, sank. Thirteen
centuries later Senegalese sailors extracted the cup
from the belly of a whale, in the Indian Ocean." "Undamaged?"
"Undamaged." Again a pause. "From Abyssinia, an Italian airman
stole it together with the treasure of the King of Kings
not long ago. . . . His plane fell into Etna."
"Into Etna!" I cried in falsetto, I straightened up
as well as I could and I raised my arms into the air,
frightening by this motion two male cardinals
that were fighting a knightly battle
on the grass, plucking at each other's beautiful scarlet crests.
"And yet Etna threw back the cup,"
unexpectedly screeched the turtle. "Like a
                              sandal?" "Of Empedocles,"

he asserted with vivid satisfaction. Again silence. The crying
of the infant had long subsided. And the laugh of the lovers.
And the hissing of the birds. I could not stand this stillness.
"Where is the blood of my ancestor?" I shouted, full of hope.
                              "Blood, blood, blood,"
he grated angrily. Adrianna got up: "I wanted, master,
to sit at your feet and imbibe the words of wisdom from your
lips. And now . . . " She sobbed, poor, dear Adriana. "Blood,
of blood, with blood," repeated the turtle, obviously unable to stop.
"You gulped the blood of my cousins, is not that enough? Seizing
them in whole fistfuls in the bulrushes by the river Ili, crushing and
smashing them with a rolling pin, on the rough table in the kitchen
of the Prokombinat where you helped the dirty woman cook to
steal food. The blood of my brothers splashed into your eyes,
bespattered your face, your rags, you waded in their blood, still you
didn't have enough. You have never had enough. Not
                              enough. Not enough. Not
enough . . . "

I was afraid that he would have a stroke, he was choking.
Ashamed, we fled across the lawns and for a long time
the gargoyles of Magdalen pursued us with their howling laughter.

Oxford, July 1962

Translated from the Polish
by Czeslaw Milosz and Leonard Nathan

LÉOPOLD SÉDAR SENGHOR □

From "Elegy for the Queen of Sheba"
(for two *koras** and a *balaphon*†)

I am black and comely . . .
> Song of Songs

III

The promised day, the festive dawn exuding the fresh-
    smelling
Trees, the armed heroes, chimes raised high, announcing
Her presence at three thousand steps, and under gleaming
    tents,
Seventy-seven elephants preceded her, dark and advancing
At a pachyderm's pace. And elephant keepers, their braids
    decorated in red-gold
Balanced their long poles while making brief, rhythmic
    shouts.
Then darker warriors on foot, numerous and tight together,
Their leopard skin strapped to their shoulders.
Then came Sheba's gifts
Carried by sixty young men, sixty young women arching
    firm breasts
Who advanced smiling more than the water lilies
Above the Trade Winds lake, and nine blacksmiths with
    hammers
On their shoulders, who taught the basic numbers
Born from the rhythm of the drum. To say nothing of other
    gifts
Whose list would be long. Such was God's plan,
When, engaged, you ascended the Holy Hill.
I remember the night of my festival when gently,
Like a flamingo taking flight, dressed in a pink *boubou*,‡
Your frail neck under the crest of plaits and braids
    constellated
In white and gold, slowly you raised your bosom,
After me, with me, at my call to close the fan of dances,
Dancing the spring dance.
Farewell cold and dry winter! The rain answers the call of
    spring

---

* *kora:* an instrument with many strings stretched along a wooden arm and extending from
a hollowed calabash
† *balaphon:* (*bala* in Manding) instrument similar to the xylophone
‡ *boubou:* a large, flowing robe worn by women and men

And spring is rain. Gently, slowly, one then two serious
    drops
And it is the flapping of the noisy clouds, shoulders shaking
To reach the virgin belly, feet pounding like clod-crushers
Beating the land in the time when—your lips barely open—
Our arms swim in the torrent like vines.

IV

The *boubou* falls. At the dry beat of the music
The clear bosom fuses under the black jumper,
Streaked with green-gold across the hips where the skirt
Opens on thighs and lively legs. It is the second movement
That grows in the ground when the soles of the feet beat,
Shakes the hips, and it is the volcanic mountain
Pitching and arching the loins to explode, the throat
    budding
In the serene burst of spring, the dark fragrance of *gongo,**
The earth of the flesh. Then under the unfettered sky
Begins the movement of golden pollen.
They are two parallel dances, watching, inhaling the air's
    breath,
But turning and advancing, one to the other, the trembling
    wave
Seizes us and pushes us one toward the other; you
    undulating
Arms and legs like a basket of flowers for an offering,
And I, around you, an ardent sandstorm in the dry season,
A brushfire. A blunt blow to the loins and I was thrown back
Abandoning you, even in spite of myself, to your empty
    waiting.
And you ran to me, trembling from your neck to your pink
    heels,
Descending low and lower, on your knees at my knees
Singing the song that shakes me down to the roots of my
    being:
"Tell me, tell me, my Sage, my Poet. Speak the golden words
That are a weight and a miracle to my soul. May your
    rhythm
And melody dispose the spheres to the magic of the golden
    section."
Turned suddenly around, I reached you in a gust of wind

---

* *gongo:* musky perfume worn by Senegalese women

And we stood together face-to-face like the moon and the
    sun,
Hand in hand, brow-to-brow, breathing in unison.
Again your knees pointed to the end of long shapely legs,
Nervous under the shaking undulation of your shoulders.
Oh, the rhythmic rolling of our loins, the deep working
Of the sandy belly. I remember my leap to your call,
Right up to the ecstasy of faces of light when you received
In your open angle and melodious thighs the song
Of golden pollen in the joy of our death-rebirth.

V
Still we waited nine nights and nine days to enter
The Childhood Kingdom. But here we are all new, revived
In childhood's garden. Here you are under the lamp,
Under your shimmering skin, and I at your feet
In the fervor of my knees, before my statue of black basalt
And red sandstone: Your skin of blue bronze, of blue night
Under the moon, your skin the color and aroma of palm oil,
Your bushy, steaming armpits where I burn the incense
Of my love. I remember your smiling body, your silken
    smile,
Tender caresses, Ha, in caves of ecstasy, your body of velvet
    fur,
The fleece of your little dark valley in the shade
Of a holy hillock. If she smiles at me, I feel my snows
Melting in the April sun. Her heart opens to me,
And I fall right on it like an eagle on a tender lamb.
You are my sacred wood, my temple and tabernacle,
You are my bridge of vines, my palm tree.
Your waist between my elbows, and I contemplate crossing
My bridge of harmonious curves. I mount to gather the
    fabulous
Fruits of my garden, for you are my Jacob's ladder.
When your mouth is fragrant with ripe guavas, your snaking
    arms
Imprison me against your heart and your rhythmic rattle,
Then I create the poem: the new world in the paschal joy!
Yes! she has kissed me a kiss from her mouth,
My black and comely one among the daughters of
    Jerusalem.

Translated from the French
by Melvin Dixon

WILLIAM BUTLER YEATS ☐

On Woman

May God be praised for woman
That gives up all her mind,
A man may find in no man
A friendship of her kind
That covers all he has brought
As with her flesh and bone,
Nor quarrels with a thought
Because it is not her own.

Though pedantry denies,
It's plain the Bible means
That Solomon grew wise
While talking with his queens,
Yet never could, although
They say he counted grass,
Count all the praises due
When Sheba was his lass,
When she the iron wrought, or
When from the smithy fire
It shuddered in the water:
Harshness of their desire
That made them stretch and yawn,
Pleasure that comes with sleep,
Shudder that made them one.
What else He give or keep
God grant me—no, not here,
For I am not so bold
To hope a thing so dear
Now I am growing old,
But when, if the tale's true,
The Pestle of the moon
That pounds up all anew
Brings me to birth again—
To find what once I had
And know what once I have known,
Until I am driven mad,
Sleep driven from my bed,
By tenderness and care,
Pity, an aching head,
Gnashing of teeth, despair;

And all because of some one
Perverse creature of chance,
And live like Solomon
That Sheba led a dance.

R ▪ Elijah

1 KINGS 18:41–45a

[41]And Elijah said unto Ahab: "Get thee up, eat and drink; for there is the sound of abundance of rain." [42]So Ahab went up to eat and to drink. And Elijah went up to the top of Carmel; and he bowed himself down upon the earth, and put his face between his knees. [43]And he said to his servant: "Go up now, look toward the sea." And he went up, and looked, and said: "There is nothing." And he said: "Go again seven times." [44]And it came to pass at the seventh time, that he said: "Behold, there ariseth a cloud out of the sea, as small as a man's hand." And he said: "Go up, say unto Ahab: Make ready thy chariot, and get thee down, that the rain stop thee not." [45]And it came to pass in a little while, that the heaven grew black with clouds and wind, and there was a great rain.

Translation: JPS 1917

230

NATAN ZACH ☐

I Saw

I saw a white bird in the black night
and I knew the light of my eyes in the black night
was close to extinction.

I saw a cloud as small as a man's hand
and I knew I have not been able to tell one person
my sense of the rain.

I saw a leaf that fell, that is falling.
Time is short. I'm not complaining.

Translated from the Hebrew
by David Curzon and Gabriel Preil

1 KINGS 19:1–8

And Ahab told Jezebel all that Elijah had done, and withal how he had slain all the prophets with the sword. [2]Then Jezebel sent a messenger unto Elijah, saying: "So let the gods do [to me], and more also, if I make not thy life as the life of one of them by to-morrow about this time." [3]And when he saw that, he arose, and went for his life, and came to Beer-sheba, which belongeth to Judah, and left his servant there. [4]But he himself went a day's journey into the wilderness, and came and sat down under a broom-tree; and he requested for himself that he might die; and said: "It is enough; now, O LORD, take away my life; for I am not better than my fathers." [5]And he lay down and slept under a broom-tree; and, behold, an angel touched him, and said unto him: "Arise and eat." [6]And he looked, and, behold, there was at his head a cake baked on the hot stones, and a cruse of water. And he did eat and drink, and laid him down again. [7]And the angel of the LORD came again the second time, and touched him, and said: "Arise and eat; because the journey is too great for thee." [8]And he arose, and did eat and drink, and went in the strength of that meal forty days and forty nights unto Horeb the mount of God.

Translation: JPS 1917

ANNA KAMIENSKA □

The Weariness of the Prophet Elijah

Lord
You understand such immense weariness
when one only whispers
release your servant now
deliver me from the scraps of hunger and thirst
called life
I don't need more than
the shade of a broom-tree to rest my head
a shawl of darkness for eyes
call back the angel
who hastens with bread and a jar of water
send me a long purifying
issueless sleep
lift my loneliness above its cumber
above every bereavement
Lord
You know the weariness of your prophets
You wake them with a jolt of new hurt
to place a new desert beneath their feet
to give them a new mouth a new voice
and a new name

11 August 1985

Translated from the Polish
by Grażyna Drabik and David Curzon

³⁰Jehu went on to Jezreel. When Jezebel heard of it, she painted her eyes with kohl and dressed her hair, and she looked out of the window. ³¹As Jehu entered the gate, she called out, "Is all well, Zimri, murderer of your master?"* ³²He looked up toward the window and said, "Who is on my side, who?" And two or three eunuchs leaned out toward him. ³³"Throw her down," he said. They threw her down; and her blood spattered on the wall and on the horses, and they trampled her.

³⁴Then he went inside and ate and drank. And he said, "Attend to that cursed woman and bury her, for she was a king's daughter." ³⁵So they went to bury her; but all they found of her were the skull, the feet, and the hands. ³⁶They came back and reported to him; and he said, "It is just as the LORD spoke through His servant Elijah the Tishbite: The dogs shall devour the flesh of Jezebel in the field of Jezreelᴾ; ³⁷and the carcass of Jezebel shall be like dung on the ground, in the field of Jezreel, so that none will be able to say: 'This was Jezebel.' "

* See 1 Kings 16:8–10
ᴾ See "Notes on the Poems," p. 335

THOMAS HARDY ☐

Jezreel

On Its Seizure by the English under Allenby,
September 1918

Did they catch as it were in a Vision at shut of the day—
When their cavalry smote through the ancient Esdraelon Plain,
And they crossed where the Tishbite stood forth in his enemy's way—
His gaunt mournful Shade as he bade the King haste off amain?

On war-men at this end of time—even on Englishmen's eyes—
Who slay with their arms of new might in that long-ago place,
Flashed he who drove furiously? . . . Ah, did the phantom arise
Of that queen, of that proud Tyrian woman who painted her face?

Faintly marked they the words "Throw her down!" from the Night
    eerily,
Spectre-spots of the blood of her body on some rotten wall?
And the thin note of pity that came: "A King's daughter is she,"
As they passed where she trodden was once by the chargers' footfall?

Could such be the hauntings of men of to-day, at the cease
Of pursuit, at the dusk-hour, ere slumber their senses could seal?
Enghosted seers, kings—one on horseback who asked "Is it peace?" . . .
Yea, strange things and spectral may men have beheld in Jezreel!

24 September 1918

S ▪ Prophets

ISAIAH 6:1–7

In the year that King Uzziah died, I beheld my Lord seated on a high and lofty throne; and the skirts of His robe filled the Temple. ²Seraphs stood in attendance on Him. Each of them had six wings: with two he covered his face, with two he covered his legs, and with two he would fly.

³And one would call to the other,
"Holy, holy, holy!
The LORD of Hosts!
His presence fills all the earth!"

⁴The doorposts* would shake at the sound of the one who called, and the House kept filling with smoke. ⁵I cried,
"Woe is me; I am lost!
For I am a man †⁻of unclean lips⁻†
And I live among a people
Of unclean lips;
Yet my own eyes have beheld
The King LORD of Hosts."

⁶Then one of the seraphs flew over to me with a live coal, which he had taken from the altar with a pair of tongs. ⁷He touched it to my lips and declared,
"Now that this has touched your lips,
Your guilt shall depart
And your sin be purged away."

* Meaning of Heb. uncertain
†⁻† I.e., speaking impiety; cf. Isa. 9:16, and contrast "pure of speech (lit. 'lip')" in Zeph. 3:9

WILLIAM BUTLER YEATS □

From "Vacillation"

VII

The Soul. Seek out reality, leave things that seem.
The Heart. What, be a singer born and lack a theme?
The Soul. Isaiah's coal, what more can man desire?
The Heart. Struck dumb in the simplicity of fire!
The Soul. Look on that fire, salvation walks within.
The Heart. What theme had Homer but original sin?

ISAIAH 21:11–12

[11]The burden of Dumah.

One calleth unto me out of Seir:
"Watchman, what of the night?
Watchman, what of the night?"
[12]The watchman said:
"The morning cometh, and also the night—
If ye will inquire, inquire ye; return, come."

Translation: JPS 1917

PRIMO LEVI □

Nachtwache

"Watchman, what of the night?"

"I've heard the owl repeat
Its hollow prescient note,
The bat shriek at its hunting,
The water-snake rustle
Under the pond's soaked leaves.
I have heard vinous voices,
Stammering, angry, as I drowsed
In the tavern near the chapel.
I have heard lovers' whispers, laughter,
And the labored breathing of absolved longings,
Adolescents murmuring in their dreams,
Others tossing, sleepless from desire.
I've seen silent heat-lightning,
The terror every night
Of the girl who lost her way
And doesn't know bed from coffin.
I've heard the hoarse panting
Of a lonely old man struggling with death,
A woman torn in labor,
The cry of a just-born child.
Stretch out and sleep, citizen.
Everything is in order; this night is half over."

10 August 1983

Translated from the Italian
by Ruth Feldman

ISAIAH 51:17

[17]Rouse, rouse yourself!
Arise, O Jerusalem,
You who from the LORD's hand
Have drunk the cup of His wrath,
You who have drained to the dregs
The bowl, the cup of reeling!

ISAIAH 60:1–3

Arise, shine, for your light has dawned;
The Presence of the LORD has shone upon you!
[2]Behold! Darkness shall cover the earth,
And thick clouds the peoples;
But upon you the LORD will shine,
And His Presence be seen over you.
[3]And nations shall walk by your light;
Kings, by your shining radiance.

PAUL CELAN ☐

YOU BE LIKE YOU, ever.[q]
Ryse up Ierosalem and
rowse thyselfe
The very one who slashed the bond unto you,
and becum
yllumyned
knotted it new, in memoraunce,
spills of mire I swallowed, inside the tower,
speech, dark-selvedge,
kumi
ori.

Translated from the German
by John Felstiner

[q] See "Notes on the Poems," p. 335

ISAIAH 54:7–8

⁷For a small moment have I forsaken thee; but with great mercies will I gather thee.

⁸In a little wrath I hid my face from thee for a moment; but with everlasting kindness will I have mercy on thee, saith the LORD thy Redeemer.

Translation: King James Version

HOWARD NEMEROV   □

Small Moment

Isaiah 54:7

Death is serious,
or else all things are serious
except death. A player who dies
automatically disqualifies
for the finals. If there were no death
nothing could be taken seriously,
not truth, not beauty, but that is not
a situation which we need to face.
Men invented the gods, but they
discovered death; therefore, although
the skull is said to grin, the flesh
is serious, and frowns, for the world
is not a stage. And the gay spirit, gone
through wisdom to absurdity,
welcomes the light that shudders in the leaves
in all weathers and at any season,
since love, the pure, unique, and useless virtue,
climbs in the stalk and concentrates this dust
until it takes the light and shines
with the fat blood of death. So men say
that flowers light the sun, and so also,
when Theseus fought Antiope,[r]
the battlefield became the marriage bed.
When you have known how this may be
you have already lived forever,
forsaken once in the small moment,
but gathered with great mercies after.

[r] See "Notes on the Poems," p. 335

ISAIAH 56:5

⁵I will give them, in My House
And within My walls,
A monument and a nameˢ
Better than sons or daughters.
I will give them an everlasting name
Which shall not perish.

ˢ See "Notes on the Poems," p. 335

PAUL CELAN □

JUST THINK.[t]
the peat-bog soldier of Masada
makes a home for himself, most
undestroyably,
against
every barb in the wire.

Just think:
the eyeless ones with no shape
lead you free through the tumult, you
grow stronger and
stronger.

Just think: your
own hand
has held
this piece of
habitable earth,
again suffered
up into life.

Just think:
that came toward me,
name-awake, hand-awake
for ever,
from the unburiable.

Translated from the German
by John Felstiner

[t] See "Notes on the Poems," p. 335

ANTHONY HECHT □

Destinations

The harvest is past, the summer is ended, and we are not saved.

Jeremiah 8:20

The children having grown up and moved away,
One day she announced in brisk and scathing terms
That since for lo, as she said, these many years
She had thanklessly worked her fingers to the bone,
Always put him and the children first and foremost,
(A point he thought perhaps disputable)
She had had it up to here, and would be leaving
The following day, would send him an address
To which her belongings could be forwarded
And to which the monthly payments could be sent.
He could see her point. It was only tit for tat.
After all the years when the monthly pains were hers
They now were to be his. True to her word,
Which she commanded him to mark, she packed
And left, and took up shifting residence,
First with a barber, then with a state trooper:
From the scissors of severance to the leather holster
Of the well-slung groin—the six-pack, six-gun weapon
Of death and generation. He could see the point.
In these years of inflation ways and means
Had become meaner and more chancy ways
Of getting along. Economy itself
Urged perfect strangers to bed down together
Simply to make ends meet, and so ends met.
Rather to his surprise, his first reaction
Was a keen sense of relief and liberation.
It seemed that, thinking of her, he could recall
Only a catalogue of pettiness,
Selfishness, spite, a niggling litany
Of minor acrimony, punctuated
By outbursts of hysteria and violence.
Now there was peace, the balm of Gilead,
At least at first. Slowly it dawned upon him
That she had no incentive to remarry,
Since, by remaining single and shacking up,
She would enjoy two sources of income.

In the house of her deferred and mortgaged dreams
Two lived as cheaply as one, if both had funds.
He thought about this off and on for years
As he went on subsidizing her betrayal
In meek obedience to the court decree,
And watered the flowers by his chain-link fence
Beside the railroad tracks. In his back yard
He kept petunias in a wooden tub
Inside the white-washed tire of a tractor trailer,
And his kitchen steps of loose, unpainted boards
Afforded him an unimpeded view
Of the webbed laundry lines of all his neighbors,
Rusted petroleum tins, the buckled wheels
Of abandoned baby-carriages, and the black-
Sooted I-beams and girders of a bridge
Between two walls of rusticated stonework
Through which the six-fifteen conveyed the lucky
And favored to superior destinies.
Where did they go, these fortunates? He'd seen
Blonde, leggy girls pouting invitingly
In low-cut blouses on TV commercials,
And thought about encountering such a one
In a drugstore or supermarket. She
Would smile (according to his dream scenario)
And come straight home with him as if by instinct.
But in the end, he knew, this would be foreplay
To the main event when she'd take him to the cleaners.

EZEKIEL 37:1–14

The hand of the LORD came upon me. He took me out by the spirit of the LORD and set me down in the valley. It was full of bones. [2]He led me all around them; there were very many of them spread over the valley, and they were very dry. [3]He said to me, "O mortal, can these bones live again?" I replied, "O Lord GOD, only You know." [4]And He said to me, "Prophesy over these bones and say to them: O dry bones, hear the word of the LORD! [5]Thus said the Lord GOD to these bones: I will cause breath to enter you and you shall live again. [6]I will lay sinews upon you, and cover you with flesh, and form skin over you. And I will put breath into you, and you shall live again. And you shall know that I am the LORD!"

[7]I prophesied as I had been commanded. And while I was prophesying, suddenly there was a sound of rattling, and the bones came together, bone to matching bone. [8]I looked, and there were sinews on them, and flesh had grown, and skin had formed over them: but there was no breath in them. [9]Then He said to me, "Prophesy to the breath, prophesy, O mortal! Say to the breath: Thus said the Lord GOD: Come, O breath, from the four winds, and breathe into these slain, that they may live again." [10]I prophesied as He commanded me. The breath entered them, and they came to life and stood up on their feet, a vast multitude.

[11]And He said to me: O mortal, these bones are the whole House of Israel. They say, "Our bones are dried up, our hope is gone; we are doomed." [12]Prophesy, therefore, and say to them: Thus said the Lord GOD: I am going to open your graves and lift you out of the graves, O My people, and bring you to the land of Israel. [13]You shall know, O My people, that I am the LORD when I have opened your graves and lifted you out of your graves. [14]I will put My breath into you and you shall live again, and I will set you upon your own soil. Then you shall know that I the LORD have spoken and have acted— declares the LORD.

DAN PAGIS □

Draft of a Reparations Agreement

All right, gentlemen who cry blue murder as always,
nagging miracle-makers,
quiet!
Everything will be returned to its place,
paragraph after paragraph.
The scream back into the throat.
The gold teeth back to the gums.
The terror.
The smoke back to the tin chimney and further on and inside
back to the hollow of the bones,
and already you will be covered with skin and sinews and you will live,
look, you will have your lives back,
sit in the living room, read the evening paper.
Here you are. Nothing is too late.
As to the yellow star: immediately
it will be torn from your chest
and will emigrate
to the sky.

Translated from the Hebrew
by Stephen Mitchell

JOEL 4:2 and 4:12–14

²I will gather all the nations
And bring them down to the Valley of Jehoshaphat.*
There I will contend with them. . . .
. . .

¹²Let the nations rouse themselves and march up
To the Valley of Jehoshaphat;†
For there I will sit in judgment
Over all the nations round about.
¹³Swing the sickle,
For the crop is ripe:
Come and tread,
For the winepress is full,
The vats are overflowing!
For great is their wickedness.

¹⁴Multitudes upon multitudes
In the Valley of Decision!
For the day of the LORD is at hand
In the Valley of Decision.
¹⁵Sun and moon are darkened,
And stars withdraw their brightness.

* Here understood as "The LORD contends"; contrast v. 12
† Here understood as "The LORD judges"; contrast v. 2

ZBIGNIEW HERBERT □

At the Gate of the Valley[u]

After the rain of stars
on the meadow of ashes
they all have gathered under the guard of angels

from a hill that survived
the eye embraces
the whole lowing two-legged herd

in truth they are not many
counting even those who will come
from chronicles fables and the lives of the saints

but enough of these remarks
let us lift our eyes
to the throat of the valley
from which comes a shout

after a loud whisper of explosion
after a loud whisper of silence
this voice resounds like a spring of living water
it is we are told
a cry of mothers from whom children are taken
since as it turns out
we shall be saved each one alone

the guardian angels are unmoved
and let us grant they have a hard job

she begs
—hide me in your eye
in the palm of your hand in your arms
we have always been together

you can't abandon me
now when I am dead and need tenderness

a higher ranking angel
with a smile explains the misunderstanding

[u] See "Notes on the Poems," p. 335

an old woman carries
the corpse of a canary
(all the animals died a little earlier)
he was so nice—she says weeping
he understood everything
and when I said to him—
her voice is lost in the general noise

even a lumberjack
whom one would never suspect of such things
an old bowed fellow
catches to his breast an axe
—all my life she was mine
she will be mine here too
she nourished me there
she will nourish me here
nobody has the right
—he says—
I won't give her up

those who as it seems
have obeyed the orders without pain
go lowering their heads as a sign of consent
but in their clenched fists they hide
fragments of letters ribbons clippings of hair
and photographs
which they naïvely think
won't be taken from them

so they appear
a moment before
the final division
of those gnashing their teeth
from those singing psalms

Translated from the Polish
by Czeslaw Milosz

STEVIE SMITH ☐

Magnificent Words

"Ye shall be a blessing; fear not, but let your hands be strong."

Zechariah 8:13

These magnificent words that I read today
Are what the Daily Telegraph had chosen, to display
From the bible.

Who is it who chooses at the Daily Telegraph each day
Magnificent words out of all of them, to display
From the bible?

This unknown person's hand is strong, he is a blessing,
Everyday
He chooses magnificent words in the Daily Telegraph, to display
From the bible.

T • Jonah

JONAH 1:1–16

The word of the LORD came to Jonah* son of Amittai: ²Go at once to Nineveh, that great city, and proclaim judgment upon it; for their wickedness has come before Me.

³Jonah, however, started out to flee to Tarshish from the LORD's service. He went down to Joppa and found a ship going to Tarshish. He paid the fare and went aboard to sail with the others to Tarshish, away from the service of the LORD.

⁴But the LORD cast a mighty wind upon the sea, and such a great tempest came upon the sea that the ship was in danger of breaking up. ⁵In their fright, the sailors cried out, each to his own god; and they flung the ship's cargo overboard to make it lighter for them. Jonah, meanwhile, had gone down into the hold of the vessel, where he lay down and fell asleep. ⁶The captain went over to him and cried out, "How can you be sleeping so soundly! Up, call upon your god! Perhaps the god will be kind to us and we will not perish."

⁷The men said to one another, "Let us cast lots and find out on whose account this misfortune has come upon us." They cast lots and the lot fell on Jonah. ⁸They said to him, "Tell us, you who have brought this misfortune upon us, what is your business? Where have you come from? What is your country, and of what people are you?" ⁹"I am a Hebrew," he replied. "I worship the LORD, the God of Heaven, who made both sea and land." ¹⁰The men were greatly terrified, and they asked him, "What have you done?" And when the men learned that he was fleeing from the service of the LORD—for so he told them—¹¹they said to him, "What must we do to you to make the sea calm around us?" For the sea was growing more and more stormy. ¹²He answered, "Heave me overboard, and the sea will calm down for you; for I know that this terrible storm came upon you on my account." ¹³Nevertheless, the men rowed hard to regain the shore, but they could not, for the sea was growing more and more stormy about them. ¹⁴Then they cried out to the LORD: "Oh, please,

---

* Mentioned in 2 Kings 14:25

254

LORD, do not let us perish on account of this man's life. Do not hold us guilty of killing an innocent person! For You, O LORD, by Your will, have brought this about." [15]And they heaved Jonah overboard, and the sea stopped raging.

[16]The men feared the LORD greatly; they offered a sacrifice to the LORD and they made vows.

GABRIEL PREIL ☐

Then, Too, It Was Autumn

Planes pass over avenues of air
and Jonah set out from this very city
on a journey that ended in
the innards of the fish.

Had the same sky also turned festive,
had the same waves also conversed?
Had the landscapes of history
kept repeating themselves—
and all remained as is?

Even Auden's poisoned glass
in a dive on fifty-second street[v]
is the glass that scalds my hand.
Then, too, autumn was in full melancholy
and a picture on a wall slipped from its frame.

Only the viewer of things is another.

Jaffa, October 1967

Translated from the Hebrew
by Gabriel Preil and David Curzon

[v] See "Notes on the Poems," p. 336

JONAH 2:1–11

The LORD provided a huge fish to swallow Jonah; and Jonah re-
mained in the fish's belly three days and three nights. ²Jonah prayed
to the LORD his God from the belly of the fish. ³He said:
> In my trouble I called to the LORD,
> And He answered me;
> From the belly of Sheol I cried out,
> And You heard my voice.
> ⁴You cast me into the depths,
> Into the heart of the sea,
> The floods engulfed me;
> All Your breakers and billows
> Swept over me.
> ⁵I thought I was driven away
> Out of Your sight:
> Would I ever gaze again
> Upon Your holy Temple?
> ⁶The waters closed in over me,
> The deep engulfed me.
> Weeds twined around my head.
> ⁷I sank to the base of the mountains;
> The bars of the earth closed upon me forever.
> Yet You brought my life up from the pit,
> O LORD my God!
> ⁸When my life was ebbing away,
> I called the LORD to mind;
> And my prayer came before You,
> Into Your holy Temple.
> ⁹They who cling to empty folly
> Forsake their own welfare,*
> ¹⁰But I, with loud thanksgiving,
> Will sacrifice to You;
> What I have vowed I will perform.
> Deliverance is the LORD's!

¹¹The LORD commanded the fish, and it spewed Jonah out upon
dry land.

* Meaning of Heb. uncertain

DAN PAGIS □

Tidings

The great fish that vomited out Jonah
swallowed nothing more.
Without any prophecy in his guts, he pined away.

The great fish died and the sea vomited him out onto dry land,
three hundred cubits of disappointed and forsaken flesh
in the light of the end of day.

Then they were merciful to him, an omen of things to come in a
    moment:
gangs of crabs
surrounded him, delighted in him, picked him clean.

After all the tidings, there remained on the deserted beach
the skeleton: caverns, columns, gates, secret entranceways—
a city of refuge[w] for an escaped wind. Everything has been fulfilled.

Translated from the Hebrew
by Stephen Mitchell

ZBIGNIEW HERBERT □

Jonah[x]

Now the Lord had prepared a great fish to swallow up Jonah

Jonah son of Amittai
running away from a dangerous mission
boarded a ship sailing
from Joppa to Tarshish

the well-known things happened
great wind tempest
the crew casts Jonah forth into the deep
the sea ceases from her raging
the foreseen fish comes swimming up

---

[w] See "Notes on the Poems," p. 336
[x] See "Notes on the Poems," p. 336

three days and three nights
Jonah prays in the fish's belly
which vomits him out at last
on dry land

the modern Jonah
goes down like a stone
if he comes across a whale
he hasn't time even to gasp

saved
he behaves more cleverly
than his biblical colleague
the second time he does not take on
a dangerous mission
he grows a beard
and far from the sea
far from Nineveh
under an assumed name
deals in cattle and antiques

agents of Leviathan
can be bought
they have no sense of fate
they are the functionaries of chance

in a neat hospital
Jonah dies of cancer
himself not knowing very well
who he really was

the parable
applied to his head
expires
and the balm of the legend
does not take to his flesh

Translated from the Polish
by Czeslaw Milosz

STEPHEN MITCHELL   □

Jonah

After the first few hours he came to feel quite at ease inside the belly of the whale. He found himself a dry, mildly fluorescent corner near one of the ribs, and settled down there on some huge organ (it was springy as a waterbed). Everything—the warmth, the darkness, the odor of the sea— stirred in him memories of an earlier comfort. His mother's womb? Or was it even before that, at the beginning of the circle which death would, perhaps soon, complete? He had known of God's mercy, but he had never suspected God's sense of humor. With nothing to do now until the next installment, he leaned back against the rib and let his mind rock back and forth. And often, for hours on end, during which he would lose track of Ninevah and Tarshish, his mission, his plight, himself, resonating through the vault: the strange, gurgling, long-breathed-out, beautiful song.

GABRIEL PREIL   □

Jonah

The prophet Jonah ran from his angry Master
and I to my ship empty of God and man
from a certain nightness which strikes root,
from a net spread to maim,
from a shadow that swallows me
   like Jonah in the belly of the fish.

All the black things envisioned by the prophets,
tangible, as in a returning mirror, penetrate to me;
all words of consolation are white petals
that flutter, fragile, on over-calm waters.

I, God willing, while escaping my Master, hope to find
a minute of refuge in a season of faith and ripeness.

Translated from the Hebrew
by Gabriel Preil and David Curzon

HART CRANE □

After Jonah[y]

In my beginning was the memory, somehow
contradicting Jonah, that essential babe
of unbaptised digestion, being a nugget
to call pity on Jerusalem and on Nature, too.

We have his travels in the snare so widely
ruminated,—of how he stuck there, was reformed,
forgiven, also—
and belched back like a word to grace us all.

There is no settling tank in God. It must be borne
that even His bowels are too delicate to board
a sniping thief that has a pious beard.
We must hail back the lamb that went unsheared.

O sweet deep whale as ever reamed the sky
with high white gulfs of vapor, castigate
our sins, but be hospitable as Hell.
And keep me to the death like ambergris,
sealed up, and unforgiven in my cell.

[y] See "Notes on the Poems," p. 336

JONAH 3:1–4:4

The word of the LORD came to Jonah a second time: [2]"Go at once to Nineveh, that great city, and proclaim to it what I tell you." [3]Jonah went at once to Nineveh in accordance with the LORD's command.

Nineveh was *⁻an enormously large city⁻* a three days' walk across. [4]Jonah started out and made his way into the city the distance of one day's walk, and proclaimed: "Forty days more, and Nineveh shall be overthrown!"

[5]The people of Nineveh believed God. They proclaimed a fast, and great and small alike put on sackcloth. [6]When the news reached the king of Nineveh, he rose from his throne, took off his robe, put on sackcloth, and sat in ashes. [7]And he had the word cried through Nineveh: "By decree of the king and his nobles: No man or beast— of flock or herd—shall taste anything! They shall not graze, and they shall not drink water! [8]They shall be covered with sackcloth—man and beast—and shall cry mightily to God. Let everyone turn back from his evil ways and from the injustice of which he is guilty. [9]Who knows but that God may turn and relent? He may turn back from His wrath, so that we do not perish."

[10]God saw what they did, how they were turning back from their evil ways. And God renounced the punishment He had planned to bring upon them, and did not carry it out.

4 This displeased Jonah greatly, and he was grieved. [2]He prayed to the LORD, saying, "O LORD! Isn't this just what I said when I was still in my own country? That is why I fled beforehand to Tarshish. For I know that You are a compassionate and gracious God, slow to anger, abounding in kindness, renouncing punishment. [3]Please, LORD, take my life, for I would rather die than live." [4]The LORD replied, "Are you that deeply grieved?"

⁻ Lit. "a large city of God"

ROBERT FROST □

From "A Masque of Mercy"

A bookstore late at night. The Keeper's wife
Pulls down the window curtain on the door
And locks the door. One customer, locked in,
Stays talking with the Keeper at a showcase.
The Keeper's wife has hardly turned away
Before the door's so violently tried
It makes her move as if to reinforce it.

JESSE BEL. You can't come in! (*Knock, knock*) The store is closed!

PAUL. Late, late, too late, you cannot enter now.

JESSE BEL. We can't be always selling people things.
He doesn't go.

KEEPER.   You needn't be so stern.
Open enough to find out who it is.

JESSE BEL. Keeper, you come and see. Or you come, Paul.
Our second second-childhood case tonight.
Where do these senile runaways escape from?
Wretchedness in a stranger frightens me
More than it touches me.

PAUL.   You may come in.

FUGITIVE. (*Entering hatless in a whirl of snow*)
God's after me!

JESSE BEL.   You mean the Devil is.

FUGITIVE. No, God.

. . .

KEEPER. Now we are hearing from the Exegete.
You don't know Paul: he's in the Bible too.
He is the fellow who theologized
Christ almost out of Christianity.
Look out for him.

PAUL.   "Look out for me" is right.
I'm going to tell you something, Jonas Dove.
I'm going to take the nonsense out of you
And give you rest, poor Wandering Jew.

JONAH.   I'm not
The Wandering Jew—I'm who I say I am,
A prophet with the Bible for credentials.

PAUL. I never said you weren't. I recognized you.
You are the universal fugitive—
Escapist, as we say—though you are not
Running away from Him you think you are,
But from His mercy-justice contradiction.
Mercy and justice are a contradiction.
But here's where your evasion has an end.
I have to tell you something that will spoil
Indulgence in your form of melancholy
Once and for all. I'm going to make you see
How relatively little justice matters.

JONAH. I see what you are up to: robbing me
Of my incentive—canceling my mission.

. . .

KEEPER. One minute, may I, Paul?—before we leave
Religion for these philosophic matters.
That's the right style of coat for prophecy
You're sporting there. I'll bet you're good at it.
Shall it be told we had a prophet captive
And let him get off without prophesying?
Let's have some prophecy. What form of ruin
(For ruin I assume was what it was)
Had you in mind to visit on the city,
Rebellion, pestilence, invasion?

JONAH.   Earthquake
Was what I thought of.

. . .

PAUL. Now if we've had enough of sacrilege,
We can go back to where we started from.
Let me repeat: I'm glad to hear you say
You can't trust God to be unmerciful.
What would you have God if not merciful?

JONAH. Just, I would have Him just before all else,
To see that the fair fight is really fair.
Then he could enter on the stricken field
After the fight's so definitely done
There can be no disputing who has won—
Then he could enter on the stricken field
As Red Cross Ambulance Commander-in-Chief
To ease the more extremely wounded out
And mend the others up to go again.

PAUL. I thought as much. You have it all arranged,
Only to see it shattered every day.
You should be an authority on Mercy.
That book of yours in the Old Testament
Is the first place in literature, I think,
Where Mercy is explicitly the subject.
I say you should be proud of having beaten
The Gospels to it. After doing Justice justice
Milton's pentameters go on to say,
But Mercy first and last shall brightest shine—
Not only last, but first, you will observe;
Which spoils your figure of the ambulance.

KEEPER. Paul only means you make too much of justice.
There's some such thing and no one will deny it—
Enough to bait the trap of the ideal
From which there can be no escape for us
But by our biting off our adolescence
And leaving it behind us in the trap.

. . .

JONAH 4:5–11

⁵Now Jonah had left the city and found a place east of the city. He made a booth there and sat under it in the shade, until he should see what happened to the city. ⁶The LORD God provided a ricinus plant,* which grew up over Jonah, to provide shade for his head and save him from discomfort. Jonah was very happy about the plant. ⁷But the next day at dawn God provided a worm, which attacked the plant so that it withered. ⁸And when the sun rose, God provided a sultry† east wind; the sun beat down on Jonah's head, and he became faint. He begged for death, saying, "I would rather die than live." ⁹Then God said to Jonah, "Are you so deeply grieved about the plant?" "Yes," he replied, "so deeply that I want to die."

¹⁰Then the LORD said: "You cared about the plant, which you did not work for and which you did not grow, which appeared overnight and perished overnight. ¹¹And should not I care about Nineveh, that great city, in which there are more than a hundred and twenty thousand persons who do not yet know their right hand from their left, and many beasts as well!"‡

---

* Meaning of Heb. uncertain; others "gourd"
† Meaning of Heb. uncertain
‡ Infants and beasts are not held responsible for their actions

ENRIQUE LIHN □

Jonah

I could damn everything equally, just don't ask me in the name
of what.
In the name of Isaiah, the prophet, yet with the grotesque and
unfinished gesture of his colleague Jonah
who never managed to go through with his simple task, given to
the ups and downs
of good and evil, to the fickle circumstances of history
that plunged him into the whale's belly.
Like Jonah, the clown of heaven, always obstinate in going
through with his simple task, the explosive briefcase
tucked under a sweaty armpit, an umbrella worn down like
a lightning rod.
And Jehovah's doubts about him, wavering between mercy and
anger, grabbing him and tossing him, that old instrument
whose use is doubtful
no longer used at all any more.

I too will end my days under a tree
but like those old drunken tramps who detest everything
equally, don't ask me
anything, all I know is that we'll be destroyed.
Blindly, I see the hand of a lord whose name I don't remember,
his delicate fingers clenched awkwardly. And also something else
that has nothing to do with it. I remember something like . . .
no, it's only that. Just a thought, it doesn't matter. I just don't
know where I am going again.
"Help me Lord in thy abandonment."

Translated from the Spanish
by Jonathan Cohen

HOWARD NEMEROV □

On a Text: Jonah 4:11

The Lord might have spared us the harsh joke;
Many that live in Nineveh these days
Cannot discern their ass from a hot rock.
Perhaps the word "cattle" refers to these?

U ▪ Psalms

PSALM 1

Blessed is the man who walks not in the counsel of the wicked, nor stands in the way of sinners, nor sits in the seat of scoffers; [2]but his delight is in the law of the LORD, and on his law he meditates day and night. [3]He is like a tree planted by streams of water, that yields its fruit in its season, and its leaf does not wither. In all that he does, he prospers. [4]The wicked are not so, but are like chaff which the wind drives away. [5]Therefore the wicked will not stand in the judgement, nor sinners in the congregation of the righteous; [6]for the LORD knows the way of the righteous, but the way of the wicked will perish.

Translation: Revised Standard Version

MARIANNE MOORE ☐

Blessed Is the Man

who does not sit in the seat of the scoffer—
    the man who does not denigrate, depreciate, denunciate;
        who is not "characteristically intemperate,"
who does not "excuse, retreat, equivocate; and will be heard."

(Ah, Giorgione! there are those who mongrelize
    and those who heighten anything they touch; although it
                                                may well be
        that if Giorgione's self-portrait were not said to be he,
it might not take my fancy. Blessed the geniuses who know

that egomania is not a duty.)
    "Diversity, controversy; tolerance"—in that "citadel
        of learning" we have a fort that ought to armor us well.
Blessed is the man who "takes the risk of a decision"—asks

himself the question: "Would it solve the problem?
    Is it right as I see it? Is it in the best interests of all?"
        Alas. Ulysses' companions are now political—
living self-indulgently until the moral sense is drowned,

having lost all power of comparison,
    thinking license emancipates one, "slaves whom they
                                        themselves have bound."
        Brazen authors, downright soiled and downright spoiled, as
                                                if sound
and exceptional, are the old quasi-modish counterfeit,

mitin-proofing conscience against character.
    Affronted by "private lies and public shame," blessed is the
                                                author
        who favors what the supercilious do *not* favor—
who will not comply. Blessed, the unaccommodating man.

Blessed the man whose faith is different
    from possessiveness—of a kind not framed by "things which
                                        do appear"—
        who will not visualize defeat, too intent to cower;
whose illumined eye has seen the shaft that gilds the sultan's
                                                tower.

YEHUDA AMICHAI ☐

I Am a Man "Planted beside Streams of Water"

I am a man "planted beside streams of water,"
but I'm not "blessed be the man."
The desert is calm all around me, but there's no peace
    in me.
Two sons I have, one still small,
and whenever I see a child crying
I want to make another one
as if I hadn't got it right
and wanted to start afresh.
And my father is dead, and God is only one, like me.
And the Hill of Evil Counsel[z] sails into the night
all covered with antennae up to heaven.

I'm a man planted beside streams of water,
but I can only weep it,
and sweat it, and urinate it
and spill it from my wounds—
all this water.

Translated from the Hebrew
by Yehuda Amichai

NISSIM EZEKIEL ☐

From "Latter-Day Psalms"

I
Blessed is the man that walketh
not in the counsel of the con-
ventional, and is at home with
sin as with a wife. He shall
listen patiently to the scorn-
ful, and understand the sources
of their scorn.

---

[z] See "Notes on the Poems," p. 336

He does not meditate day and
night on anything; his delight
is in action.

Rare is the man whose fruit is
in his season. Yet, his leaf
must wither, and that which
appears to prosper, is often
dying at the root.

The ungodly are in the same con-
dition, no more like the chaff
which the wind driveth away
than the godly.

The godly and the ungodly shall
not stand in the judgement, for
neither are worthy of their true
potential. In the congregation
of the righteous, the sinners
are well disguised. Do not seek
to count them.

For the Lord only knows how the
way to him is found: therefore
the way of the ungodly shall ne-
ver perish on the earth.

DAVID CURZON □

Psalm 1

Blessed is the man not born
in Lodz in the wrong decade,
who walks not in tree-lined shade
like my father's father in this photo, *nor
stands in the way of sinners* waiting for
his yellow star,
nor sits, if he could sit, in their cattle car,

but his delight is being born
as I was, in Australia, far away,
and on God's law he meditates night and day.

He is like a tree that's granted
the land where it is planted,
that yields its fruit by reason
of sun and rain in season.

The wicked are not so, they
burn their uniforms and walk away.

Therefore the wicked are like Cain
who offered fruit which God chose to disdain.

And *the way of the righteous* is Abel's, whose
slaughtered lambs God chose to choose
and who was murdered anyway.

PSALM 23

A Psalm of David.

The LORD is my shepherd; I shall not want.
²He maketh me to lie down in green pastures;
He leadeth me beside the still waters.
³He restoreth my soul;
He guideth me in straight paths for His name's sake.
⁴Yea, though I walk through the valley of the shadow of death,
I will fear no evil,
For Thou art with me;
Thy rod and Thy staff, they comfort me.
⁵Thou preparest a table before me in the presence of mine enemies;
Thou hast anointed my head with oil; my cup runneth over.
⁶Surely goodness and mercy shall follow me all the days of my life;
And I shall dwell in the house of the LORD for ever.

Translation: JPS 1917

LOUIS MacNIECE ☐

Whit Monday

Their feet on London, their heads in the grey clouds,
The Bank (if you call it a holiday) Holiday crowds
Stroll from street to street, cocking an eye
For where the angel used to be in the sky;
But the Happy Future is a thing of the past and the street
Echoes to nothing but their dawdling feet.
The Lord's my shepherd—familiar words of myth
Stand up better to bombs than a granite monolith,
Perhaps there is something in them. *I'll not want*—
Not when I'm dead. *He makes me down to lie*—
Death my christening and fire my font—
The quiet (Thames, or Don's or Salween's) *waters by.*

1941

NATAN ZACH ☐

Song of a Womanizer

I have in my room
    a bed made of wood
which is always in bud.
Night unto night utters speech.
From season to season
my couch is leafy.
I shall not want.

Translated from the Hebrew
by Gabriel Preil and David Curzon

PSALM 34:1–8

A Psalm of David, when he changed his behavior before Abimelech; who drove him away, and he departed.

I will bless the LORD at all times: his praise *shall* continually *be* in my mouth.
[2]My soul shall make her boast in the LORD: the humble shall hear *thereof,* and be glad.
[3]O magnify the LORD with me, and let us exalt his name together.
[4]I sought the LORD, and he heard me, and delivered me from all my fears.
[5]They looked unto him, and were lightened: and their faces were not ashamed.
[6]This poor man cried, and the LORD heard *him,* and saved him out of all his troubles.
[7]The angel of the LORD encampeth round about them that fear him, and delivereth them.
[8]O taste and see that the LORD *is* good: blessed *is* the man *that* trusteth in him.

Translation: King James Version

DENISE LEVERTOV □

O Taste and See

The world is
not with us enough.[aa]
O taste and see

the subway Bible poster said,
meaning *The Lord,* meaning
if anything all that lives
to the imagination's tongue,

grief, mercy, language,
tangerine, weather, to
breathe them, bite,
savor, chew, swallow, transform

into our flesh our
deaths, crossing the street, plum, quince,
living in the orchard and being

hungry, and plucking
the fruit.

[aa] See "Notes on the Poems," p. 336

PSALM 42:1–4

For the Leader; Maschil of the sons of Korah.

^{2}As the hart panteth after the water brooks,
So panteth my soul after Thee, O God.
^{3}My soul thirsteth for God, for the living God:
'When shall I come and appear before God?'
^{4}My tears have been my food day and night,
While they say unto me all the day: 'Where is thy God?'

Translation: JPS 1917

SEAMUS HEANEY ☐

From "Clearances"

6

In the first flush of the Easter holidays
The ceremonies during Holy Week
Were highpoints of our *Sons and Lovers* phase.
The midnight fire. The paschal candlestick.
Elbow to elbow, glad to be kneeling next
To each other up there near the front
Of the packed church, we would follow the text
And rubrics for the blessing of the font.
As the hind longs for the streams, so my soul . . .
Dippings. Towellings. The water breathed on.
The water mixed with chrism and with oil.
Cruet tinkle. Formal incensation
And the psalmist's outcry taken up with pride:
Day and night my tears have been my bread.

PSALM 45:1–2

To the chief Musician upon Shoshannim, for the sons of Korah, Maschil, A Song of loves.

My heart is inditing a good matter: I speak of the things which I have made touching the king: my tongue *is* the pen of a ready writer.
²Thou art fairer than the children of men: grace is poured into thy lips: therefore God hath blessed thee for ever.

Translation: King James Version

DONALD DAVIE ☐

Inditing a Good Matter

I find nothing to say,
I am heavy as lead.
I take small satisfaction
in anything I have said.

Evangelists want your assent,
be it cringing, or idle, or eager.
God shrugs. We taste dismay,
as sharp as vinegar.

He shrugs. How can He care
what *billets-doux* we send Him,
how much we applaud? Such coxcombs
inclined to commend Him!

My heart had been inditing
a good matter. My tongue
was the pen of a ready writer
who had been writing too long.

Whoever supposes his business
is to commend and bless
is due for this comeuppance:
feeling it less and less.

But I find something to say.
I pump it out, heavy as lead:
'Buoy me up out of the shadow
of your ramparts overhead.'

Like one of those vanished performers
on an afternoon-matinée console,
I arise:
　　　'Admit to your rock
this ready, this shriven, soul.'

PSALM 71:1–9

In Thee, O LORD, have I taken refuge;
Let me never be ashamed.
²Deliver me in Thy righteousness, and rescue me;
Incline Thine ear unto me, and save me.
³Be Thou to me a sheltering rock, whereunto I may continually resort,
Which Thou hast appointed to save me;
For Thou art my rock and my fortress.
⁴O my God, rescue me out of the hand of the wicked,
Out of the grasp of the unrighteous and ruthless man.
⁵For Thou art my hope;
O Lord GOD, my trust from my youth.
⁶Upon Thee have I stayed myself from birth;
Thou art He that took me out of my mother's womb;
My praise is continually of Thee.
⁷I am as a wonder unto many;
But Thou art my strong refuge.
⁸My mouth shall be filled with Thy praise,
And with Thy glory all the day.
⁹Cast me not off in the time of old age;
When my strength faileth, forsake me not.

Translation: JPS 1917

ANNA KAMIENSKA □

Psalm

Cast me not off in the time of old age.
Psalm 71

Cast us not off in the time of old age
when photos of the dead are fading
when we are no longer able to remember
mother's face
trams pursue us on the street
canes and eyeglasses get lost
there's no present tense any more
darkness has its hands on the doorknob
the rickety wagon of sleep rattles
climbing up the sheer mountain into the past
the body becomes merely the body
nothing else
so we turn from ourselves toward the wall
we die to ourselves
sons daughters are always late
it's their right
and for us now
all the trees whisper
in the time of weakness do not desert us

Translated from the Polish by
Grażyna Drabik and David Curzon

PSALM 119: GIMEL AND TAV

ג GIMEL

¹⁷Deal bountifully with Thy servant that I may live,
And I will observe Thy word.
¹⁸Open Thou mine eyes, that I may behold
Wondrous things out of Thy law.
¹⁹I am a sojourner in the earth;
Hide not Thy commandments from me.
²⁰My soul breaketh for the longing
That it hath unto Thine ordinances at all times.
²¹Thou hast rebuked the proud that are cursed,
That do err from Thy commandments.
²²Take away from me reproach and contempt;
For I have kept Thy testimonies.
²³Even though princes sit and talk against me,
Thy servant doth meditate in Thy statutes.
²⁴Yea, Thy testimonies are my delight,
They are my counsellors.

ת TAV

¹⁶⁹Let my cry come near before Thee, O LORD;
Give me understanding according to Thy word.
¹⁷⁰Let my supplication come before Thee;
Deliver me according to Thy word.
¹⁷¹Let my lips utter praise:
Because Thou teachest me Thy statutes.
¹⁷²Let my tongue sing of Thy word;
For all Thy commandments are righteousness.
¹⁷³Let Thy hand be ready to help me;
For I have chosen Thy precepts.
¹⁷⁴I have longed for Thy salvation, O LORD;
And Thy law is my delight.
¹⁷⁵Let my soul live, and it shall praise Thee;
And let Thine ordinances help me.
¹⁷⁶I have gone astray like a lost sheep; seek Thy servant;
For I have not forgotten Thy commandments.

Translation: JPS 1917

PAUL CLAUDEL □

From "Meditation on Psalm 118"[bb]

Gimel

Open Your hand, give me life, revivify Your word in me.
> Open my eyes that I may see, through Your miracles,
> clearly.
> I am an exile in the earth, do not leave me alone.
> Summon me and ceaselessly I will use the hours to reach You.
> You keep some thing reserved for the wicked, all those whose
> dreams take them outside Your law.
> Spare me that shame because I have done my best to stay on
> Your path who You are.
> There is no lack of people who hear themselves talking: Me,
> teeth clenched, I have toiled.
> I have pondered this incessant noise Your counsels have made
> in my heart.

Tav

Step by step, slowly I have reached You.
> I have chewed this enormous way of words to reach You.
> And here I stand at the end in the vast reach of my
> expostulation.
> And here I stand before You, hymn, scale, in the utter
> depths of my restitutions.
> You have put a tongue of fire in my mouth and the elocution
> of scorching flame in my heart.
> I stand beneath Your hand which creates, considers, O my
> God, because it is You who have written me, to all my
> length, and I may be read.
> Read my heart, with all I have learned from You to proclaim.
> O sentence of mine on me, recorded slowly, word by word,
> find me worthy of all that the Grace in me deserves.

[bb] See "Notes on the Poems," p. 336

You are The Lamb, and I, it is true somewhere I was the sheep, O present actuality, scarcely more than one with memory, injunction scarcely more than one with Grace.

Translated from the French
by Jeffrey Fiskin

PSALM 119: HAY

ה HAY

³³Teach me, O Lord, the way of Thy statutes;
And I will keep it at every step.
³⁴Give me understanding, that I keep Thy law
And observe it with my whole heart.
³⁵Make me to tread in the path of Thy commandments;
For therein do I delight.
³⁶Incline my heart unto Thy testimonies,
And not to covetousness.
³⁷Turn away mine eyes from beholding vanity,
And quicken me in Thy ways.
³⁸Confirm Thy word unto Thy servant,
Which pertaineth unto the fear of Thee.
³⁹Turn away my reproach which I dread;
For Thine ordinances are good.
⁴⁰Behold, I have longed after Thy precepts;
Quicken me in Thy righteousness.

Translation: JPS 1917

ANNA KAMIENSKA □

Vanity

Turn away mine eyes from beholding vanity
Psalm 119:37

But give me too a little bit of vanity
the sky an etching of branches
the call of a bird
the touch of a hand

But do not deprive me of a pinch of vanity
of poems music smiles

Try to see at least once through granny's eyeglasses
when she was mending brown wool stockings
and rocking all night long her grandson covered with measles

Vanities mean a lot at times for vanity
the feast of childhood
dinner special from soup to compote
and wishing the cake would rise
and wishing the wrinkles on the dress
were carefully ironed out

Vanity of vanities
everything
to which the heart clings
so that it seems to break
the taste of domestic afternoons
the daughter-in-law bustling in the kitchen
the little boy on his father's lap

Two fingers on the lids in any case
will soothe the eyes
will avert sight from vanity
for it to see from then on only grand things
I cannot see

So give me the vanity of a departing moment
always as tender as wisdom itself

Translated from the Polish
by Grażyna Drabik and David Curzon

PSALM 121:1

A Song of Ascents.

> I will lift up mine eyes unto the mountains:
> From whence shall my help come?

Translation: JPS 1917

GABRIEL PREIL □

Like David

Like David the pursued I raise my eyes to the mountains:
so slight are the differences of the valleys that indicate
the map of helplessness in his days and in mine.

Like David the submissive I raise my eyes to a woman:
so similar are the transitions in her blood and her flowering
in a city of love in his days and in mine.

From the mountains the rain beats, tall and dreary, like Goliath,
and even the sun, small as David the shepherd boy,
withholds its light from me.

Translated from the Hebrew
by Laya Firestone

PSALM 122:1–2

A Song of ascents. Of David.

I rejoiced when they said to me,
"We are going to the house of the LORD."
²Our feet stood inside your gates, O Jerusalem.

PAUL CELAN □

THERE STOOD[cc]
a sliver of fig on your lip,

there stood
Jerusalem around us,

there stood
the bright pine scent
above the Danish ship we thanked,

I stood
in you.

> Translated from the German
> by John Felstiner

[cc] See "Notes on the Poems," p. 336

PSALM 126

A Song of Ascents.

> When God returned
> the turned-to-Zion
> we seemed then
> like those who dream.
> [2]Our mouth then
> filled with laughter,
> our tongue with singing,
> and among the nations
> it was said then
> "For them, God
> did great things."

> [3]For us, God
> did great things;
> we were joyful.

> [4]Return our release, Lord,
> like streams in the Negev!

> [5]Those who sow with tears
> will reap with joy!

> [6]Those who go weeping
> on their way bearing
> seed, and sowing,
> will surely come bearing
> their sheaves with joy!

> Translated from the Hebrew
> by Ya'acov Hanoch and David Curzon

YEHUDA AMICHAI   □

Like the Streams in the Negev

I sit in a café in the afternoon hours.
My sons are grown, my daughter is dancing
    somewhere else.
I have no baby carriage, no newspaper, no God.

I saw a woman whose father was with me in the
    battles of the Negev,
I saw his eyes gaping in a time of trouble
and dread of death. Now they are in the face of his
    daughter,
quiet, beautiful eyes. The rest of her body—
from other places, her hair grew in a time of peace,
a different genetics, generations and times I didn't
    know.

I have many times, like many watches
on the walls of a clock shop, each one shows a
    different time.
My memories are scattered over the earth
like ashes of a person who willed before his death
to burn his body
and scatter his ashes over seven seas.

I sit. Voices talking around me
like fine ironwork on a banister,
beyond it I hear the street. The table before me
is built for easy access like a bay,
like a dock in a port, like God's hand, like bride and
    groom.

Sometimes suddenly tears of happiness well up in me
as an empty street suddenly fills up with cars
when the light changes at a distant intersection,
or like the streams in the Negev
that suddenly fill up with torrents of water from a
    distant rain.
Afterward, again silence, empty
Like the streams in the Negev, like the streams in the Negev.

Translated from the Hebrew
by Barbara and Benjamin Harshav

PSALM 150

Hallelujah.
Praise God in His sanctuary;
Praise Him in the firmament of His power.
²Praise Him for His mighty acts;
Praise Him according to His abundant greatness.
³Praise Him with the blast of the horn;
Praise Him with the psaltery and harp.
⁴Praise Him with the timbrel and dance;
Praise Him with stringed instruments and the pipe.
⁵Praise Him with the loud-sounding cymbals;
Praise Him with the clanging cymbals.
⁶Let every thing that hath breath praise the LORD.
Hallelujah.

Translation: JPS 1917

ERNESTO CARDENAL   □

The Cosmos Is His Sanctuary (Psalm 150)

Praise the Lord in the cosmos
                     His sanctuary
with a radius of a hundred thousand million light years
Praise Him through the stars
                     and the interstellar spaces
Praise Him through the galaxies
                     and the intergalactic spaces
Praise Him through the atoms
                     and the interatomic voids
Praise Him with the violin and the flute
                     and with the saxophone
Praise Him with the clarinets and with the horn
     with bugles and trombones
                     with cornets and trumpets
Praise Him with violas and cellos
                     with pianos and pianolas
Praise Him with blues and jazz
                     and with symphonic orchestras
with Negro spirituals
            and with Beethoven's Fifth
     with guitars and marimbas
Praise Him with record players
                     and with magnetic tapes
Let everything that breathes praise the Lord
     every living cell
            Hallelujah

Translated from the Spanish
by Donald D. Walsh

V • Proverbs

PROVERBS 3:1–3

My son, forget not my teaching;
But let thy heart keep my commandments;
[2]For length of days, and years of life,
And peace, will they add to thee.
[3]Let not kindness and truth forsake thee;
Bind them about thy neck,
Write them upon the table of thy heart.

Translation: JPS 1917

DAVID CURZON □

Proverbs 3:1

My son, forget not my teaching—recall

our conversation on the word "sadism," when I
maintained the main medical definition
was pain inflicted while making love
and how you insisted (as if important
to you at fourteen!) the meaning was broader;
and recall my advice to forego your affection
for physics and become a physician so that
if you failed at research you could have a recourse;
and recall that I never remarried and lived alone,
and recall your visits to my sparse rented
furnished rooms, our common silence
filled in with games of chess, and recall
coming into the kitchen in your mother's house
to be told I was dead and how it happened
and the hours over years of meditation on
your part in the silence that led to suicide—

and let your heart keep my commandments.

W ▪ Job

THE BOOK OF JOB

DAN PAGIS ☐

Homily

From the start, the forces were unequal: Satan a grand seigneur in heaven, Job mere flesh and blood. And anyway, the contest was unfair. Job, who had lost all his wealth and had been bereaved of his sons and daughters and stricken with loathsome boils, wasn't even aware that it was a contest.

Because he complained too much, the referee silenced him. So, having accepted this decision, in silence, he defeated his opponent without even realizing it. Therefore his wealth was restored, he was given sons and daughters—new ones, of course—and his grief for the first children was taken away.

We might imagine that this compensation was the most terrible thing of all. We might imagine that the most terrible thing was Job's ignorance: not understanding whom he had defeated, or even that he had won. But in fact, the most terrible thing of all is that Job never existed and was just a parable.

Translated from the Hebrew
by Stephen Mitchell

WISLAWA SZYMBORSKA □

Summary

Job, tested severely in body and property, curses human fate. It is grand poetry. Friends arrive. Tearing their robes, they examine Job's guilt before the Lord. Job cries that he has been a just man. Job does not want to talk with them. Job wants to talk with the Lord. The Lord appears riding on a gale. In front of this man torn open to the bone, the Lord praises His works: heaven, seas, earth and animals. And especially Behemoth, and in particular Leviathan, beasts which fill one with pride. It is grand poetry. Job listens—the Lord does not speak to the subject, because the Lord does not want to speak to the subject. Promptly then, Job humbles himself before the Lord. Now things happen quickly. Job recovers his donkeys and camels, his mules and sheep, doubled in number. His skin grows back on his bared skull. And Job accepts it. Job is reconciled. Job does not want to spoil the masterpiece.

Translated from the Polish
by Grażyna Drabik and Sharon Olds

JOB 3:20–26

^{20}Wherewith is light given to him that is in misery,
And life unto the bitter in soul—
^{21}Who long for death, but it cometh not;
And dig for it more than for hid treasures;
^{22}Who rejoice unto exultation,
And are glad, when they can find the grave?—
^{23}To a man whose way is hid,
And whom God hath hedged in?
^{24}For my sighing cometh instead of my food,
And my roarings are poured out like water.
^{25}For the thing which I did fear is come upon me,
And that which I was afraid of hath overtaken me.
^{26}I was not at ease, neither was I quiet, neither had I rest;
But trouble came.

Translation: JPS 1917

A. E. HOUSMAN □

From "More Poems"

VI

I to my perils
　　Of cheat and charmer
Came clad in armour
　　　By stars benign.
Hope lies to mortals
　　And most believe her,
But man's deceiver
　　　Was never mine.

The thoughts of others
　　Were light and fleeting,
Of lovers' meeting
　　　Or luck or fame.
Mine were of trouble,
　　And mine were steady,
So I was ready
　　　When trouble came.

JOB 5:6–7

⁶For affliction cometh not forth from the dust,
Neither doth trouble spring out of the ground;
⁷But man is born unto trouble,
As the sparks fly upward.

Translation: JPS 1917

JOHN HOLLANDER □

As the Sparks Fly Upward

As of an ungrounded grief,
Bluish sparks fly upward from
Under the shadow-thickened,
Tree-covered, part of night toward
What can yet be construed as
Dimmed azure, while the summer
Glow of soft streetlamp light hums
Along the wide sidewalk through
Listening leaves: fireflies
Far from the sea rise in an
Untroubled-looking midland,
Soundless, their gaps in the dark
Soundless, and the thunder soon
Coming with a crash across
Glistening eaves will be no
Answer, echo, or noisy
Amplifying of echo.
I will await what the ground,
The great, grass-skinned ground, will say.

JOB 19:23–26

[23]Oh that my words were now written!
   Oh that they were inscribed in a book!
[24]That with an iron pen and lead
   They were graven in the rock for ever!
[25]But as for me, I know that my Redeemer liveth,
   And that He will witness at the last upon the dust;
[26]And when after my skin this is destroyed,
   Then without my flesh shall I see God.

Translation: JPS 1917

NELLY SACHS   □

O the Chimneys

*And though after my skin worms destroy this body, yet in
my flesh shall I see God.*

Job 19:26

O the chimneys
On the ingeniously devised habitations of death
When Israel's body drifted as smoke
Through the air—
Was welcomed by a star, a chimney sweep,
A star that turned black
Or was it a ray of sun?

O the chimneys!
Freedomway for Jeremiah and Job's dust—
Who devised you and laid stone upon stone
The road for refugees of smoke?

O the habitations of death,
Invitingly appointed
For the host who used to be a guest—
O you fingers
Laying the threshold
Like a knife between life and death—

O you chimneys,
O you fingers
And Israel's body as smoke through the air!

Translated from the German
by Michael Roloff

JOB 39:19–30

¹⁹Hast thou given the horse his strength?
Hast thou clothed his neck with fierceness?
²⁰Hast thou made him to leap as a locust?
The glory of his snorting is terrible.
²¹He paweth in the valley, and rejoiceth in his strength;
He goeth out to meet the clash of arms.
²²He mocketh at fear, and is not affrighted;
Neither turneth he back from the sword.
²³The quiver rattleth upon him,
The glittering spear and the javelin.
²⁴He swalloweth the ground with storm and rage;
Neither believeth he that it is the voice of the horn.
²⁵As oft as he heareth the horn he saith: "Ha, ha!"
And he smelleth the battle afar off,
The thunder of the captains, and the shouting.

²⁶Doth the hawk soar by thy wisdom,
And stretch her wings toward the south?
²⁷Doth the vulture mount up at thy command,
And make her nest on high?
²⁸She dwelleth and abideth on the rock,
Upon the crag of the rock, and the stronghold.
²⁹From thence she spieth out the prey;
Her eyes behold it afar off.
³⁰Her young ones also suck up blood;
And where the slain are, there is she.

Translation: JPS 1917

ROBINSON JEFFERS □

Birds and Fishes[dd]

Every October millions of little fish come along the shore,
Coasting this granite edge of the continent
On their lawful occasions: but what a festival for the
    seafowl.
What a witches' sabbath of wings
Hides the dark water. The heavy pelicans shout "Haw!"
    like Job's friend's warhorse
And dive from the high air, the cormorants
Slip their long black bodies under the water and hunt
    like wolves
Through the green half-light. Screaming, the gulls watch,
Wild with envy and malice, cursing and snatching. What
    hysterical greed!
What a filling of pouches! the mob
Hysteria is nearly human—these decent birds!—as if
    they were finding
Gold in the street. It is better than gold,
It can be eaten: and which one in all this fury of wildfowl
    pities the fish?
No one certainly. Justice and mercy
Are human dreams, they do not concern the birds nor
    the fish nor eternal God.
However—look again before you go.
The wings and the wild hungers, the wave-worn skerries,
    the bright quick minnows
Living in terror to die in torment—
Man's fate and theirs—and the island rocks and immense
    ocean beyond, and Lobos
Darkening above the bay: they are beautiful?
That is their quality: not mercy, not mind, not goodness,
    but the beauty of God.

[dd] See "Notes on the Poems," p. 336

JOB 42:10–17

[10]And the LORD changed the fortune of Job, when he prayed for his friends; and the LORD gave Job twice as much as he had before. [11]Then came there unto him all his brethren, and all his sisters, and all they that had been of his acquaintance before, and did eat bread with him in his house; and they bemoaned him, and comforted him concerning all the evil that the LORD had brought upon him; every man also gave him a piece of money, and every one a ring of gold. [12]So the LORD blessed the latter end of Job more than his beginning; and he had fourteen thousand sheep, and six thousand camels, and a thousand yoke of oxen, and a thousand she-asses. [13]He had also seven sons and three daughters. [14]And he called the name of the first, Jemimah*; and the name of the second, Keziah†; and the name of the third, Kerenhappuch.‡ [15]And in all the land were no women found so fair as the daughters of Job; and their father gave them inheritance among their brethren. [16]And after this Job lived a hundred and forty years, and saw his sons, and his sons' sons, even four generations. [17]So Job died, being old and full of days.

Translation: JPS 1917

* That is, "Dove"
† That is, "Cassia"
‡ That is, "Horn of eye-paint"

ANNA KAMIENSKA □

From "The Second Happiness of Job"

The Return of Job

Job didn't die
didn't throw himself under a train
didn't croak in a vacant lot
the chimney didn't spew him out
despair didn't finish him off
he arose from everything
from misery dirt
scabs loneliness

How much more authentic a dead Job would be
even after death shaking his fist at the God of pain
But Job survived
washed his body of blood sweat pus
and lay down in his own house again
New friends came running
A new wife was breathing new love into his mouth
new children were growing up with soft hair
for Job to touch with his hands
new sheep donkeys oxen were bellowing
shaking new shackles in the stable
kneeling down on the straw

But happy Job didn't have strength to be happy
afraid by another happiness to betray happiness
afraid by another life to betray life
Wouldn't it be better for you Job
to rot in a lost paradise with the dead
than to wait now for their nightly visit
in dreams they come they envy you life
Wouldn't it be better happy Job
to remain offal since you are offal
the pus washed off your hands and face
ate through you to heart and liver
You will die Job
Wouldn't it have been better for you to die
with the others in the same pain and mourning
than to depart now from a new happiness
You walk in the dark wrapped in darkness

among new people superfluous as a pang of conscience
you suffered by pain now suffer by happiness

And Job whispered stubbornly Lord Lord

Translated from the Polish
by Grażyna Drabik and David Curzon

ROBERT FROST □

From "A Masque of Reason"

A fair oasis in the purest desert.
A man sits leaning back against a palm.
His wife lies by him looking at the sky.

. . .

WIFE.   Go over
And speak to Him before the others come.
Tell Him He may remember you: you're Job.

GOD. Oh, I remember well: you're Job, my Patient.
How are you now? I trust you're quite recovered,
And feel no ill effects from what I gave you.

JOB. Gave me in truth: I like the frank admission.
I am a name for being put upon.
But, yes, I'm fine, except for now and then
A reminiscent twinge of rheumatism.
The letup's heavenly. You perhaps will tell us
If that is all there is to be of Heaven,
Escape from so great pains of life on earth
It gives a sense of letup calculated
To last a fellow to Eternity.

GOD. Yes, by and by. But first a larger matter.
I've had you on my mind a thousand years
To thank you someday for the way you helped me
Establish once for all the principle
There's no connection man can reason out
Between his just deserts and what he gets.
Virtue may fail and wickedness succeed.

'Twas a great demonstration we put on.
I should have spoken sooner had I found
The word I wanted. You would have supposed
One who in the beginning *was* the Word
Would be in a position to command it.
I have to wait for words like anyone.
Too long I've owed you this apology
For the apparently unmeaning sorrow
You were afflicted with in those old days.
But it was of the essence of the trial
You shouldn't understand it at the time.
It had to seem unmeaning to have meaning.
And it came out all right. I have no doubt
You realize by now the part you played
To stultify the Deuteronomist
And change the tenor of religious thought.
My thanks are to you for releasing me
From moral bondage to the human race.
The only free will there at first was man's,
Who could do good or evil as he chose.
I had no choice but I must follow him
With forfeits and rewards he understood—
Unless I liked to suffer loss of worship.
I had to prosper good and punish evil.
You changed all that. You set me free to reign.
You are the Emancipator of your God,
And as such I promote you to a saint.

. . .

JOB. All very splendid. I am flattered proud
To have been in on anything with You.
'Twas a great demonstration if You say so.
Though incidentally I sometimes wonder
Why it had had to be at my expense.

GOD. It had to be at somebody's expense.
Society can never think things out:
It has to see them acted out by actors,
Devoted actors at a sacrifice—
The ablest actors I can lay my hands on.
Is that your answer?

JOB.   No, for I have yet
To ask my question. We disparage reason.

But all the time it's what we're most concerned with.
There's will as motor and there's will as brakes.
Reason is, I suppose, the steering gear.
The will as brakes can't stop the will as motor
For very long. We're plainly made to go.
We're going anyway and may as well
Have some say as to where we're headed for;
Just as we will be talking anyway
And may as well throw in a little sense.
Let's do so now. Because I let You off
From telling me Your reason, don't assume
I thought You had none. Somewhere back
I knew You had one. But this isn't it
You're giving me. You say we groped this out.
But if You will forgive me the irreverence,
It sounds to me as if You thought it out,
And took Your time to it. It seems to me
An afterthought, a long-long-after-thought.
I'd give more for one least beforehand reason
Than all the justifying ex-post-facto
Excuses trumped up by You for theologians.
The front of being answerable to no one
I'm with You in maintaining to the public.
But, Lord, we showed them what. The audience
Has all gone home to bed. The play's played out.
Come, after all these years—to satisfy me.
I'm curious. And I'm a grown-up man:
I'm not a child for You to put me off
And tantalize me with another "Oh, because."
You'd be the last to want me to believe
All Your effects were merely lucky blunders.
That would be unbelief and atheism.
The artist in me cries out for design.
Such devilish ingenuity of torture
Did seem unlike You, and I tried to think
The reason might have been some other person's.
But there is nothing You are not behind.
I did not ask then, but it seems as if
Now after all these years You might indulge me.
Why did You hurt me so? I am reduced
To asking flatly for the reason—outright.

GOD. I'd tell you, Job—

JOB.   All right, don't tell me, then,
If you don't want to. I don't want to know.
But what is all this secrecy about?
I fail to see what fun, what satisfaction
A God can find in laughing at how badly
Men fumble at the possibilities
When left to guess forever for themselves.
The chances are when there's so much pretense
Of metaphysical profundity
The obscurity's a fraud to cover nothing.
I've come to think no so-called hidden value's
Worth going after. Get down into things,
It will be found there's no more given there
Than on the surface. If there ever was,
The crypt was long since rifled by the Greeks.
We don't know where we are, or who we are.
We don't know one another; don't know You;
Don't know what time it is. We don't know, don't we?
Who says we don't? Who got up these misgivings?
Oh, we know well enough to go ahead with.
I mean we seem to know enough to act on.
It comes down to a doubt about the wisdom
Of having children—after having had them,
So there is nothing we can do about it
But warn the children they perhaps should have none.
You could end this by simply coming out
And saying plainly and unequivocally
Whether there's any part of man immortal.
Yet You don't speak. Let fools bemuse themselves
By being baffled for the sake of being.
I'm sick of the whole artificial puzzle.

JOB'S WIFE. You won't get any answers out of God.

GOD. My kingdom, what an outbreak!

JOB'S WIFE.   Job is right.
Your kingdom, yes, Your kingdom come on earth.
Pray tell me what does that mean? Anything?
Perhaps that earth is going to crack someday
Like a big egg and hatch a heaven out
Of all the dead and buried from their graves.
One simple little statement from the throne
Would put an end to such fantastic nonsense;

And, too, take care of twenty of the four
And twenty freedoms on the party docket.
Or is it only four? My extra twenty
Are freedoms from the need of asking questions.
(I hope You know the game called twenty questions.)
For instance, is there such a thing as Progress?
Job says there's no such thing as Earth's becoming
An easier place for man to save his soul in.
Except as a hard place to save his soul in,
A trial ground where he can try himself
And find out whether he is any good,
It would be meaningless. It might as well
Be Heaven at once and have it over with.

GOD. Two pitching on like this tend to confuse me.
One at a time, please. I will answer Job first.
I'm going to tell Job why I tortured him,
And trust it won't be adding to the torture.
I was just showing off to the Devil, Job,
As is set forth in Chapters One and Two.
(*Job takes a few steps pacing.*) Do you mind?
(*God eyes him anxiously.*)

JOB.   No. No, I mustn't.
'Twas human of You. I expected more
Than I could understand and what I get
Is almost less than I can understand.
But I don't mind. Let's leave it as it stood.
The point was it was none of my concern.

. . .

X · The Song of Songs

SONG OF SONGS 2:1–7

I am a rose of Sharon,
A lily of the valleys.

²As a lily among thorns,
So is my love among the daughters.

³As an apple-tree among the trees of the wood,
So is my beloved among the sons.
Under its shadow I delighted to sit,
And its fruit was sweet to my taste.
⁴He hath brought me to the banqueting-house,
And his banner over me is love.
⁵"Stay ye me with dainties, refresh me with apples;
For I am love-sick."
⁶Let his left hand be under my head,
And his right hand embrace me.
⁷"I adjure you, O daughters of Jerusalem,
By the gazelles, and by the hinds of the field,
That ye awaken not, nor stir up love,
Until it please."

Translation: JPS 1917

DAHLIA RAVIKOVITCH □

Poem of Explanations

Some people know how to love,
for others it's just not right.
Some people kiss in the street,
others find it unpleasant
—and not only in the street.

I think it's a talent like any other,
perhaps that's an advantage.
Like the rose of Sharon with its gift for blooming,
like the lily of the valley
that chooses its colors.
A rose or a lily in bloom
is blinding.
I don't mean to offend: I know
there are other kinds.

Hummingbirds are the loveliest of birds
in my opinion,
but if you like, you can go to the sparrow.

Even so, I keep telling myself,
I'm not a bird of paradise,
I'm not a three-headed calf,
I'm not an apple that doesn't ripen.

Translated from the Hebrew
by Chana Bloch and Ariel Bloch

SONG OF SONGS 7:1

Return, return, O Shulammite;
Return, return, that we may look upon thee.

What will ye see in the Shulammite?
As it were a dance of two companies.

Translation: JPS 1917

PAUL CELAN □

Deathsfugue[cc]

Black milk of daybreak we drink it at evening
we drink it at midday and morning we drink it at night
we drink and we drink
we shovel a grave in the air   there you won't lie too cramped
A man lives in the house he plays with his vipers he
      writes
he writes when it grows dark to Deutschland your golden
      hair Marguerite
he writes it and steps out of doors and the stars are all
      sparkling
                        he whistles his hounds to come close
he whistles his Jews into rows has them shovel a grave in
      the ground
he orders us play up for the dance

Black milk of daybreak we drink you at night
we drink you at morning and midday we drink you at
      evening
we drink and we drink
A man lives in the house he plays with his vipers he
      writes
he writes when it grows dark to Deutschland your golden
      hair Marguerite
your ashen hair Shulamith we shovel a grave in the air
                    there you won't lie too cramped
He shouts jab this earth deeper you lot there you others
      sing up and play
he grabs for the rod in his belt he swings it his eyes they
      are blue
jab your spades deeper you lot there you others play on
      for the dancing

Black milk of daybreak we drink you at night
we drink you at midday and morning we drink you at
      evening
we drink and we drink
a man lives in the house your goldenes Haar Marguerite

[cc] See "Notes on the Poems," p. 336

your aschenes Haar Shulamith he plays with his vipers
He shouts play death more sweetly this Death is a master
    from Deutschland
he shouts scrape your strings darker then rise up as
    smoke to the sky
you'll have a grave then in the clouds there you won't lie
    too cramped

Black milk of daybreak we drink you at night
we drink you at midday Death is a master aus Deutschland
we drink you at evening and morning we drink and we drink
this Death is ein Meister aus Deutschland his eye it is blue
he shoots you with shot made of lead shoots you level and true
a man lives in the house your goldenes Haar Margarete
he looses his hounds on us grants us a grave in the air
he plays with his vipers and daydreams
                der Tod ist ein Meister aus Deutschland

dein goldenes Haar Margarete
dein aschenes Haar Sulamith

1944–45

Translation from the German
by John Felstiner

IAKOVOS KAMBANELIS   ☐

Song of Songs

Have you seen the one I love?
Song of Songs 3:3

How lovely is my love
in her everyday dress
with a little comb in her hair.
No one knew how lovely she was.
Girls of Auschwitz
girls of Dachau
have you seen the one I love?

We saw her on the long journey.
She wasn't wearing her everyday dress
or the little comb in her hair.

How lovely is my love
caressed by her mother,
kissed by her brother.
No one knew how lovely she was.
Girls of Belsen
girls of Mauthausen
have you seen the one I love?

We saw her in the frozen square
with a number on her white arm
and a yellow star over her heart.

Translated from the Greek
by Gail Holst Warhaft

Y · Ruth

RUTH 1:1–17

In the days when the chieftains* ruled, there was a famine in the land; and a man of Bethlehem in Judah, with his wife and two sons, went to reside in the country of Moab. ²The man's name was Elimelech, his wife's name was Naomi, and his two sons were named Mahlon and Chilion—Ephrathites of Bethlehem in Judah. They came to the country of Moab and remained there.

³Elimelech, Naomi's husband, died; and she was left with her two sons. ⁴They married Moabite women, one named Orpah and the other Ruth, and they lived there about ten years. ⁵Then those two—Mahlon and Chilion—also died; so the woman was left without her two sons and without her husband.

⁶She started out with her daughters-in-law to return from the country of Moab; for in the country of Moab she had heard that the Lord had taken note of His people and given them food. ⁷Accompanied by her two daughters-in-law, she left the place where she had been living; and they set out on the road back to the land of Judah.

⁸But Naomi said to her two daughters-in-law, "Turn back, each of you to her mother's house. May the Lord deal kindly with you, as you have dealt with the dead and with me! ⁹May the Lord grant that each of you find security in the house of a husband!" And she kissed them farewell. They broke into weeping ¹⁰and said to her, "No, we will return with you to your people."

¹¹But Naomi replied, "Turn back, my daughters! Why should you go with me? Have I any more sons in my body who might be husbands for you? ¹²Turn back, my daughters, for I am too old to be married. Even if I thought there was hope for me, even if I were married tonight and I also bore sons, ¹³should you wait for them to grow up? Should you on their account debar yourselves from marriage? Oh no, my daughters! My lot is far more bitter than yours, for the hand of the Lord has struck out against me."

¹⁴They broke into weeping again, and Orpah kissed her mother-

* I.e., the leaders who arose in the period before the monarchy. Others "judges"

324

in-law farewell. But Ruth clung to her. [15]So she said, "See, your sister-in-law has returned to her people and her gods. Go follow your sister-in-law." [16]But Ruth replied, "Do not urge me to leave you, to turn back and not follow you. For wherever you go, I will go; wherever you lodge, I will lodge; your people shall be my people, and your God my God. [17]Where you die, I will die, and there I will be buried. [†-]Thus and more may the LORD do to me[-†] if anything but death parts me from you."

MARGE PIERCY   ☐

The Book of Ruth and Naomi

When you pick up the Tanakh and read
the Book of Ruth, it is a shock
how little it resembles memory.
It's concerned with inheritance,
lands, men's names, how women
must wiggle and wobble to live.

Yet women have kept it dear
for the beloved elder who
cherished Ruth, more friend than
daughter. Daughters leave. Ruth
brought even the baby she made
with Boaz home as a gift.

Where you go, I will go too,
your people shall be my people,
I will be a Jew for you,
for what is yours I will love
as I love you, oh Naomi
my mother, my sister, my heart.

Show me a woman who does not dream
a double, heart's twin, a sister
of the mind in whose ear she can whisper,
whose hair she can braid as her life
twists its pleasure and pain and shame.
Show me a woman who does not hide

[†-†] A formula of imprecation

in the locket of bone that deep
eye beam of fiercely gentle love
she had once from mother, daughter,
sister; once like a warm moon
that radiance aligned the tides
of her blood into potent order.

At the season of first fruits we recall
two travellers, co-conspirators, scavengers
making do with leftovers and mill ends,
whose friendship was stronger than fear,
stronger than hunger, who walked together
the road of shards, hands joined.

ANNA KAMIENSKA □

Naomi

*And she said unto them: "Call me not Naomi [that is,
pleasant], call me Marah [that is, bitter]; for the Almighty hath
dealt very bitterly with me."*

Ruth 1:20

Naomi my sister
everyone here knew you
you were like a skylark
on your husband's cheeks
the down had barely begun to appear
holding hands like children
you left the town

Naomi is it you Naomi
life really rolled over you
and you come back alone
as if you never had
a husband two sons
what weighs you down
an empty house on your back

You are not alone
there is after all this youngster Ruth
who attached herself to you
go away daughter you tell her

there everything will be strange to you
she persisted
I know you said nothing and walked on in silence
you accepted her eagerness
in place of love

Naomi perhaps you thought
I'm still not so old
I still may give birth
didn't he ask about me
let my daughter-in-law go to him
perhaps she'll remind him of the young Naomi

Perhaps waiting in the dark you thought
he himself will come
heavy-set with a golden beard
but he only sent a measure of barley
Naomi my sister you'll never
give birth to a son
accept a grandson on your lap
for the man did enter the woman
and He through whom there flows
the stream of life
again caused
a man to be born

Surely she herself is better
than seven sons
who'd abandon you in old age and pain

And so she brings you your grandson
rejoice you'll be his nurse
you'll still be useful here
his soft little head
tiny hands
rosy ears
sobs of emotion
tug at your guts

Naomi don't cry
O Naomi

Translated from the Polish
by Grażyna Drabik and David Curzon

Z ▪ Ecclesiastes

ECCLESIASTES 1:1–9

The words of Koheleth, the son of David, king in Jerusalem.

²Vanity of vanities, saith Koheleth;
Vanity of vanities, all is vanity.

³What profit hath man of all his labour
Wherein he laboureth under the sun?
⁴One generation passeth away, and another generation cometh;
And the earth abideth for ever.
⁵The sun also ariseth, and the sun goeth down,
And hasteth to his place where he ariseth.
⁶The wind goeth toward the south,
And turneth about unto the north,
It turneth about continually in its circuit,
And the wind returneth again to its circuits.
⁷All the rivers run into the sea,
Yet the sea is not full;
Unto the place whither the rivers go,
Thither they go again.
⁸All things toil to weariness;
Man cannot utter it,
The eye is not satisfied with seeing,
Nor the ear filled with hearing.
⁹That which hath been is that which shall be,
And that which hath been done is that which shall be done;
And there is nothing new under the sun.

Translation: JPS 1917

JORGE LUIS BORGES ☐

Ecclesiastes 1:9

If I run my hand over my brow,
if I caress the spines of books,
if I recognize the Book of the Nights,
if I turn the resistant lock,
if I stay too long on the uncertain threshold,
if the terrible pain leaves me crushed,
if I remember the Time Machine,
if I remember the Unicorn Tapestry,
if I change my position in sleep,
if memory returns a verse to me,
I repeat what I have finished
many times in my set ways.
I cannot perform a new act.
I spin spindles to weave the same fable,
repeat a repeated pentameter,
speak what others have spoken to me,
feel the same things at the same
hour of the day or, in the abstract, night.
Each night the same nightmares,
each night the rigor of the labyrinth.
I have the lethargy of an immobile mirror
or the dust of a museum.
I'm only I hope a thing not tasteful,
an offering, a gold of the shadow,
this virgin, death. (The Spanish language
permits this metaphor.)

> Translated from the Spanish
> by David Curzon and Leonor Maia-Sampaio

NOTES ON THE POEMS
INDEX OF TRANSLATORS
INDEX OF POETS
INDEX OF TITLES

Notes on the Poems

a. (Robinson Jeffers, "The Great Explosion") Line 1 states that "The universe expands and contracts like a great heart." Some versions of the big bang model have the universe expanding forever, while others have it eventually collapsing back again into the dense chaos that preceded the big bang, to be followed by another vast cycle of expansion and contraction, and so on.

b. (Eugenio Montale, "Big Bang or Whatever") Line 4 alludes to the steady-state cosmological model developed in the late 1940s by Hermann Bondi, Thomas Gold, and Fred Hoyle (of A. D. Hope's poem, "Protest to Fred Hoyle"). To be consistent with observations that indicate the universe is expanding, the steady-state model requires new matter to be created at a rate that preserves the existing distribution of matter. And so, in Montale's accurate formulation, as translated by Ruth Feldman, it is a model of "a swarming stagnation."

c. (Howard Nemerov, "Creation Myth on a Moebius Band") The title: A moebius band can be made by taking a thin strip of paper, giving it a half twist, and then joining the ends. This construction appears to have two surfaces but a line traced along its length will be continuous, showing that it has only one surface.

d. (A. D. Hope, "Protest to Fred Hoyle") Line 6: The "Bridgewater Treatises" are, perhaps, those of the eighteenth-century British Catholic theologian John Bridgewater.

e. (Paul Celan, "Psalm") *Translator's note:* "The stubborn echoes of Creation here, 'earth', and 'clay' and 'dust,' struggle against hopelessness and thus feed into the paradox that follows. Celan, like many another, could live neither with nor without intimations of sacredness" (John Felstiner, "Mother Tongue/Holy Tongue: Celan into Hebrew," *Tel Aviv Review* 3 [1991]: 155).

f. (Jaroslav Seifert, "Lost Paradise") Some of the etymologies of Hebrew names in the poem are problematical. Stanza 5, for example, states "Orpah/is a Hind." In the Book of Ruth, 1:14–15, we are told that Orpah returned to her people, the Moabites, while Ruth continued on with Naomi, their Israelite mother-in-law. The Midrash (Ruth Rabbah 2.9) derives Orpah's name from the Hebrew "Oref" or nape because she turned her back (i.e., the nape of her neck) on Naomi. However, if Orpah was a Moabite name the actual derivation would presumably have been from that language. Speculation by Israeli friends as to what Seifert might have had in mind or been told yielded the transposition of the second and third letters of "Orpah" to give the Hebrew "Ofra," a word in use as a name and meaning a small female deer.

g. (Robert Graves, "The Ark") Line 3: "the arch-fiend Samael" (often spelled Sammael) is Satan.

h. (Allen Afterman, "Covenant") Line 4: A *mohel* is a person trained and authorized to perform circumcisions.

i. (Stanley Moss, "Lot's Son") One of the riddles Sheba asked Solomon (see Introduction, n. 21) was "Who is the woman who says to her son, 'Your father is my father, your grandfather is my husband, you are my son and I am your sister?' Solomon answered 'One of Lot's daughter's.'"

j. (Melech Ravitch, "Twelve Lines about the Burning Bush") Line 10: "Not for nothing is one of your thousand names—thorn, . . . " In rabbinic tradition the burning bush was identified as a thorn-bush, as this midrash makes clear:

> A heathen once asked R. Joshua b. Karah (others say R. Gamaliel): "Why did God choose a thorn-bush from which to speak to Moses?" He replied: "If it had been a carob tree or a sycamore tree you would have asked the same question; but to dismiss you without reply is not right, so I will tell you why. To teach you that no place is devoid of God's presence, not even a thorn-bush." (*Midrash Rabbah*, 3d ed., 10 vols. [London: Soncino Press, 1983], 3:53)

k. (Jacob Glatstein, "Dead Men Don't Praise God") The title is from Psalm 115:17 (18 in Christian canons). Line 2: The Maidenek concentration camp was at Lublin. Glatstein was born in Lublin and emigrated to the United States when he was 18 in 1914. His parents remained in Lublin and died in the Holocaust. Lines 5 and 6 and 17–20 allude to and summarize a rabbinic midrash. Cf. Deut. 29:14 and *Midrash Rabbah*, 3d ed., 10 vols. (London: Soncino Press, 1983), 3:335–36.

l. (D. H. Lawrence, "The Old Idea of Sacrifice") I doubt if Lawrence had a specific biblical passage in mind, so that the poem is not, strictly speaking, midrashic. Since Leviticus opens with a detailed account of the laws of sacrifice, I chose the first few verses as the text.

m. (Deuteronomy 8:1–3) In verse 3, the phrase "Man doth not live by bread only" has become proverbial in English as "man shall not live by bread alone." This version, used in the poem opposite, occurs in the King James translation of Matthew 4:4: "It is written, Man shall not live by bread alone. . . ."

n. (Rainer Maria Rilke, "The Death of Moses") This poem is remarkable for its selection and use of traditional midrashic material. These components of the poem are from the Midrash:

- the refusal of the angels to gather Moses to his death
- the agreement of Sammael (i.e., Satan) to do so
- Sammael's defeat
- Moses writing the Name of God when Sammael arrived
- the brightness of Moses' eyes
- God himself descending with angels
- the making of a bed by God and the angels
- the debate with Moses' soul
- death by a kiss from God
- closing up the mountain

J. B. Leishman annotates his translation of this poem (Rilke, *Selected Works*, 2 vols. [London: Hogarth Press, 1960], 2:316) as follows: "Lines 1–14 Paris, summer 1914; lines 15–22 Munich, October 1915. 'With reference to a passage in the Talmud about the death of Moses, translated by Herder.'"

Rilke, however, is drawing on a number of different midrashim in this poem, some of which are not in the Talmud at all, let alone in one passage. The full set of Jewish legends on the death of Moses can be found, with detailed notes and citations, in Louis Ginsberg, *The Legends of the Jews*, 7 vols. (Philadelphia: Jewish Publication Society, 1909–38), 3:466–73. Ginsberg's third volume was published in German in 1911, three years before the earliest date Leishman gives for the composition of the poem. Rilke was presumably using Ginsberg's *Legends* or a similar compilation as his source.

The New Testament, in Jude 1:9, contains a cryptic allusion to a variant on the legend with which Rilke starts his poem. In this variant "the archangel Michael, contending with the devil, disputed about the body of Moses" (Revised Standard Version).

o. (Alicia Ostriker, "The Story of Joshua") The quotation ten lines from the end is from Deut. 10:19. Similar formulations are to be found at Exod. 22:21, 23:9; Lev. 19:33; Deut. 23:7.

p. (2 Kings 9:30–37) The reference in verse 36 is to 1 Kings 21:23.

q. (Paul Celan, "You Be Like You") *Translator's note:* "Celan explains that Jewishness is 'a concern less thematic than spiritual.' Yet during the late 1960s, he wrote several poems that explicitly have Judaism at stake. This poem is on rebinding a severed bond. In the poem, Celan quotes the medieval German of Meister Eckhart's vernacular version of Isaiah 51 and 60. For an archaic tone in English I adapted the Wycliffe Bible. His darkened speech makes it all the more gratifying when his poem finally converts to Isaiah's Hebrew, *kumi ori*, 'arise, shine,' evoking the Sabbath hymn *Lecha Dodi* and promising redemption from exile. Celan wrote lodged in exile: his *kumi ori*, even transliterated as he published it, gets its purifying tone by contrast with German speech that has verged on darkness. Not long after writing 'You Be Like You,' he made a long-deferred visit to Israel. One day, he wrote out this poem for a friend in Jerusalem, and there he put *kumi ori* not in transliterated form (of course not!), but in fluent Hebrew script—the poem and now the poet borne upstream to the source" (John Felstiner, "Mother Tongue/Holy Tongue: Celan into Hebrew," *Tel Aviv Review* 3 [1991]: 156–159).

r. (Howard Nemerov, "Small Moment") Reference to Theseus and Antiope six lines from the end: "Some say that Theseus took part in Heracles' successful expedition against the Amazons, and received as his share of the booty their queen Antiope, also called Melanippe; but that this was not so unhappy a fate for her as many thought, because . . . of the passion he had already kindled in her heart" (Robert Graves, *The Greek Myths*, 2 vols. [Baltimore: Penguin Books, 1955], 1, sec. 100).

s. (Isaiah 56:5) Heb., *yad vashem;* lit. "a hand and a name." The Holocaust memorial and museum in Jerusalem is named Yad Vashem.

t. (Paul Celan, "Just Think") *Translator's note:* "The strain of Celan's Judaic affiliation alters with the Six-Days War. On June 7th and 8th, 1967, he wrote this poem on 'the peat-bog soldier of Masada' that leads from ancient heroism through Nazi-camp inmates to Israelis repossessing the land" (John Felstiner, "Mother Tongue/Holy Tongue: Celan into Hebrew," *Tel Aviv Review* 3 [1991]: 155–156).

u. (Zbigniew Herbert, "At the Gate of the Valley") "The scenery of the Last Judgement is presented by a speaker who uses the style of a modern radio announcer, as if he were covering a soccer match. . . . The scenery of the Valley of

Jehoshaphat reveals a distressing similarity to a concentration camp. In other words, both the realm of heritage condensed into myth (in this case, biblical eschatology) and the realm of modern disinheritance appear equally cruel and inhuman" (Stanislaw Baranczak, *A Fugitive from Utopia: The Poetry of Zbigniew Herbert* [Cambridge, Mass.: Harvard University Press, 1987] 100–101).

v. (Gabriel Preil, "Then, Too, It Was Autumn") Lines 10 and 11 refer to W. H. Auden's poem "September 1, 1939."

w. (Dan Pagis, "Tidings") Last line: On the biblical "cities of refuge," see Exod. 21:13; Num. 35:9–15; Josh. 20:7–9.

x. (Zbigniew Herbert, "Jonah") "Any attempt to sum up what this poem presents as the nature of the incompatibility between the biblical and the 'modern' Jonahs must certainly begin with the opposition of 'fate' and 'chance.' The past's heritage seems to have been determined by a providential order of things, while the modern disinheritance is the domain of blind chance. . . . Today's Jonah . . . cannot become a hero of myth, which would give significance to his experience by sanctifying it or at least preserving it in posterity's collective memory" (Stanislaw Baranczak, *A Fugitive from Utopia: The Poetry of Zbigniew Herbert* [Cambridge, Mass.: Harvard University Press, 1987] 19–20; see also pages 94–95).

y. (Hart Crane, "After Jonah") This poem is to be found in *The Poems of Hart Crane*, ed. by Marc Simon (New York: Liveright, 1986); it was not published by Crane. The editor's note on the poem reads: "Composed c. 1922–1926. The present text is based on HC's one extant typescript of 'After Jonah.'"

z. (Yehuda Amichai, "I Am a Man 'Planted beside Streams of Water'") Line 10: "The Hill of Evil Counsel" is the hill above Jerusalem where British government offices were located during the Mandate period; now occupied by United Nations offices.

aa. (Denise Levertov, "O Taste and See") Lines 1 and 2 echo the sonnet of Wordsworth which begins "The world is too much with us."

bb. (Paul Claudel, "Meditation on Psalm 118") Vulgate numbering.

cc. (Paul Celan, "There Stood") *Translator's note:* "On Celan's return to Paris from his only visit to Israel in October 1969, there followed a spate of short lyrics. The first ones written name various places in Jerusalem. 'There Stood,' my favorite in this sequence, the most hopeful, underpins a loving encounter with a memory of the Danes' 1943 rescue of the Jews" (John Felstiner, "Mother Tongue/Holy Tongue: Celan into Hebrew," *Tel Aviv Review* 3 [1991]: 160).

dd. (Robinson Jeffers, "Birds and Fishes") Robinson Jeffers's poem contains only a passing allusion to "Job's friend's warhorse" and so does not appear to be, at first glance, a midrashic poem. But the "friend" is God, who, in the passage alluded to, speaks to Job from the whirlwind and points out the brutal beauty of Creation, as Jeffers does in his poem. Czeslaw Milosz's "Theodicy" and Jeffers's "Birds and Fishes" strike me as complementary to each other.

ee. (Paul Celan, "Deathsfugue") *Translator's note:* "The *Todesfuge* is one of those poems by Celan—the first such, in fact—that culminate in a Hebrew term. Throughout its fugal structure the commandant's beloved Marguerite, namesake of Faust's Nordic heroine, is played off against Shulamith, the comely maiden who in the Song of Songs can personify Israel. By the poem's closing couplet these two seem in Germanic-Judaic concord: 'your golden hair Marguerite/your ashen hair Shulamith.' Yet the parallelism of these quasi-Biblical verses ironically drives the 'ashen' Shulamith out of any coexistence. The poem ends on a millennial (if tragic) Hebraic note" (John Felstiner, "Mother Tongue/Holy Tongue: Celan into Hebrew," *Tel Aviv Review* 3 [1991]: 152–153).

Index of Translators

Index of Poets

Several of the poets were exiles. The language in which they wrote is given in parentheses when this differs from the one implied by the preceding information.

Index of Titles

DATE DUE